JAMES JOYC

return

Irish Writers in their Time

Series Editor: Stan Smith

This innovative series meets the urgent need for comprehensive new accounts of Irish writing across the centuries which combine readability with critical authority and information with insight. Each volume addresses the whole range of a writer's work in the various genres, setting its vision of the world in biographical context and situating it within the cultural, intellectual, and political currents of the age, in Ireland and the wider world. This series will prove indispensable for students and specialists alike.

1. Patrick Kavanagh
(Editor: STAN SMITH)

2. Elizabeth Bowen
(Editor: EIBHEAR WALSHE)

3. John Banville
(JOHN KENNY)

FORTHCOMING

4. Jonathan Swift
(BREAN HAMMOND)

5. James Joyce
(Editor: SEAN LATHAM)

6. Sean O'Casey
(JAMES MORAN)

James Joyce

Edited by
SEAN LATHAM
University of Tulsa

IRISH ACADEMIC PRESS
DUBLIN • PORTLAND, OR

First published in 2010 by Irish *Academic Press*

2 Brookside,
Dundrum Road,
Dublin 14, Ireland

920 NE 58th Avenue, Suite 300
Portland, Oregon,
97213-3786, USA

www.iap.ie

British Library Cataloguing-in-Publication Data
An entry can be found on request

978 0 7165 2906 4 (cloth)
978 0 7165 2907 1 (paper)

Library of Congress Cataloging-in-Publication Data
An entry can be found on request

Printed by MPG Books Group, King's Lynn and Bodmin

This book is dedicated to
David G. Wright (1952–2008)

Contents

Contributors

Tim Conley is Associate Professor of English and Comparative Literature at Brock University in Canada. He is the author of *Joyces Mistakes: Problems of Intention, Irony, and Interpretation* (2003) and, with Stephen Cain, *The Encyclopedia of Fictional and Fantastic Languages* (2006).

Kevin J.H. Dettmar is W.M. Keck Professor and Chair of the Department of English at Pomona College. His research focuses on the institutional politics of modernist writing and culture, and on the cultural dynamics of rock & roll. He is the author of *The Illicit Joyce of Postmodernism* and *Is Rock Dead?*

Michael Groden is Distinguished University Professor at the University of Western Ontario and the author of *'Ulysses' in Progress* (1977), general editor of *The James Joyce Archive* (sixty-three volumes, 1977–79), as well as editor of two volumes on *Dubliners* and the sixteen volumes on *Ulysses*, and compiler of *James Joyce's Manuscripts: An Index* (1980). He also co-edited *The Johns Hopkins Guide to Literary Theory and Criticism* (1994; 2nd edition, 2005) and *Genetic Criticism: Texts and Avant-textes* (2004). On Bloomsday 2004 he received an honorary doctorate from the National University of Ireland.

Miranda Hickman is an Associate Professor of English at McGill University in Montreal. She is the author of *The Geometry of Modernism* (2006) and has published on modernist literature and detective fiction, chiefly on the work of Pound, HD and Raymond Chandler. She is currently at work on an edition of letters between Ezra Pound and London publisher Stanley Nott, as well as a book about early twentieth-century women critics and the construction of critical authority.

Aaron Jaffe is Associate Professor of English at the University of

Louisville. He is the author of Modernism and the Culture of Celebrity (2005) and is currently working on a book project entitled Modernist Event Horizons.

Sean Latham is Professor of English at the University of Tulsa where he serves as editor of the James Joyce Quarterly and director of the Modernist Journals Project <www.modjourn.org>. He is the author of Am I a Snob? Modernism and the Novel (2003), Joyce's Modernism (2005) and The Art of Scandal: Modernism, Libel Law, and the Roman à Clef (2009). He is President of the Modernist Studies Association and a trustee of the International James Joyce Foundation.

Katherine Mullin is Senior Lecturer in Modern Literature at the University of Leeds. She is the author of James Joyce, Sexuality and Social Purity (2003) and several articles on Joyce. She is currently working on a book on representations of typists, shop-girls, barmaids and other working women in late Victorian, Modernist and popular fiction.

Christine van Boheemen-Saaf is Professor (Chair) of English at the University of Amsterdam, trustee of the International James Joyce Foundation and founding editor of European Joyce Studies, which has appeared annually since 1989. She has published widely on the relations between narrative fiction and philosophy, gender studies and post-colonial fiction.

Bruce Stewart is Reader in Anglo-Irish Literature at the University of Ulster and author of James Joyce (2007). He has edited numerous conference collections for the Orincess Grace Irish Library, including The Supernatural and Fantastic in Irish Literature and its Contexts (1998) and volumes onJoyce and Beckett. In 2004 he issued a selection from the Irish Book Lover (1909–59). He maintains an online Irish Studies archive at >http://www.ricorso.net.>

David G. Wright taught English and Irish literature, including a graduate course on Joyce, at the University of Auckland, New Zealand. He is the author of Characters of Joyce (1983), Ironies of 'Ulysses' (1992), many articles on Joyce, and Yeats's Myth of Self: The Autobiographical Prose (1987). He died in 2008.

Abbreviations

CW	*The Critical Writings of James Joyce*, ed. Ellsworth Mason and Richard Ellmann (New York: Viking, 1959).
D	*Dubliners: Text, Criticism, and Notes*, ed. Robert Scholes and A. Walton Litz (New York: Penguin, 1976).
E	*Exiles*, with Author's Own Notes and an Introduction by Padraic Colum (London: Jonathan Cape, 1968).
FW	*Finnegans Wake* (New York: Viking, 1939).
GJ	*Giacomo Joyce*, ed. Richard Ellmann (New York: Viking, 1968).
JJ	Richard Ellmann, *James Joyce: Revised Edition* (New York: Oxford University Press (1982).
LI	*Letters of James Joyce*, Vol. I, ed. Stuart Gilbert (New York: Viking, 1957).
LII and LIII	*Letters of James Joyce*, Vols. II and III, ed. Richard Ellmann (New York: Viking, 1966).
P	*A Portrait of the Artist as a Young Man: Text, Criticism, and Notes*, ed. Chester G, Anderson (New York: Viking, 1968).
PSW	*Poems and Shorter Writings, including 'Epiphanies', 'Giacomo Joyce' and 'A Portrait of the Artist'*, ed. Richard Ellmann, A. Walton Litz and John Whittier-Ferguson (London: Faber and Faber, 1991).
SH	*Stephen Hero*, ed. Theodore Spencer, John J. Slocum and Herbert Cahoon (New York: New Directions, 1963).
SL	*Selected Letters of James Joyce*, ed. Richard Ellmann (New York: Viking, 1975).
U	*Ulysses*, ed. Hans Walter Gabler (New York: Garland, 1984).

CHAPTER ONE

Introduction: Joyce's Modernities

SEAN LATHAM

In the perplexing opening pages of *Finnegans Wake*, we come across the description of the fallen giant, Finn Mac Cool, whose archaic corpse now forms Dublin's modern topography. This monstrous figure's head sticks out into the bay forming the Howth peninsula while his body stretches across the city to his 'tumptytumtoes' (*FW*, 3.21) in Chapelizod. *Ulysses* too creates its own mythic geography, transforming the city of Dublin into the epic Greek landscapes – from the enchanted island of Circe to the rocky shores of Ithaca – through which Leopold Blooms travels. In his famous essay, '*Ulysses*, Order, and Myth', T.S. Eliot finds himself deeply drawn to this reassuring element of Joyce's art, insisting that these symbolic structures provide a means of 'controlling, of ordering, of giving a shape and a significance to the immense panorama of futility and anarchy which is contemporary history'.[1] So nostalgic and pessimistic a reading of Joyce's work, however, requires us to suppress its most vital element: a wilful and creative engagement with a 'contemporary history' that actually seems full of Utopian promise. The 'Wandering Rocks' episode of *Ulysses*, for example, plunges us into the heart of an urban metropolis where unexpected connections and juxtapositions explode off the page, marking a clear turning point in the larger novel. Similarly, in *Finnegans Wake* we find passages on television, radio and media more generally that seem both to promise, and simultaneously to enact, a fundamentally new mode of human communication, what the text playfully calls 'a sentence with surcease' (*FW*, 129.8). Indeed, when we look closely at the mythic structures Eliot identifies, they often seem rather brittle. Bloom, after all, is by no means Odysseus and the text deliberately rejects any kind of

1

reconciliation between symbolic father and son. Similarly, the giant, Finn Mac Cool, is 'nowhemoe' (*FW*, 7.15) vanquished from both space (nowhere) and time (no more) as he becomes 'Only a fadograph of a yestern scene' (*FW*, 7.15).

This rich and redolent term 'fadograph' captures the paradoxical temporalities of Joyce's texts in which mythic and modern time collide. A photograph, like an epic narrative, attempts to suspend time, preserving a single moment, 'rescuing it', as André Bazin writes, 'from its proper corruption'.[2] This very act of preservation, however, does violence to the inescapably temporal nature of human experience and is doomed to failure as the frozen moment and even the photograph itself inevitably begins to fade, succumbing to the very flow of time they seek to counter. So too the mythic topoi Joyce employs – which appear to preserve a frozen and unchanging world – become blurred and deformed when subjected to a modernity Baudelaire associates with 'that which is ephemeral, fugitive, contingent'.[3] Looking at the 'fadographs' of Joyce's canon therefore requires a compound vision in which myth is shot through with modernity, creating the bewildering array of distortions that generate both the difficulty and the power of these works. Focusing only on the binocular tension between myth and modernity, however – between Odysseus and Bloom or Finn and HCE – tightly restricts our critical vision. Stereoscopically compounding the everyday contingencies of Edwardian Dublin and the timeless epics of Greek and Gaelic myth produces only the illusion of depth. By attempting to 'revision' Joyce, this volume passes the major and minor texts through a series of critical prisms capable of revealing richly layered composites. Indeed, the pleasures of Joyce's work lie precisely in their ability to become 'fadographs': sedimentary records of a modernity at once intimately familiar and troublingly alien.

'Modernity', Anthony Giddens writes, 'is not just one civilization among others'; it is instead a complex social, economic, cultural and subjective set of structures which has grown to encompass the entire globe.[4] Living and working in Dublin, Trieste, Paris and Zurich throughout the first half of the twentieth century, Joyce witnessed and recorded its complex expansion, which Dilip Parameshwar Gaonkar describes in this way:

> Modernity is now everywhere. It has arrived not suddenly, but

slowly, bit by bit, over the long durée – awakened by contact; transported through commerce; administered by empires, bearing colonial descriptions; propelled by nationalism; and now increasingly steered by global media, migration, and capital.[5]

Yet rather than a singular or monolithic structure, modernity must be understood as always already divided against itself; its own insistence on constant change introduces contradictions that paradoxically render it a global structure mutating through an ever-spinning kaleidoscope of local experience. Joyce might best be seen, therefore, less as a modernist writer than as a writer of modernities, some of which have already begun to fade while others remain stubbornly and even surprisingly alive. His work powerfully seizes our imaginations because it potently encodes the contradictions so readily inherent at the intersections of these multiple and discontinuous modernities.

We may, in fact, have become too comfortable with Joyce as a modernist writer, comfortably attributing the complex challenges his texts present to the deliberate difficulty of their form. Rich analytical insights have unquestionably been produced by linking Joyce to other formally innovative writers of the early twentieth century, ranging from Wyndham Lewis and T.S. Eliot to Marcel Proust and Virginia Woolf. As a card-carrying member of what Hugh Kenner famously calls 'a supranational movement called International Modernism', Joyce has become familiar to us as an experimental writer engaged in an attempt to challenge the prevailing codes of realism by inventing new modes of literary and linguistic representation.[6] The problem with treating Joyce simply as a modernist, however, is that such a moniker now provides a convenient way of bypassing the very real challenges his work presents to us, allowing us lazily to chalk them up to the contingent concerns of a now rapidly receding place and time. Indeed, the fact that we now depend so heavily on lengthy annotations and even critical introductions (like this very book) suggests that Joyce's modernism no longer has much connection to our own modern moment. That is, we can attribute those places where the texts become particularly opaque to the widening gap between Joyce's poverty-stricken, 'semi-colonial' Dublin and the wealthy, cosmopolitan capital of today's Irish Republic. Joyce's modernism thus becomes increasingly isolated from the very concept of modernity itself, his work preserved in the mummifying amber of literary canonization.

Salvaging Joyce's works from mere aesthetic difficulty requires us to position them instead at the intersection of discordant, competing and often contradictory modernities – including our own. In her attempt to articulate what she calls 'a polycentric, planetary concept of modernity', Susan Stanford Friedman argues that it generates 'velocity, acceleration, and dynamism of shattering change across a wide spectrum of societal institutions ... change that interweaves the cultural, economic, political, religious, familial, sexual, aesthetic, technological, and so forth'.[7] As sociologists such as Max Weber, Pierre Bourdieu and Jürgen Habermas argue, however, these various spheres of human experience are themselves created by the forces of this same explosive modernity which blow apart the lifeworld and subject its increasingly autonomous elements to differential types and rates of change.[8] Just as we make a mistake in attempting to create a generalized concept of modernism, therefore, so too does a narrow or monolithic idea of modernity limit our interpretive and analytical horizons. Thus, when I argue that Joyce is a writer of modernities, I mean that he engages both the uneven differentiation of these fields as well as the dynamic and often unsettling changes within them. The richness of a book like Ulysses or even a short story like 'The Dead' lies precisely in Joyce's attempt to develop the aesthetic, linguistic and narrative resources necessary to represent these radical changes. They are difficult texts, but the difficulty arises directly from the challenge of negotiating these discontinuous modernities in which both the writer and his texts are constantly created and destroyed. Finnegans Wake turns precisely on this very pattern of genesis and apocalypse as its story of a family – father, mother, two sons and a daughter – unfolds simultaneously in a single night's dream and across the entire span of human history. Seemingly mythic patterns of the kind Eliot sought to identify in Ulysses emerge endlessly from the text and are just as quickly submerged again beneath the funferal (FW, 120.10 – both funeral and fun for all) of the text's language. The book itself thus comes to depend on an ever-recurring cycle of destruction and reinvention that forms the deep structures of family, history, language and the individual psyche. Rather than turning to myth, as Eliot suggests, in order to bring order to chaos, Joyce instead renders mythic the radical instabilities of modernity itself.

To read Joyce's work – from the very first poem he published in the *Dana* to the final publication of *Finnegans Wake* just under two years before his death – we must engage with the paradoxical contradictions of these discordant modernities. Such temporal dissonance generates moments of both profound beauty and troubling alienation as we struggle to make sense of a story, a chapter or even a single sentence. The most mundane details become luminous with meaning yet shot through with doubt and anxiety, riven by the competing claims of sexuality, empire, gender and technology. Each of these possess their own modernity, their own internal and increasingly autonomous logic of meaning, organization and intention; yet in Joyce's work they are made to intersect – sometimes jarringly – in a single object or experience. In *Stephen Hero*, the abandoned version of a semi-autobiographical narrative that would eventually be transformed into *A Portrait of the Artist as a Young Man*, the text's protagonist attempts to define this experience in purely aesthetic terms:

> By an epiphany he meant a sudden spiritual manifestation, whether in the vulgarity of speech or of gesture or in a memorable phase of the mind itself. He believed that it was for the man of letters to record these epiphanies with extreme care, seeing that they themselves are the most delicate and evanescent of moments. He told Cranly that the clock of the Ballast Office was capable of an epiphany. (SH, 211)

The theory Stephen articulates actually seems rather dull, essentially repackaging as it does the romantic aestheticism of Wilde, Pater and Ruskin. By focusing on the clock, however, Stephen transforms the epiphany from a timeless moment of poetic experience into an encounter with the rational, mechanized temporality of modernity. Marking out an objective and essentially empty time, the clock thus condenses for Stephen a concept of epiphany which is registered in the 'ephemeral, fugitive' contingency Baudelaire argues is so essential to modernity.[9]

By selecting the Ballast Office clock as the site for potential revelation, however, Joyce simultaneously insists that modernity itself is fractured, its structure defined less by a coherent rationality than by a competing array of differential experiences, ideologies and logics. After all, this clock – as we later learn when Bloom passes this same spot in *Ulysses* – is 'worked by an electric clock from Dunsink' (*U*, 8.572) and thus runs twenty-five minutes behind Greenwich Mean Time, itself marked by a timeball atop the same building. Thus, far from an empty marker of the passing moments, time itself is fractured on this building, split between Irish and British standards. In tracing the implications of this discrepancy, Luke Gibbons emphasizes 'the breakdown of simultaneity in Joyce's Dublin, the dislocation of synchronicity by aberrant senses of time'.[10] This temporal rupture records an essentially imperial logic: the imposition on Ireland of an alternative measurement of time which ties the colony and its ports into a global economic network. Yet the clock Stephen sees and embeds in his theory of epiphany is visible primarily from the street, registering an alternative temporality, a local modernity that at once co-exists and competes with the one measured by the larger timeball atop the building. And it is here, in the gap between these two clocks, that the Joycean epiphany emerges – at the interface between a prismatic array of competing modernities.

Insisting simultaneously on the local and global nature of modernity, Joyce deliberately lodges his work at the site of richly generative paradox. On the one hand, we can read his texts as part of an essentially international aesthetic movement directly engaged with a world and history which we ourselves continue to negotiate. In this sense we attempt, as Richard Ellmann writes, 'to become Joyce's contemporaries, to understand our interpreter'.[11] On the other hand, his work remains tightly focused on the colonial city of Dublin in a narrow window roughly between the death of Parnell in 1891 and the passage of the Home Rule Bills through the British Commons in 1914. Rather than Joyce's contemporaries, we here become his interpreters, struggling to make sense of a text so deeply rooted in a particular place and time that it sends us endlessly in search of guidebooks and annotations. Insisting on too narrow or unified a conception of modernity essentially requires us to choose one of these options, selecting either a global frame of reference or a local one. As that encounter with the Ballast Office clock suggests, however, we need a critical vision that accommodates both of these options. Joyce the international modernist is as confining an interpretive paradigm as Joyce the Irishman, since each can articulate only one part of a differential modernity defined precisely by its power to shatter any single optic. This requires us, of course, to negotiate some rather complicated contradictions as we – like Joyce – try to make sense of the interplay between local and global modernities in the text itself as well as in our own contemporary reading of it. Like Leopold Bloom trying to tell the time by looking at the two clocks on the Ballast Office simultaneously, we must proceed by a critical parallax that calibrates the fractured structures of modernity.

*   *   *

One of the things that continues to make Joyce's works so compelling is that they attempt to enact precisely this kind of critical reading, their subtle and complicated forms entangling us in this prismatic modernity. While such moments abound, I want to focus here by way of example on one particularly odd and somewhat jarring moment in *A Portrait of the Artist as a Young Man*, when Stephen Dedalus accompanies his father on a brief trip to Cork city in order to execute the final sale of the family's heavily mortgaged properties. While there, Stephen makes the following discovery: 'On the desk before him he read the word *Foetus* cut several times in the dark stained wood. The sudden legend startled his blood' (P, 89). Like the song, 'The Lass of Aughrim', which Gretta hears in 'The Dead', this word unexpectedly resurrects ghostly images of the past – in this case the 'the absent students of the college ... which his father's words had been powerless to evoke' (P, 89). Stephen then finds himself trying desperately to fight back this epiphanic vision, which locks him in a ghostly world where the boundaries between past and present rupture.

He encounters the word while looking for his father's initials in an anatomy theatre at Queen's University – a seemingly charged search symbolizing the young man's attempt to claim the name of the father and with it some stable sense of self. The paternal name, however, even once found, evokes nothing for Stephen, who is still staggered by his vision. Instead, only the word 'foetus' brings his father's history into sharp focus, even as it simultaneously becomes a signifier of his own miscarriage and the aborted possibilities of his life as his father's son. The word, however, operates powerfully beyond these symbolic and psychoanalytic registers as well, signifying not just the collapse of the future into the past, but the 'trace of what he had deemed till then a brutish and individual malady of his own mind' (P, 90). Issues of paternity and inheritance thus give way to sexuality and desire as Stephen's body becomes a site of anxiety and contradiction. This effect is further heightened by the setting in an anatomy amphitheatre where the desks all hover over a central dissecting table. In this space, Stephen is both aware of the concrete, material existence of the body and simultaneously terrified of its reproductive power. Within his psyche the word becomes a sign of subjective instability, evidence of a failure to be born into the world of his father that is at once invoked, mourned and ridiculed in this section of the novel. This discovery itself is both traumatic and disorienting, forcing Stephen to deploy an already familiar strategy of self-authentication. Echoing the words written on the flyleaf of his geography textbook years earlier at Clongowes, he says to himself, 'I am Stephen Dedalus. I am walking beside my father whose name is Simon Dedalus. We are in Cork, in Ireland. Cork is a city. Our room is in the Victoria Hotel. Victoria and Stephen and Simon. Simon and Stephen and Victoria. Names' (P, 92). This attempt at mapping, however, leads only to more confusion, since rather than firmly locating Stephen, they only further disorient him. They are, as he notes, 'names', mere words like 'foetus' itself, which are as unstable as they are powerful.

What Marjorie Howes provocatively calls the 'perverse modernity' of Edwardian Ireland here leaves Stephen caught at the intersection of differential and often contradictory changes in the organization of social, sexual, psychic and familial life.[12] Unable to access the sort of identity drunkenly mourned by his father, Stephen finds his very sense of self dissected in the amphitheatre as he struggles to master languages that no longer cohere. His disorientation, furthermore, is not a purely individual or fully psychological experience, but the product of modernity's reorganization of time and space. This brief episode in *A Portrait* is, in fact, nearly unique in Joyce's work not only because it is set outside Dublin and its suburbs, but because it directly records an extended journey. The change of scene, in fact, is quite abrupt as we move from Stephen standing amid the 'horse piss and rotted straw' of Dublin across a line of asterisks to find him seated 'once more' beside his father in a carriage in Kingsbridge Station, the main terminus of Ireland's southern railways (P, 86). Just getting our own bearings here is difficult, since that temporal marker 'once more' seems to have no actual antecedent in the text. When was the last time Stephen sat beside his father on a train and why is that scene not narrated? It is possible that the last time Stephen took a railway journey with his father was when he was sent to Clongowes Wood – a connection reinforced by Stephen's allusion to 'his childish wonder of years before' as 'the train steamed out of the station' (P, 86). This may also explain why Stephen ends up attempting to map himself in Cork as he did at Clongowes, the repetition suggesting that there is something risky and disorienting in life outside of metropolitan Dublin. Then there is the railway journey itself, so evocative of the 'perverse modernity' that matches telegraph poles to the depopulated countryside Stephen surveys: a seemingly foreign country that is nevertheless his own.

The unique quality of this section demands close consideration. Why record this journey and no other? And why Cork rather than say Paris, London or Galway? Biography, of course, offers one easy answer: this is merely a retelling of one of the trips Joyce himself made with his father in 1894. Cork, however, was more than just the ancestral home of the Joyces. As Ireland's 'second city' it was a modern and relatively wealthy metropolis with a customs-house, a major university and a bustling port. It was, furthermore, deeply associated with nationalist and liberationist causes, playing a far more vital role in the Irish anti-imperial imaginary than Dublin (at least until the Easter Uprising focused attention once more on the capital city). Unlike Galway, furthermore, it was not a part of the Gaeltacht and could only very loosely be associated with the romanticized 'West' of Ireland so important to revivalist fantasies.

Most significantly, Cork was also deeply affected by the Famine – far more so than metropolitan Dublin. This event – so distinctive of Ireland's 'perverse modernity' – is curiously absent from Simon Dedalus's memories of the place. The Illustrated London News of 1847 records the horrors of the event as they unfolded in Cork, describing the 15,000 people in

9

the county deemed destitute and the families who staggered into the city to take soup or enter the workhouses.[13] As a key terminus on what Howes (borrowing a term from Paul Gilroy) calls the 'Irish Atlantic', Cork was also the largest point of departure for Irish emigration to North America.[14] It was through this city's ports more than any other that the Famine and post-Famine generations passed in their flight from the blighted countryside and a colonial modernity that left them starved, grief-stricken and homeless. Simon, of course, would have been too young to witness these events first-hand, but they do not register in his history or memory of the place at all. Instead, he recalls the handsome and sporting image of his own father who rode to hounds and turned the heads of women throughout the city. He takes Stephen on a tour of the university, his favourite pubs and his old haunts, but nowhere does this otherwise ardent nationalist and cheap sentimentalist evoke the memory of the Famine and its close ties to Cork.

Although this catastrophe and its after-effects may not be directly recorded in the narrative, it nevertheless hovers just beneath the surface, emerging first in Stephen's description of the trip itself. Looking out the window of his railway carriage, he sees 'the unpeopled fields and the closed cottages' of the Ireland beyond Dublin, an image which – like the word 'foetus' – brings to life disturbing ghosts of an unmanageable history: 'The neighborhood of unseen sleepers filled him with strange dread as though they could harm him; and he prayed that the day might come quickly' (P, 87). Like the ghost of Michel Furey in 'The Dead' or the students who suddenly surround Stephen in the amphitheatre, these spectres mark his traumatic encounter with a painfully fractured modernity. Traces of the Famine and of the waves of Irish emigration it spawned surface not just here, but throughout this short section of the text. Stephen, for example, thinks insistently of his own 'dispossession', a term that denotes his father's failures and his own disrupted sense of self. Yet this loaded term makes him an heir to the Famine generations as well who walked away from farms and cottages to this same city of Cork.

We can see additional traces of such unsought exile in the song Simon sings about leaving for 'Amerikay', a tune that Stephen says is 'much prettier than any of your other come-all-yous' (P, 88) and it potently links

Ireland itself to an old, abandoned love. Later in the section, Simon again inadvertently touches on this same theme when he tells Stephen that his father once offered him a cigar from an 'American captain' – a captain likely in command of a boat of emigrants (P, 92). Stephen's subsequent attempt to calm his enflamed imagination by reciting his geographical location also suggests the sense of disorientation provoked by the barely suppressed traces of the Famine. After all, his younger self first makes the imaginative list stretching from the Class of Elements at Clongowes Wood to the Universe when he 'could not learn the names of places in America' (P, 15). 'They were all different places that had those different names', he thinks to himself, yet they nevertheless have a vital connection to Ireland itself – indeed constitute part of his own national identity as somewhere within the 'Irish Atlantic'. This same geographical dispersion is evoked once more in the opening page of *Finnegans Wake*, which explicitly links Ireland to America where 'topsawyer's rocks by the stream Oconee exaggerated themselse to Laurens County's gorgios while they went doubling their mumper all the time' (*FW*, 3.7–9). Thus, when Stephen recites his geographical location in Cork, the exercise seems increasing fraught since, instead of a great chain of being stretching from his body to the universe, he instead finds only transitive 'names' that cannot fix him properly in a national space. Indeed, Stephen (like the city of Cork itself) is poised here at the intersection where the promise of a distant America meets the disaster of the Famine, unable finally to assimilate or reconcile the competing claims of these densely entwined yet seemingly irreconcilable modernities.

Struggling to create a sense of self clearly located in space and time, Stephen's thoughts finally turn from his own father and the useless incantation of the names 'Simon and Stephen and Victoria' to an acknowledgement of his interpretive predicament: 'He recalled only names: Dante, Parnell, Clane, Clongowes. A little boy had been taught geography by an old woman who kept two brushes in her wardrobe. Then he had been sent away from home to a college' (P, 92, 93). This epiphanic moment finds Stephen suddenly aware of the differential modernities in which he is lodged, the names he recalls all encoding discrete aspects of a lifeworld that simply cannot be integrated into a single and self-consistent narrative. At this moment of crisis, he returns to one of the formative experiences of his youth: the death of Parnell (himself the MP for Cork), which he had imaginatively shared in the infirmary at Clongowes:

> There had been no mass for the dead in the chapel and no procession. He had not died but he had faded out like a film in the sun. He had been lost or had wandered out of existence for he no longer existed. How strange to think of him passing out of existence in such a way, not by death but by being lost and forgotten somewhere in the universe! (P, 93)

As in the *Wake's* 'fadograph', here too space, history and memory all collide with one another in Stephen's imagination, each entangled in a spectral array of modernities that cannot be fully synthesized or integrated either by the aspiring artist or even by the text itself.

Joyce's works remain so powerful and so immediate because they evocatively place us in the same difficult condition as Stephen in this brief episode: at once open to the promise and the terror of a lifeworld that can be neither fixed nor foreclosed. This unquestionably makes his works extremely difficult, precisely because they attempt to operate within and across a fragmented series of modernities, some as desperately archaic as others are startlingly immediate. In doing so, however, they open up new visions of our own encounter with the past and present as we too seek to organize and simultaneously to embrace the 'fugitive' contingencies Baudelaire so presciently identified. The essays in this volume provide an introduction to Joyce's major works and the critical contexts which have shaped their reception. In so doing, they also engage Joyce's disparate modernities, each holding a distinct and carefully ground prism up to the works in order to reveal their dazzling richness. The individual studies create distinct images of Joyce's writings and offer simultaneously a revision of the modernities in which these fictions emerged and through which they continue to pass.

* * *

The collection begins by looking at Joyce's own complicated life and the ways in which it was so deftly woven into his fiction. From the writer's earliest essays and sketches to the daunting complexities of *Ulysses* and *Finnegans Wake*, Bruce Stewart traces the writer's ongoing fascination with subjectivity and the powers of the artistic mind. Stephen Dedalus in *A Portrait* struggles to develop a method whereby he might somehow capture 'the reality of experience', the very instability and contradiction, that is, of the shifting modernities seeming to pull the self in so many directions. In Stewart's own portrait of Joyce as an artist, this project emerges as the persistent attempt to 'trace the *curve* or *rhythm* of the artist as he emerges through the workings of his own immanent development'. This interplay between artist and text, between subject and object, between psychology and history itself forms the essence of Joyce's aesthetic project – and makes the artist's biography itself a crucial part of the art he creates. But mapping the contours of Joyce's biography is difficult, in part, because so much of his work deliberately muddies the boundaries between fiction and autobiography. In the major and minor works alike beginning with *A Portrait of the Artist*, we encounter figures like Stephen, Bloom and Shem who all echo aspects of the author's own life. In the short stories of *Dubliners*, however, a clearer sense of distance between author and text persists as Joyce seeks 'to betray the soul of that hemiplegia or paralysis which many consider a city' (LI, 55).

In 'The Curious Language of *Dubliners*', David G. Wright explores the ways in which this collection at once plunges into the fragmented modernities of the colonial city even as Joyce attempts to shield himself from its contradictions. By carefully controlling the language and form of both the individual stories and the collection as a whole, Wright contends, Joyce develops a series of narrative strategies designed to satirize the desires of his first publisher who sought something that would not 'shock the readers'. Operating at a carefully cultivated distance from his characters and from the city itself, each story forms part of a 'mosaic', which only the reader and Joyce are allowed to see as a whole. Indeed, as Wright explains, 'the series of stories suggests that such social inadequacies thrive in a situation where nobody looks outside immediate contexts for a solution'. Only Joyce's readers, however, are finally permitted this commanding, authorial view and the collection itself marks the last time we are offered so singular and integral a view of Dublin's modernity.

The narrative voice so characteristic of *Dubliners* survives only into the now fragmentary remains of *Stephen Hero*, an autobiographical novel started in 1904 then abandoned three years later. Joyce began revising it with astonishing speed into the novel that would become *A Portrait of the Artist as a Young Man*, and in doing so he opens himself and the text to the very contradictions so carefully suppressed in the short stories. Satire effectively gives way to irony and we find ourselves at once too close and too far from Stephen, struggling to figure out whether he is indeed a portrait of the artist or another hemiplegic Dubliner. Multiple interpretive frames emerge simultaneously that become increasingly disorienting since they radiate out to implicate not only Edwardian Dublin but the disparate modernities which characterize our own reading moment. As Kevin J.H. Dettmar insists in 'The Materiality and Historicity of Language in *A Portrait of the Artist as a Young Man*', these multiple frames capture the dynamic forces shaping the emerging consciousness of Stephen Dedalus, but they also inject a destabilizing irony into the novel itself. Like Stephen himself, we find ourselves pulled simultaneously into an array of competing interpretive frames, the reading experience riven by some of the same differential forces that decimate the self-confident Stephen on that trip to Cork.

The ironies of *A Portrait* were themselves not always so readily visible as they are now, and as Dettmar notes, they first began to emerge only when the surviving pieces of *Stephen Hero* were published in 1944. That these drafts of an earlier text proved so influential, in fact, suggests that any attempt to 'revision' Joyce must itself negotiate the complexities of the canon itself. After all, even as we celebrate the unique power and vision of works like *Ulysses* and *Finnegans Wake*, there remain those neglected works – the poems, a play, a notebook sketch – which are generally ignored or marginalized. A full understanding of Joyce's modernities, however, requires that we think carefully about these works, as Miranda Hickman does here in '"Not love-verses at all, I perceive": Joyce's Minor Works'. Indeed, the works she considers offer a powerful counterpoint to the coolly ironic Joyce of *A Portrait*, exposing the differential effects of a sexual modernity which 'distil out … a non-ironic "other" Joyce, a kind of alterity, perhaps even a kind of "minor literature", within the Joycean canon'. *Exiles*, *Chamber Music* and *Giacomo Joyce* may be anomalous texts, but this is less a sign of their failure than a symptom of the anomaly of modernity itself.

Joyce's modernities coalesce most powerfully in *Ulysses*, his epic of modern life, which captures what Andrew Gibson calls the author's staggering 'will to modernity'.[15] Yet this book – perhaps the most famous and influential novel of the last century – simultaneously remains for many readers a forbidding text, shrouded in a cloak of difficulty that is only further darkened by the vast array of guides, introductions and readers offering a way through it. In 'The Complex Simplicity of *Ulysses*', Michael Groden argues that the text's challenges are constitutive of its modernity, enacting an endlessly unfolding dialectic between freedom and form, liberation and constraint. The book itself relates a relatively simple story about a day in the life of Leopold Bloom, his wife (Molly) and an aspiring artist named Stephen Dedalus. Moving through Edwardian Dublin, these characters encounter a world structured as much by the contingency of modernity itself as by the fixity of epic. We are constantly challenged to sort the details of everyday life, piecing together fleeting meanings from them that are constantly open to revision, evolution and even epiphany. We only err, in fact, by imagining that we have somehow mastered the text since, as Groden argues, *Ulysses* itself is 'based on rich ambiguities that cannot be reduced to clear answers'. The pleasure lies more in the pursuit of meaning than in its arrest, and the work's difficulty is less a deliberate challenge than a daring attempt to encode the endless visions and revisions of modernity itself.

Ulysses continues to lure readers, in part because, despite its formal challenges, it still retains the formal apparatus of a novel: stable characters developing through a recognizable and distinctly human time and space. *Finnegans Wake*, however, the book which absorbed fifteen years of Joyce's life and closed his eerily complete body of work, offers no such compensations. Far from difficult, it has long been seen as an essentially impossible text: the first work of an emerging postmodernism for some and for others the absurd death rattle of a hopelessly abstract modernism. In '*Finnegans Wake*: Some Assembly Required', Tim Conley links it to another strain of Joyce's multifaceted modernity – an insistent and faithful Utopianism. 'Because', he contends, 'the *Wake* attempts to emulate a collective unconscious, so its ideal reader is necessarily a collective capable of dreaming its dream'. This collective, however, is inherently unstable, the dream it weaves evoking a sense of replenished hope that is as fleeting as it is redemptive. In assembling the text together as readers – either in groups or by opening ourselves to the chorus of voices embedded in the book's seemingly endless and 'omnivocal' language – we enact the teleogical faith of modernity in an ever-expanding future while simultaneously encountering its inevitable contradiction and collapse.

As I have insisted through this introduction, Joyce is lodged in a series of *discontinuous* modernities, many of which extend well beyond the books themselves and into the ever-evolving process of reading and circulation. This collection therefore concludes with three essays which broadly survey some crucial aspects of that reception, beginning with Christine van Boheemen-Saaf's 'Joyce in Theory/Theory in Joyce'. A wide-ranging survey of key theoretical approaches to Joyce's work, it begins in the Paris of the late 1940s – where some of the initial roots were set down that would later emerge in the work of Lacan, Derrida and other post-structuralists – and concludes with recent ethical, queer and cultural studies models. For new readers, of course, this very critical diversity makes Joyce's work seem that much more daunting as library catalogues, information databases and web searches reveal the vast scholarly web in which even a single book like *Ulysses* is now lodged. This may, I argue elsewhere, give us good reason 'to hate Joyce properly',[16] but it simultaneously illustrates this volume's larger claim: these texts so insistently multiply new modes of reading and thinking precisely because we can still recognize ourselves in the blurring lines of the Joycean 'fadograph'. Rather than anticipating aspects of our modernity, in other words, his texts preserve fragments of a lifeworld we continue to fracture and reassemble.

These fragments can be pulled into a rich array of constellations, and Katherine Mullin in 'Joyce's Bodies' emphasizes the importance of the physical, sexual body as a key site for exposing the contradictions of a differential modernity. Bloom's famous trip to the outhouse at the beginning of *Ulysses* and the book's perhaps even more scandalous record of his masturbation on Sandymount Strand provocatively reveal the ways in which even the body becomes diffused across a tangled array of social, political and psychic networks, each pulling it into different shapes and configurations. Exploring the 'the complex and modulating relationship between bodies and texts', Mullin both traces the intricate careers of Joyce's bodies and insists on the importance of these bodies in fashioning his career as a modernist writer. Identifying what she calls a strand of 'low modernism', in fact, the essay insists on the vitality of Joyce's engagement with the body and the raw power it still retains to upset our critical attempts to discipline it.

James Joyce: Visions and Revisions concludes by turning from Joyce's physical bodies to the body of Joyce's work as Aaron Jaffe, in 'Joyce's Afterlives' asks 'Why didn't he win the Nobel Prize?' This may seem like a puerile question about public honours, but as the essay argues, it reveals the constitutive role Joyce – as both author and icon – plays in the maintenance of literary prestige. In considering how Joyce's name came 'to serve as a leading synecdoche for the kind of world-class literary value ... enshrined *par excellence* in the Nobel', Jaffe moves deftly between an array of different cultural, historical and textual registers from the scenes of prize-winning in Joyce's works to the speeches of various Nobel laureates. In so doing, he traces 'the drift of Joyce's name in a post-literary social system', opening up a new set of connections and discontinuities between Joyce's modernities and our own. In this essay, as in the others, contradictions again abound, but they are of the same kind that afflict Stephen as he struggles to fix himself in place while standing in Cork. That is, they are the very stuff not only of the Joycean aesthetic, but of his own engagement with a fractured modernity that, although it may be everywhere, is nevertheless constitutively unable to congeal into a single structure or pattern. Trying to fix Joyce in his 'afterlife', therefore, is as impossible a task as fixing the texts themselves. Instead, we are left with the Penelopean task of weaving and unweaving the 'nowhemoe' of Joyce's modernities – as well as our own.

NOTES

1. T.S. Eliot, '*Ulysses*, Order, and Myth', *The Dial*, 75 (1923), p.480.
2. See A. Bazin, *What Is Cinema?* (Berkeley, CA: University of California Press, 1967).
3. C. Baudelaire, 'The Painter of Modern Life', in *The Painter of Modern Life and Other Essays*, trans. and ed. J. Mayre (New York: Dacapo Press, 1964), p.13.
4. A. Giddens, *The Consequences of Modernity* (Palo Alto, CA: Stanford University Press, 1990), p.51.
5. D. Gaonkar, 'On Alternative Modernities', in *Alternative Modernities*, ed. D. Gaonkar (Durham, NC: Duke University Press, 2001), p.1.

6. H. Kenner, 'The Making of the Modernist Canon', *Chicago Review*, 34, 2 (1984), pp.53–7.

7. S. Stanford Friedman, 'Periodizing Modernism: Postcolonial Modernities and the Space/Time Borders of Modernist Studies', *Modernism/Modernity*, 13, 3 (2006), p.433.

8. See, M. Weber, 'Politics as a Vocation', in *From Max Weber: Essays in Sociology*, ed. Hans Gerth and C. Wright Mills (Oxford: Oxford University Press, 1958), pp.77–128; J. Habermas, *Toward a Rational Society: Student Protest, Science and Politics* (Boston, MA: Beacon Press, 1970); and P. Bourdieu, 'The Market for Symbolic Goods', in *The Field of Cultural Production* (New York: Columbia University Press, 1993), pp.112–41.

9. For a discussion of clock-time and its implications for Joyce's work, see L.E.J. Hornby, 'Visual Clockwork: Photographic Time and the Instant in 'Proteus', *James Joyce Quarterly*, 42–43 (2004–6), pp.49–68.

10. L. Gibbons, '"Spaces of Time Through Times of Space": Joyce, Ireland and Colonial Modernity', *Field Day Review*, 1 (2005), p.79.

11. R. Ellmann, *James Joyce* (New York: Oxford University Press, 1982), p.3.

12. M. Howes, '"Goodbye Ireland I'm going to Gort": Geography, Scale, and Narrating the Nation', in *Semicolonial Joyce*, ed. D. Attridge and M. Howes (Cambridge: Cambridge University Press, 2000), p.64.

13. *Illustrated London News*, 16 January 1847. For a useful collection of such articles see http://departments.vassar.edu/~sttaylor/FAMINE/ILN/.

14. Howes, '"Goodbye Ireland I'm going to Gort"', p.65. See also P. Gilroy, *The Black Atlantic: Modernity and Double Consciousness* (Cambridge, MA: Harvard University Press, 1993).

15. A. Gibson, *James Joyce* (London: Reaktion Books, 2006), p.15.

16. S. Latham, 'Hating Joyce Properly', *Journal of Modern Literature*, 26, 1 (2002), pp.119–31.

CHAPTER TWO

A Short Literary Life of James Joyce

BRUCE STEWART

I: THE DUBLIN YEARS

James Joyce was born on 2 February 1882 in the respectable Dublin suburb of Rathgar, the son of John Stanislaus Joyce, who had inherited £500 a year from building interests in Cork. Joyce *père* could claim remote descent from an Anglo-Norman family and a nearer kinship, through his mother, with Daniel O'Connell, the political champion of Catholic rights in colonial Ireland. He was a gifted singer and raconteur, and – like his fictional counterpart Simon Dedalus – latterly a 'praiser of his own past' (P, 245). He commenced medicine in Queen's College, Cork, but devoted himself to amateur dramatics and sport instead, shining at both. In his mid-20s his widowed mother removed him to Monkstown, Co. Dublin, to curtail his Fenian associations. In 1877 the capital he had put into a distillery venture at Chapelizod was embezzled by a partner named Alleyn, but John was soon appointed to a post in the Dublin Rates Office in 1880, having managed a polling victory for the Liberals. By the time the post was abolished in 1893 he had seriously dented his pension through misdemeanours including a trip to Cork to canvas his tenants for Parnell. In the year of his appointment he married Mary Jane ("May") Murray, the daughter of a vintner from Co. Longford and his junior by ten years. The union was disapproved of on both sides. In later years John Joyce took to proclaiming that he had demeaned himself, but his troubles were of his own making. In *Stephen Hero* we are told, 'he knew his own ruin had been his own handiwork, but he had talked himself into believing that it had been the handiwork of others', and also that '(h)e had his son's distaste for responsibility without his son's courage' (SH, 101). In a letter of 1904 Joyce similarly told to his future partner Nora Barnacle that his home life had been 'the usual middle-class affair ruined by spendthrift habits which I have inherited' (SL, 25–7). At his father's death in 1931, he called him 'the silliest man I ever knew and yet cruelly shrewd' besides being the source of his own 'good tenor voice, and an extravagant licentious disposition' (SL, 360–1).

By comparison with the large place occupied by his father in Joyce's works his mother's is distinctly narrow, if only because she died on 13 August 1903 some time before the events of Ulysses on 16 June 1904.[1] While John Joyce provided an increasingly groundless air of grandeur, it was May Joyce who supplied the familial network of his childhood. Like others in her family she played the piano and was cultured in the way of the newly emergent Irish Catholic middle class. Her Flynn aunts, who would provide the models for the Miss Morkans in 'The Dead', taught music at Usher's Island. Joyce later told his friend Arthur Power that his youth had been 'exceptionally violent; painful and violent'.[2] It had been more so for his mother, who endured fifteen pregnancies and bore six boys and six girls at numerous addresses on the family's downward course. She suffered the death of the first and last in infancy and lost another, George, from peritonitis before dying from cancer of the liver at 44. In 1894, soon after the death in infancy of the last-born child Freddie, Joyce had to stop his father beating her by jumping on his back. Yet John Joyce was not the sole source of grief. Writing to Nora on the same occasion in 1904 Joyce said: 'My mother was slowly killed, I think, by my father's ill-treatment, by years of trouble, and by my cynical frankness of conduct', adding characteristically that he 'cursed the system which had made her a victim' (SL, 25). A loving mother, she was awed by her son's intelligence and saddened by his apostasy. In Ulysses she makes a gruesome appearance as a 'corpsechewer' (U, 15.4213) but is more justly represented by her wish for Stephen on his first departure from Ireland: 'She prays I may learn in my own life and away from home and friends what the heart is and what it feels' (P, 257).

When Joyce was 5 the family moved to a large house on the esplanade in Bray and the following year he was sent to Clongowes Wood College, a Jesuit boarding school in Co. Kildare that was deemed the best in Ireland. There he suffered from homesickness as well as the injustice recorded in *A Portrait of the Artist as a Young Man* when he was 'pandy-batted' on account of broken glasses. In taking his grievance to the Rector Father John Conmee, he established a principle that would serve a lifetime: always confront authority at the highest level. Joyce's return home from school following an attack of fever coincided with the death of Parnell in autumn 1891 and also with a 'sudden flight from the comfort and revery of Blackrock' (P, 67), the first of many moon-lit migrations prompted by the family's growing financial distress. At Bray Joyce had witnessed the dinner-table quarrel about Parnell memorialized in the first chapter of *A Portrait*; at Blackrock he wrote 'Et Tu, Healy', an elegy attacking Tim Healy, the man who ousted Parnell from the Irish Parliamentary Party. His father had this specimen of literary Parnellism printed and claimed to have sent a copy to the Vatican though none survive today. By the end of 1892 the family was living at Fitzgibbon Street adjacent to the Nighttown area of *Ulysses*. Like Stephen Dedalus, Joyce was 'cast down by the dull phenomenon of the Dublin' (P, 80) but soon rallied by making 'a skeleton map' (68) for use on lengthy treks through the city while he 'strove to pierce to the motive centre of its ugliness' (SH, 33), as Joyce would have it later on.

In Blackrock he had conducted his own education with assistance from his mother who set tests on the books he read. In the city he briefly attended the Christian Brothers but was rescued after a chance meeting between his father and Father Conmee resulting in entrance to the Jesuit day school Belvedere College for the gifted boy and his younger brother Stanislaus. There Joyce maintained his reputation for brilliance, shining in English, Latin and modern languages. In 1894 he won an award in the Intermediate Examinations and took his parents to a fashionable restaurant on the proceeds. His piety resulted in his being elected Prefect in Sodality of Blessed Virgin in December 1895. When probed about a possible vocation for the priesthood by Father William Henry, the then rector, he reached a realization about himself something like the one that Joyce attributes to Stephen Dedalus in *A Portrait*: '(h)is destiny was to be elusive of social or religious orders ... to learn his own wisdom apart from others ... wandering among the snares of the world [which] were its ways of sin' (P, 165). A scarifying retreat conducted by

Father James Cullen soon brought him back to religious devotions but the rebellion against 'nationality, language (and) religion'[3] – the dominant forces in Irish life according to Stephen Dedalus – had already begun. (The corresponding 'weapons' of 'silence, exile and cunning' (P, 251) that Stephen adopts against those forces were purloined from Lucien de Rubempré in Honoré Balzac's novel *Splendeurs et misères des courtisanes*, 1847.[4]) In *A Portrait* the sermon that terrifies Stephen follows hard on his first encounter with a prostitute; in real life it was not until the summer he left school in 1898 that Joyce lost his virginity in this fashion, but the connection between sexual experience and freedom of spirit was nonetheless fundamental to his mentality at this and later times.

Joyce's final school year was filled with extra-curricular reading including works by Thomas Hardy, George Meredith and G.B. Shaw, which he met with in the Capel Street Library or the Dublin book-barrows. On encountering the works of Henrik Ibsen he felt his spirit merge with the most shocking modernist of the age 'in a moment of radiant simultaneity' (SH, 41). Henceforth his mind was to be firmly set on literature as his heart was to be set on liberation from the 'stale maxims of the Jesuits' (SH, 39). Unlike Stephen, however, the schoolboy Joyce was on good terms with his contemporaries – notably Richard and Eugene Sheehy, sons of a nationalist MP whose home on North Great George's Street was the scene of charades and burlesques of well-known stage productions. One of the Sheehy sisters, Mary, is generally regarded as the prototype of Emma Clery in *Stephen Hero* and her counterpart E.C. in *A Portrait* (though this is by no means certain).[5] Yet Joyce's dealings with sisters of his peers were constrained by an unspoken understanding that his family life did not admit room for thoughts of marriage. Ultimately this meant that he was more likely to form a permanent relationship beneath his social class. Already he was tending in that direction, though any alteration in his conduct or disposition went unnoticed by his teachers since he only fell out with the Sodality when he refused to sit the bishops' Cathecism Examination, preferring to study for the Senior Intermediate instead. He must not have studied very hard since he took a prize as usual but did not win an exhibition. It was a bequest from a maternal uncle, Phillip McCann, that funded his entrance to the Royal University of Ireland (later University College, Dublin), a Jesuit-run establishment on St Stephen's Green, in October 1898.

Joyce read Modern Languages along with Latin and Logic and graduated with an ordinary pass in 1901. To his contemporaries he seemed an extraordinarily self-possessed young man pursuing an independent syllabus with the assistance of the National Library of Ireland on nearby Kildare Street.[6] Although increasingly agnostic, he continued to make his Easter duties until the sudden death of his younger brother George in May 1902 when he parted with the Church forever – except insofar as the 'chemistry' of 'his own rare thoughts' resembled the 'slow growth and change of rite and dogma' he had known so well amongst the Jesuits, as Stephen reflects in Ulysses (1.652). This affinity resulted in 'a genuine predisposition in favour of all but the premises of scholasticism' (SH, 72); yet, contrary to the impression in A Portrait, Joyce's knowledge of theology was no greater than that of his contemporaries since, as Constantine Curran recalled, all the 'sentences' he quoted from St Thomas Aquinas were ready to hand in John Rickaby's General Metaphysics (1888), a textbook known to all Jesuit pupils.[7] The English empiricists had no attraction for him yet he read neo-Hegelians such as Bernard Bosanquet with attention.[8] One result was the strong Hegelian tincture of 'Ecce Homo', an essay about a painting by Michael Munkácsy exhibited at the Royal Hibernian Academy in 1899. Munkácsy's busy account of Christ brought before Pontius Pilate is taken as proof that 'it is a mistake to limit drama to the stage' (CW, 32). In this Joyce expressed a very modern antipathy to the theory about the separate domains of pictorial and dramatic arts canonically expressed in Lessing's 'Laocoön'. He displayed a precocious command of the new philosophical idiom in writing that 'drama is strife, evolution, movement, in whatever way unfolded' while arguing that it exists in any work of art 'as an independent thing, conditioned but not controlled by its scene' (CW, 32). More importantly, he shows himself unwilling to embrace any form of art that is not fundamentally dialectical or that offers opinions in place of dynamic images of living consciousness. In this sense Ulysses and Finnegans Wake are Hegelian works of art.

On 20 January 1900 Joyce enlarged on these ideas in a paper called 'Drama and Life' delivered before the students' Literary and Historical Society. According to Stephen Hero – into which he substantially transcribed the essay – his aim was 'to define his own position for himself'

(SH, 72). The whole can be read as a homage to Ibsen whether in its strictures on a 'boyish instinct to dive under the blankets at the mention of the bogey of realism' (CW, 44) or its insistence that we must accept life 'as we see it before our eyes, men and women as we meet them in the real world, not as we apprehend it in the world of faery' (45). In such a view, 'literary drama' is to 'dramatic drama' as 'literature' is to 'drama' (40) since only the last-named arises 'spontaneously out of life and is coeval with it' (43). Soon after this, Joyce defined his position for a much wider audience in an unsolicited review of *When We Dead Awaken* that appeared as 'Ibsen's New Drama' in *Fortnightly Review* (1 April 1900) – a coup that caused the Dublin literati to notice him. Joyce took his father on a spree to London on the fee and paid a visit to Ibsen's translator, William Archer, in the process. When Archer told him that the playwright had liked the article, Joyce wrote to Ibsen in his own language, mugged up for the occasion. In August he sent Archer a play of his own entitled 'A Brilliant Career'. This was dedicated 'To My Own Soul' and dealt with a young doctor's struggle against an epidemic in Mullingar, where Joyce travelled with his father about that time. Archer condemned the characters as lacking individuation and was equally discouraging about 'Shine and Dark', a collection of poems Joyce put together in September 1901. Nor did his translations of plays by Gerhart Hauptmann secure the contract from the Irish Literary Theatre that he hoped for.

In future years he would write both poetry and drama, but prose was to be his *métier* – albeit informed to an exceptional degree by elements of those others. His growing admiration for the poetry of W.B. Yeats prevented him, in any case, from attempting to compete in that medium.[9] Fiction-writing came to him almost accidentally, beginning with the first 'epiphanies', a species of brief prose records of things seen and heard that he began to collect in early 1901,[10] and later continuing with his 'epicleti', as he called the first stories of *Dubliners* commissioned by *The Irish Homestead* in July 1904 (SL, 22).[11] When Joyce inserted the putatively (though not actually) first 'epiphany' into *Stephen Hero*, he defined it as 'a sudden spiritual manifestation, whether in the vulgarity of speech or of gesture or in a memorable phase of the mind itself', adding that 'it was for the man of letters to record these epiphanies with extreme care, seeing that they themselves are the most delicate and evanescent of moments' (SH, 188). In the immediately ensuing episode Stephen describes to Cranly the manner in which a given object 'achieves its epiphany' (or *epiphanises*):[12] 'when the parts are adjusted to the special point we recognize that it is that thing which it is' (SH, 190). For some reason – certainly an important one – the term *epiphany* is absent from the otherwise closely corresponding passage in *A Portrait of the Artist*.

In October 1901 Joyce issued 'The Day of the Rabblement', a pamphlet attacking the populist tendency of the National Literary Theatre. This was occasioned by the news that the company would produce a Gaelic play by Douglas Hyde and a stage version of Irish myth by George Moore and Yeats, contrary to its stated policy of bringing the best continental drama to an Irish audience. Joyce's polemic shared its cover with another by Francis Skeffington on a feminist theme, both having been rejected by the college journal *St Stephens'*. In 'James Clarence Mangan', a college paper given on 15 February 1902, Joyce lamented that Ireland's *poète maudit* had written for an audience that only cared about political injustice – the 'nightmare of history' (U, 1.652) from which Stephen Dedalus seeks to awake in *Ulysses*. In arguing that Mangan is 'the type of his race' whom as '(h)istory encloses ... so straitly that even his fiery moments do not set him free from it' (CW, 81), Joyce took the opportunity to state his reasons for refusing to jeer at Yeats's *The Countess Cathleen* (1899) as the other students had done at its premiere in May 1899. Here his phrasing echoes their rhetoric in a newspaper letter that Joyce had refused to sign accusing Yeats of portraying 'the type of our people (as) a loathesome brood of apostates'.[13] In *A Portrait* Joyce would conclude the matter to his own satisfaction by identifying the 'type' of the Irish race with 'the batlike soul' of the Irish countrywomen 'waking to the consciousness of itself' (P, 86–7) in an illicit sexual encounter. The kind of liberation that counted for him was psychological rather than political, the former occurring before the latter.

The Mangan paper concludes with this *caveat* for nationalists: 'The poet who hurls his anger against tyrants would establish upon the future an intimate and far more cruel tyranny' (CW, 83). It also contains a famous distinction between the 'romantic temper' and the 'classical temper' as between two traditions that direct their gaze respectively towards 'insensible figures' and 'present things' (74). W.B. Yeats and George ('Æ') Russell were the chief contemporary exponents of romanticism in Dublin and Joyce was keen to set a boundary between himself and them. He also wished to impress them with his abilities, and in August 1902 he walked across Dublin at a late hour to introduce himself to Russell at his Rathgar home, afterwards providing him with copies of epiphanies and at least one chapter of *Stephen Hero* in summer 1904. Russell listened patiently before telling him that he had not enough chaos in him to be a poet.[14] He did, however, arrange a meeting with Yeats that resulted in Joyce's telling his elder that he was too old for help (Yeats was 37). The literary set snubbed Joyce socially though he did on one occasion crash a literary evening given by Lady Gregory. George Moore called Joyce 'nothing but a beggar'[15] yet he nevertheless turned to Russell, Yeats and Lady Gregory for subsidy when he decided to study medicine in Paris. In a letter to the last-named he wrote: '(T)hough I seem to have been driven out of my country here as a misbeliever I have found no man yet with a faith like mine' (SL, 8).

Joyce reached Paris on 3 December only to discover that his qualifications were not acceptable at the Faculté de médecine. After recording some epiphanies and a meeting with Joseph Casey (a Fenian-in-exile and his father's former friend) he returned home for Christmas on a ticket that his father paid for with a further mortgage on his pension. Back in Dublin, Joyce formed a friendship with Oliver St John Gogarty, an upper middle-class Catholic whose educational march had taken him from Clongowes to Trinity College, Dublin, and thence to Oxford – and onwards into *Ulysses* where he models for the 'gay betrayer' Buck Mulligan (U, 1.405). In the new year Joyce set out for Paris once again and took a reader's ticket for the Bibliothèque Nationale before moving to the smaller Bibliothèque de Ste Geneviève. There he concentrated on Aristotle's *Psychology* (*De Anima*) in J. Barthélemy Sainte-Hilaire's French translation of 1847.[16] The fruits of this research would fill some pages of his 'Paris Notebook' and feed the aesthetic theory associated with the term 'epiphany' in *Stephen Hero*.[17] His inevitable return was precipitated by a telegram of 10 April 1903 with the words: 'MOTHER DYING COME HOME FATHER'. The ensuing months were grim. At one point John Joyce shouted at his wife, 'If you can't get well, die and be damned to you!'[18]

May Joyce died on 13 August but not before her eldest son had refused her request to take the sacraments or kneel at her deathbed – an intimate *non serviam* that shocks Buck Mulligan in *Ulysses* ('You could have knelt down ... when you dying mother asked you' [1.91]). In the ensuing months Joyce fell more and more deeply into a dissolute way of life involving visits to the 'kips' with Gogarty, who maliciously regaled friends with accounts of his behaviour. Compared to well-fed Gogarty, Joyce was ill-equipped for such a life and collapsed drunk on one occasion in the lane approaching the Mechanics' Hall where the Literary Theatre was in rehearsal.

At the beginning of 1904 he was desultorily attending classes in law and medicine along with others in Irish taught by Patrick Pearse, whose nationalist hostility to the English language repelled him. He also paid for singing lessons and narrowly missed first prize at the Feis Ceol, giving way to John McCormack. Though, like Stephen in *Ulysses*, he may have thought himself a '(s)eabedabbled, fallen, weltering' (9.954) after his Icarian flight to Paris, in reality he was about to embark on his true career. On 7 January he composed an autobiographical essay of two and a half thousand words entitled, 'A Portrait of the Artist', using a ruled exercise-book belonging to his sister Mabel.[19] This he submitted to the short-lived journal *Dana*, only to have it rejected by John Eglinton and Fred Ryan on the grounds that – as Eglinton wrote afterwards – they would not publish what they could not understand.[20] (Ironically, the essay was partly modelled on Eglinton's *Two Essays on the Remnant*.[21]) In narrative terms, the 1904 'Portrait' essay sketches a young man's passage from religious thralldom to intellectual independence. According to the irreverent trope that Joyce develops in it, that journey is made through 'the gates of Assisi' – meaning the love of nature associated with St Francis – into the 'fair courts of life'.[22] The climactic moment occurs when the anonymous protagonist encounters 'the wonder of mortal beauty' (P, 175) in the shape of a wading girl, or girls, on Dollymount Strand. Through this encounter and another set among 'yellow gaslamps', the budding artist advances from loss of sexual innocence to aesthetic self-determination along a route essentially akin to Stephen's quest for full artistic selfhood in the finished novel, *A Portrait of the Artist as a Young Man*. On the way, he experiences moods of an expressly literary nature suggestive of the fin de siècle excesses W.B. Yeats had described in 'The Tables of the Law' – a story Joyce knew by heart.[23]

Although numerous sentences from the essay were later transcribed verbatim into both Stephen Hero and A Portrait, it is the literary procedure rather than the content that gives the clue to Joyce's future development. In the opening paragraph he describes the proper modality of a portrait as 'the curve of an emotion' rather than an 'identificative paper' (PSW, 211) and linked it to the process of growth and change that marks the development of any person in Aristotle's system. The 'individualising rhythm' identified here with 'the first or formal relation of their parts' (PSW, 211) echoes what he had already written in the 'Paris Notebook' where he defined rhythm as 'the first or formal relation of part to part in any whole or of any whole to its part or parts' (CW, 145). Joyce attempts here to determine how a living being who changes in time can be represented in successive prose sentences other than by exterior description: hence the account of the autobiographical subject as 'a fluid succession of presents' and the denial that a portrait can be based on the 'iron memorial aspect' of 'beard and inches' (PSW, 211). Accordingly the 1904 'Portrait' seeks to trace the curve or rhythm of the artist as he emerges through the workings of his own immanent development – an attempt which Joyce would not bring to successful execution until he had completed the five chapters of A Portrait using the method of multiple styles that would characterize all his later work. What is strange, in this context, is how wholly absent such a method of composition is from Stephen Hero, the 'first draft version' of A Portrait. Clearly, that was a 'false start', as Forrest Read has called it[24] – or, otherwise, a stylistic cul-de-sac out of which Joyce had to reverse before he could proceed beyond Dubliners to Ulysses. Something was promised in the 1904 'Portrait' that was not fulfilled in Stephen Hero.

II: POLA, TRIESTE, ROME

On 10 June 1904 Joyce met an auburn-haired girl in Nassau Street and asked her to go out with him. She was Nora Barnacle, a working-class Galway girl who had fled her family and was employed as a chambermaid at Finn's Hotel. On their first evening out she gratified him manually and was thereafter the pivotal figure in his psycho-sexual existence. Joyce's relationship with Nora was passionate, romantic, lustful and imaginative even to the extent of experimenting with real causes of jealousy as when he thrust her at another man in 1911.[25] The educational difference between them was, for him, the contrary of a problem since he believed that 'many ... men of great genius [are] not attracted to cultured and refined women', as he said of William Blake in 1912 (CW, 217). On 9 October 1904, Joyce left Dublin with Nora. Their union, which remained unsanctioned by legal marriage until 1931, was initially troubled by her distress at living in foreign lands and not knowing the language. (Later the Joyces used the Triestino dialect of Italian in the home.) For Joyce she was at first a 'beautiful wild flower of the hedges' (SL, 195) and a symbol of 'the beauty and doom of the race of whom I am a child' (SL, 195), as well as the primary model for the forms of femininity that he variously embodied into the characters of Gretta Conroy (Dubliners), Molly Bloom (Ulysses) and Anna Livia Plurabelle (Finnegans Wake).

In the summer before departure Joyce's living arrangements had been most unsettled. During mid-September he had spent a week in the Sandycove Martello Tower with Gogarty and a certain Samuel Chenevix Trench (the Haines of Ulysses). On 22 September, Gogarty had driven Joyce out by firing his .22 rifle purportedly to quieten Trench who was dreaming of panthers. Much as in Ulysses, Joyce proceeded to the Montgomery Street 'kips' with medical students. His contemporary letters to Nora speak increasingly of a sense of isolation and betrayal as well as an implacable faith in his own talent. Lack of funds and work, frayed friendships and a sense of persecution eventually persuaded him to quit Ireland. On the basis of a doubtful undertaking from an intermediary in England, the couple departed for Zurich and a supposed teaching post on 9 October 1904, reaching Switzerland on 11 October. There, however, the job proved unavailable and Joyce was directed onwards to Trieste in Austria, only finding employment as a Berlitz teacher when he reached the naval port of Pola in Yugoslavia. By March 1905 he was back in Trieste at the invitation of the school director after a 'spy ring' had been uncovered in Pola rendering foreigners unwelcome. Joyce proved a popular if idiosyncratic teacher and established in Trieste the pattern of intensive literary labour interrupted by bouts of heavy drinking and gregariousness with

a circle of lively and appreciative students, mostly in the business community – among them the novelist Italo Svevo whose reputation Joyce
successfully promoted. His own first book, *Chamber Music*, was published
by Elkin Mathew in May 1907 (though only 200 copies sold in the
ensuing five years). Teaching revenue was fitful too and in 1905 he
brought his brother Stanislaus out to Trieste to help support the family
– a son George (or 'Giorgio') having been born in July.

In Dublin Joyce had produced three stories for the *Irish Homestead* on
Russell's invitation and these were printed under his adopted pen-name
'Stephen Daedalus' between August and December 1904.[26] In Pola he
produced three more only to be refused by the editor who had had
enough of their unsuitable tendency. Meanwhile the autobiographical
novel *Stephen Hero* made rapid progress and by the time Joyce left Dublin he
had completed eighteen chapters. In Trieste he added nine more stories
and in December 1905 Grant Richards agreed to publish the collection,
which Joyce then augmented with 'Two Gallants' and 'A Little Cloud'. At
this point the writer's easy passage towards publication abruptly halted.
On 23 April 1906 Richards wrote to say that his printer objected to the
word 'bloody' in 'Two Gallants' and, later on, to remarks about the
Prince of Wales in 'Ivy Day in the Committee Room' and the sexual
theme of 'An Encounter'. (It was the printer rather than the publisher
who would face prosecution.) Joyce conducted his side of the argument
as a studied defence of his representation of Dublin as the 'centre of
paralysis', insisting that no writer was entitled to 'alter in the presentment what he has seen or heard' (*SL*, 83) while characterizing the whole
collection as a 'first step towards the spiritual liberation of my country'
(*LI*, 63). Richards nonetheless withdrew the contract in September
1906. It was a measure of Joyce's discouragement that, in June 1905 he
privately printed fifty copies of 'The Holy Office', a gauntlet thrown
down to the Irish literati ('Thus I relieve their timid arses, / Perform my
office of Katharsis' [*PSW*, 98]), and sent them to Dublin for distribution
by his brother.

Joyce was constantly on the look-out for alternatives to teaching and
even employed a music teacher (unpaid) with a view to launching a
singing career. In the summer of 1906 when teaching dried up he
accepted a job with the bankers Nast Kolb and Schumacher in Rome and

moved there with his family. The long hours and uncongenial work depressed him while the inhabitants of the eternal city reminded him of a 'man who lives by exhibiting to travellers his grandmother's corpse' (SL, 108). By January 1907 work on *Stephen Hero* had ground to a halt – 'How long am I at it now? Is there any point continuing it?' (SL, 143). At the same time Joyce was contemplating several new stories ('The Last Supper', 'The Street', 'Vengeance', 'At Bay' and 'Catharsis') and another to be called 'Ulysses', which 'never got forrader than the title', as he told Stanislaus in February 1907 (LII, 209). In Rome, too, he decided that he had been 'unnecessarily harsh' on Dublin, not having 'reproduced its ingenuous insularity and its hospitality' (SL, 109–10) – a conviction that Gabriel Conroy echoes in his encomium to the Morkan sisters in 'The Dead'.

In November 1906 Joyce suddenly quit his banking job and turned to teaching private pupils with limited financial gain. In March 1907 he took his family back to Trieste though not before he had lost his final month's bank-salary to muggers on a drunken spree the night before departure. (The help he received from passers-by of his acquaintance who took him home on that occasion gave him the hint he needed for Stephen's rescue by Bloom in *Ulysses*.) Back in Trieste, the Joyces moved into cramped quarters with Stanislaus, a difficult situation aggravated by Nora's pregnancy. Though obliged to teach at a lower rate than before, Joyce plunged into the stream of Triestino life with new enthusiasm. Roberto Prezioso, the editor of Il *Piccolo della Sera* and a pupil of his, commissioned three articles on Ireland resulting in 'Il Fenianismo: L'Ultimo Feniano' (22 March), 'Home Rule Maggiorenne' (19 May) and 'L'Irlanda all Sbarra' (16 September 1907).[27] At the invitation of another, Attilio Tamaro, he gave two lectures at the Università Popolare: 'Irlanda, Isola dei Santi et die Savi' (April 1907) and 'Giacomo Clarenzio Mangan' (May 1907), together with a third on the Irish literary revival that is now lost.[28] In April he received a letter of reproach from his father calling his liaison with Nora 'your miserable mistake' (LII, 221). His daughter Lucia Anna Joyce was born on 26 July 1907, bizarrely in the maternity ward of the public hospital where Joyce himself was laid low with a bout of rheumatic fever. During the ensuing spell of convalescence that lasted till September he completed 'The Dead' and plotted his way forward through *A Portrait* to *Ulysses*.

While working on 'The Dead' Joyce told his brother that he would rewrite *Stephen Hero* in the five-chapter format of *A Portrait*.[29] He composed the first within a month and had completed Chapter 3 by April 1908 though beyond that point progress was slow until Joyce was galvanized by a letter from Ezra Pound in 1913. (There is a confused story about his consigning of this manuscript to the fire and its being rescued by Eileen Joyce in 1911.[30]) In April 1909 Joyce sent the manuscript of *Dubliners* to George Roberts at Maunsel, and in July he travelled to Dublin to deal with him directly. When his former friend Cosgrave intimated he had enjoyed Nora's favours, Joyce fell into a fit of jealousy that led to a feverish exchange of letters between Dublin and Trieste until Byrne persuaded him that Cosgrave had been acting in concert with Gogarty to break his spirit. Joyce set out again for Trieste on 13 September with a contract for *Dubliners* and an advance of £300. With him he brought his sister Eva, who remained in Trieste as long as she could bear it before returning home in July 1911. On a hint from Eva, Joyce persuaded two local businessmen to invest in the first Irish cinema, which he opened as the Volta Cinema on Mary Street in December 1909. It quickly closed due to his preference for Italian over Anglo-American films. Returning to Trieste in the new year, he brought with him an agency for the Irish Woollen Company and his sister Eileen. It now emerged that Roberts wanted changes to two stories but, following threats of legal action, he renewed his promise to publish in January 1911. In February he wrote with further objections, this time with 'Ivy Day in the Committee Room'. In August, Joyce wrote directly to George V for his opinion of the contested phrases about Edward VII and received a predictably anodyne answer from a secretary.

In July 1912 he permitted Nora to travel to Ireland, and followed her with Giorgio shortly afterwards when she was slow in sending news. Back in Dublin, Roberts demanded a £1,000 bond as indemnity against prosecution. Joyce called on a solicitor who disappointed him by declaring the stories actionable while Thomas Kettle, from whom Joyce sought support, called them harmful to the Irish cause and promised to slate them when they appeared. Roberts then offered to sell the galleys for £30 but the printer intervened by destroying a set of 1,000. By some means Joyce managed to secure one of these and left Dublin with his family in a hurry. At Flushing station in Holland he wrote a verse-invective on the Irish literary scene entitled 'Gas from a Burner' and had it printed on his arrival in Trieste.

Back in a city which now seemed like home, he fell under the spell of a private pupil named Amalia Popper – a timid romance that fuelled *Giacomo Joyce*, an epiphany-style writing he left in a fair copy (it did not appear in print until 1968). Between November 1912 and February 1913 he gave the series of lectures on *Hamlet* at the Università Popolare that inform Stephen Dedalus's discourse in the 'Scylla and Charybdis' chapter of *Ulysses*. Suddenly, in November 1913, Grant Richards asked for another sight of *Dubliners* and in January 1914 he agreed to publish the collection without changes. In December 1913 Joyce had heard from Ezra Pound, whom W.B. Yeats had directed to him as a possible contributor to Pound's *Imagist* anthology where Joyce's 'I Hear an Army' appeared the following year. Further enquiries on Pound's part led to Joyce's sending him the manuscript of *Dubliners* along with the first chapter of *A Portrait*. Pound immediately persuaded the proprietors of *The Egoist* – a feminist journal edited by Dora Marsden and Harriet Shaw Weaver – to serialize the latter, as they did from February 1914 to September 1915 (the issue for January 1914 having first reprinted Joyce's open letter to *Sinn Féin* of 2 September 1911 under the caption 'A Curious History'). Richards was now persuaded to bring forward the publication of *Dubliners* with the proviso that *A Portrait* would appear under his imprint also.

III: ZURICH AND ULYSSES

On 1 March 1914 Joyce began the long-meditated writing of *Ulysses*. Joyce and Nora were unaffected by the First World War – though Stanislaus was interned – until Italy declared war on Germany in May 1915. With the assistance of the American consulate and much hard work by international friends, he received a Swiss visa and moved to Zurich with his family at the end of June. With him he brought the manuscript of 'Calypso', the first Bloom chapter of *Ulysses*. Pound and Yeats arranged stipends from the Royal Literary Fund, the Civil Pension List and the Society of Authors, while substantial gifts for Joyce came in from

Harriet Shaw Weaver (at first anonymously) and Mrs Edith Rockefeller McCormack who later withdrew her monthly stipend when he refused to be psychoanalyzed by Carl Jung. Joyce spent the money he received without the least frugality and soon began to manifest the chronic eye problems that would dog him for the rest of his life. Heavy drinking had been a causal factor since the night he spent in a Triestino gutter and, after surgery for glaucoma and synechia, he experienced a nervous collapse that led to a spell of convalescence in Locarno over the winter of 1917–18. During this time he continued with *Ulysses*, which was beginning to appear chapter by chapter in Margaret Anderson and Jane Heap's *Little Review* (March 1918 to December 1920). Although the literary fame of the author of *Ulysses* grew apace, Grant Richards turned down his option on *A Portrait* in May 1914 due to the poor performance of *Dubliners*. When Edward Garnett rejected the novel for Duckworths, Benjamin W. Huebsch agreed to publish it in New York with the proviso that Miss Weaver would issue 750 sets of his sheets under the *Egoist* imprint in London. *A Portrait of the Artist as a Young Man* was thus published on 29 December 1916 in America and on 22 January 1917 in England.

In *A Portrait* Joyce traced the development of his autobiographical hero by means of the ontogenic conception of style he had forecast – at least in theory – in the 1904 'Portrait' essay. In finishing *A Portrait*, Joyce had in a sense finished with Stephen. In 1916 he told Frank Budgen that Stephen had assumed 'a shape that can't be changed'.[31] The shift in values that brought Leopold Bloom on stage as a counterbalance to Stephen in that novel plunged Joyce into an epistemological maelström. Both the plot and the technique of *Ulysses* – though primarily the latter – make it clear that the world can be actualized in different ways by different people. In *A Portrait*, Joyce had recorded Stephen's perception that every 'fellow had a different way of walking' (P, 14). It is but a step to appreciate that everyone has a different way of seeing. In *Ulysses* that perception is raised to the power of a stylistic principle, and then reduced to order by means of the broad polarity between the vision of the artist and that of the citizen respectively embodied by Stephen and by Bloom.[32] In each episode of *Ulysses* Joyce racked up the pace of literary experimentalism a little further. Not everyone was pleased with the result and accordingly his correspondence is littered with attempts to explain and exonerate such innovations. In June 1924 he wrote to his patron, Miss Weaver: 'The task I set myself technically in writing a book from eighteen different points of view and in as many styles, all apparently unknown or undiscovered by my fellow tradesmen, that and the nature of the legend chosen would be enough to upset anyone's mental balance' (SL, 284). A crucial test-case proved to be the so-called mythic parallel that the novel establishes between events in Dublin 1904 and those of Homer's *Odyssey*. For T.S. Eliot, the object of the 'mythic method' was to give shape to 'the immense panorama of futility and anarchy which is contemporary history'.[33] Similarly he thought that the lesson of 'Oxen of the Sun' was the 'futility of all styles', as he told Virginia Woolf.[34] It is now clear that Joyce had little share in the élitist viewpoint that informs this interpretation, with its anxiety about the 'dissociation of sensibility' that was supposed to have degraded Western culture after the Renaissance.[35] In summarizing recent Irish readings of *Ulysses*, Aaron Kelly has suggested that Eliot's view is 'exactly the opposite' of what Joyce intended – that is, 'using the everyday, ordinary present to indict myth and the violence of the past'.[36] However, it is equally a mistake to suppose that he was privileging the Irish present over the classical past.

Joyce's relation to the British Empire during the First World War was inevitably awkward in view of his receipt of income from the English exchequer while holding to the position of neutrality expressed in his ballad 'Dooleysprudence': 'Who is the tranquil gentleman who won't salute the State ... But thinks that every son of man has quite enough to do / To paddle down the stream of life his personal canoe' (PSW, 122). Urgings from on high to show some signs of patriotism resulted in his forming the English Players with the actor Claud Sykes. The company produced Wilde's *The Importance of Being Earnest* in April 1918 and Synge's *Riders to the Sea* in June (with Nora in the part of Maurya). Following the first, Joyce became embroiled in litigation with a junior consulate official called Henry Carr, who sought a larger share of profits on account of his success in the title role. Joyce won the first round, lost the second, and arguably won the third in a court of no appeal when he bestowed Carr's name on the obnoxious British soldier in the 'Nighttown' chapter of *Ulysses*. The efforts of Sir Horace Rumbold to obstruct a production of Purcell's *Dido and Aeneas* resulted in his name being given to the hangman in the 'Cyclops' episode of that novel. The Joyces did not return to Trieste for a full year after Armistice was signed in November 1918. In October 1919 they moved into the crowded home of Eileen and her husband Frantisek Schaurek, where Stanislaus was already lodging. Relations between the brothers had cooled considerably in the interim. In the following June, Joyce met Pound at Sirmione by arrangement and was persuaded to move to Paris, where the Joyces arrived on 8 July 1920.

IV: THE PARIS YEARS

If Zurich saw the efflorescence of Joyce's genius with *Ulysses*, Paris brought international fame with its publication on 2 February 1922. These were also the years of 'Work in Progress' – ultimately issued as *Finnegans Wake* in 1939 – during which Joyce gathered round him a new set of admirers aligned to the 'revolution of the word', an avant-garde movement centred on Eugene Jolas and his journal *transition*. They were also years of physical and mental stress due to his deteriorating eye condition and the increasingly evident psychological disarray of his daughter Lucia, who slipped into schizophrenia from 1931 onwards. After an initial spell during which Pound supplied support, Joyce settled in an apartment at Boulevard Raspail funded by Miss Weaver, who continued to be his patron and financial mainstay to the end. A chance meeting with Sylvia Beach, the owner of the bookshop, Shakespeare & Co. on rue de l'Odéon, within days of his arrival in the city set in train the events that led to the publication of *Ulysses*. Miss Beach immediately arranged a meeting with the influential critic Valèry Larbaud whose enthusiastic prelaunch lecture given in December 1921 at Adrienne Monnier's La Maison des Amis des Livres (facing Miss Beach's) established Joyce as a literary sensation among French intellectuals. Meanwhile the confiscation of the issue of the *Little Review* containing the 'Nausicaa' chapter in America frightened Huebsch out of publishing *Ulysses* in February 1921. At this point Miss Beach offered to publish the novel under the Shakespeare & Co. imprint, while Miss Weaver agreed to issue *Ulysses* from *The Egoist* directly after, using plates prepared for Beach by the printer Maurice Darentière in Marseilles. Though Joyce was distracted by drinking and conviviality, the last phase of work on *Ulysses* was marked by feverish additions to the galleys as these reached him from the printer. The book was published on his 40th birthday. On 16 June of that year he celebrated the first 'Bloomsday' and on 12 October the *Egoist* edition of *Ulysses* appeared in London. *Ulysses* immediately enjoyed a *succès de scandale* but actual sales were severely hampered by confiscations at the customs in England and America, some 500 copies being destroyed in each country. The first unlimited edition of *Ulysses* appeared from Shakespeare & Co. at the beginning of 1925.

No sooner had the novel appeared than Joyce began to sort through twelve kilos of notes, compiling unused material into a notebook known as *Scribbledehobble* with story-titles from *Dubliners* as section-headings.[37] In the ensuing years of 'Work in Progress' he would go on to produce some seventy such notebooks, now held by the University of Buffalo.[38] In the ensuing period *Finnegans Wake* was germinating in Joyce's mind, stimulated in part by revolutionary events in Ireland. (He was not pleased when Tim Healy was appointed Governor-General of the Irish Free State.) After *Ulysses* Joyce believed that he had 'come to the end of English'.[39] He also believed that he had exhausted what could be said about day as a subject and consequently needed to turn to night. In so doing he was drawing on the idea of the subconscious associated with Sigmund Freud, though – ever a sceptic about psychoanalysis – he was apt to ask: 'Why all this fuss about the mystery of the unconscious? What about the mystery of the conscious? What do they know about that?'[40] *Finnegans Wake* was thus to be a night-book, and for it Joyce needed a new language since, as he explained to Miss Weaver in 1926, '(o)ne great part of every human existence is passed in a state which cannot be rendered sensible by the use of wideawake language, cutandry grammar and goahead plot' (SL, 318).

Yet the dream-language explanation of *Finnegans Wake* falls down if pressed too hard, as do any other form of intellectual paraphrase. The book does not reflect a pre-existing philosophical framework of any kind and Joyce was insistent that he used such theories as Giordano Bruno's 'coinciding opposites' and Giambattista Vico's universal history as a 'trellis' only – as he told Mary Colum.[41] Similarly he advised Miss Weaver not to 'pay overmuch attention to these theories, beyond using them for all they are worth' (SL, 314). Samuel Beckett said that *Finnegans*

Wake is less like a 'book about something than that thing itself',[42] and Bernard Benstock has written comparably that '*Finnegans Wake* is about *Finnegans Wake*'.[43] The sense of both these judgements is that the book is radically self-reflexive and that it embodies a vision of human cognition as essentially self-generating and self-limiting. While the radically sceptical epistemology involved in all such readings is an important correlate of its textual fabric, it is hardly more than part of the answer. *Finnegans Wake* attempts a totalization of all human languages, history and cultures and, as such, it is in some sense a complete image of the 'reality of experience' (P, 257) Stephen Dedalus sets out to capture in an artistic image at the end of *A Portrait*. Considered thus, the *Wake* is no less part of that mimetic project than any of Joyce's other works – only the means are much more complicated and the scope more comprehensive. Another way of saying this is to argue that Joyce's development as a writer proceeded from his early epiphanies to the 'panepiphanal world' (FW, 611.13) of *Finnegans Wake*.[44]

'Work in Progress' advanced rapidly at first, but was soon hampered by Joyce's growing difficulty with his eyesight. In 1930 he even thought of handing over the task to the Irish writer James Stephens. He nevertheless had a clear plan from the outset and stuck to it. On 21 May 1926 he told Miss Weaver, 'I have the book fairly well planned out in my head' (LI, 241). On other occasions he compared the work involved to 'tunnelling parties' (SL, 304), digging through a mountain from two sides. The result is a 'simple equilibrium of two symmetrical half-arches supporting a keystone of greater complexity', as Roland McHugh has shown.[45] Such symmetries abound: thus Anna's soliloquy at the end of Book I ('Anna Livia Plurabelle') is answered by Earwicker's soliloquy at the end of Book III ('Haveth Childers Everywhere') while 'The Mookse and the Gripes' in Book I is a companion to 'The Ondt and the Gracehoper' in Book III. Book IV, known as the 'Ricorso', is essentially a coda involving all the themes and plots of the other parts, many in the form of their first conception since it is replete with the earliest drafts of 'Work in Progress' that Joyce composed.[46]

In June 1925 the Joyces moved to 2, Square Robiac, where they were to remain until 1931. *Exiles*, Joyce's only published play, had been unsuccessfully staged in a German translation in Berlin in 1919 and was now premièred at the Neighbourhood Playhouse in New York in February

1926, to be followed shortly by a Stage Society production in London. About this time Ezra Pound signed off as Joyce's chief publicist writing that 'nothing short of divine vision or a new cure for the clapp can possibly be worth all the circumambient peripherisation' that he met with in 'Work in Progress'.[47] Yet, if older allies fell away, younger ones took their place and throughout the 1930s Joyce received the homage of Eugene and Maria Jolas, Paul and Lucy Léon, Louis Gillet, Nino Frank and Samuel Beckett, while Stuart Gilbert – a retired colonial officer – wrote James Joyce's 'Ulysses' with chapter-by-chapter prompts from Joyce himself. A hostile review of Anna Livia Plurabelle by Sean O'Faolain in Eliot's journal Criterion led Joyce to organize an explanatory volume entitled Our Exagmination Round His Factification For Incamination Of Work In Progress with contributions by Beckett, Budgen, William Carlos Williams and ten others.

In 1930 Joyce travelled to Zurich to attend Dr Alfred Vogt's clinic and experienced a considerable improvement in his eyesight following three gruelling operations. Unable to work in earnest, he invested his energy instead in a campaign for the recognition of the Irish tenor John Sullivan, which petered out in 1933. His earlier doubts about Carl Jung were vindicated when the latter wrote a hostile preface for the German translation of Ulysses (1930), which Joyce scotched before publication. In July 1931 Joyce and Nora were married at the Kensington Registry Office for 'testimentary reasons' – albeit to the dismay of Lucia who was ignorant of her legal status. When his father, whose birthday fell on the day chosen for the wedding, died on 29 December Joyce experienced a bout of mental distress which was palliated by the birth of a grandson, Stephen, in February 1932. The coincidence of these events gave rise to a touching poem, 'Ecce Puer' ('Of the dark past / A child is born. / With joy and grief / My heart is torn.' [PSW, 67]). In 1933, on Joyce's 50th birthday, Lucia threw a chair at her mother and was placed in a sanatorium. Later incidents – including a mad escapade at Bray when she stayed there with Eileen – resulted in her being committed to a state asylum in 1935 and afterwards installed in a mental home at Ivry-sur-Seine outside Paris. Joyce was deeply disturbed by her descent into madness and at first rejected the evidence provided by friends and professionals.[48] Among several other therapeutic activities, Joyce encouraged her to pursue the art of illustration, and when his pamphlet 'The

Mime of Mick, Nick and the Maggies' was issued in the Hague in 1934, it bore her cover designs.

The first published sections of 'Work in Progress' appeared in Ford Maddox Ford's *transatlantic review* in April 1924 and Robert McAlmon's *Contact Collection of Contemporary Writers* in May 1925, while T.S. Eliot printed a sample of 'Mamafesta' in *Criterion*. Subsequent chapters appeared in journals and pamphlets, such as *Two Tales of Shem and Shaun* in 1932. Joyce wrote the final word of *Finnegans Wake* on 13 November 1938 – 'un mot qui n'est pas un mot, qui sonne à peine entre les dent, un souffle, un rien, l'article the', as he told Louis Gillet.[49] The first printed copy of *Finnegans Wake* reached him unbound on 30 January 1939, and simultaneous publication by Faber & Faber in London and Viking Press in New York ensued on 4 May 1939.

V: RETURN TO ZURICH

Joyce seemed uninterested as storm clouds gathered over Europe, telling his brother Stanislaus when they met in Zurich in the summer of 1938: 'I'm not interested in politics. The only thing that interests me is style'.[50] At the same time he was active in helping Jews he knew to escape overseas. Declaration of war in September 1939 found him in Normandy with Nora arranging for Lucia's evacuation to La Baule. While there, he sang 'La Marseillaise' atop a restaurant table to an appreciative audience of French and British soldiers.[51] After the occupation of Paris the Joyces moved frequently between Vichy and Gérand le Puy, where Maria Jolas had a school. There they were occasionally joined by Samuel Beckett and Paul Léon. The latter went to Paris to rescue Joyce's papers and lingered long enough to be arrested by the Gestapo and was subsequently murdered. In May 1940 Helen Joyce, Giorgio's wife, left for America, divorcing him soon after. For a time Stephen remained alone with his grandparents until Giorgio could rejoin them. After considerable trouble over visas, the four Joyces reached Zurich in mid-December 1940. There Joyce lived quietly among old friends, awaiting the proper reception of *Finnegans Wake*, which had been generally disparaged, though one Italian reviewer delighted him in asserting that the book was spiritual.[52] Joyce spoke of next writing a very simple book. After a dinner at the house of a former pupil on 10 January, Joyce suffered severe colitis, a malady that had been visiting him occasionally since 1933. He was taken in great pain to the Schwesterhaus vom Roten Kreuz and there underwent an operation for a perforated ulcer on 12 January. Though at first showing signs of good recovery, he slipped into a coma and died on 13 January 1941 at 2.15 a.m. before his family could arrive. On 15 January he was buried at Fluntern Cemetery, on Nora's insistence without religious rites. Miss Weaver paid for the funeral and took charge of the family's immediate financial wants as well as attending to Lucia's needs over the years ahead. A death-mask was made by the sculptor Paul Speck. When Nora died in Zurich in 1951 she was buried with him, as was Giorgio in 1977. Milton Hebald's sculpture of Joyce, legs crossed in thought, smoking a cigarette, his gaze averted from the book held loosely in one hand, and a cane resting beside him, was placed behind their grave when they were moved to a permanent resting-place within the cemetery in 1966.

NOTES

1. In *Ulysses* Joyce moved her funeral to 26 June 1903 (U, 17.952), thus placing the anniversary in the recent past on the day when the novel's events occur (16 June 1904).

2. Arthur Power, *Conversations with James Joyce* (London: Millington, 1974), pp.36–7.

3. In an alternate formulation of the oppressive trinity, Joyce tells Cranly: 'I will not serve that in which I no longer believe, whether it call itself my home, my fatherland, or my church' (P, 251). It is therefore simplest to equate 'language' with 'fatherland' although the exact meaning has more to do with the language revival movement and Irish cultural nationalism if also, more widely, with the issue of language-hegemony which Joyce broaches elsewhere in the novel (viz., 'my soul frets in the shadow of his language' [193]).

4. 'J'ai mis en pratique un axiome avec lequel on est sûr de vivre tranquille: *Fuge ... Late ... Tace.*' Richard Ellmann writes that Stuart Gilbert brought this source to his attention in Ellmann, *James Joyce. New and Revised Edition* (New York: Oxford University Press, 1982), p.65.

5. Peter Costello has suggested a fellow-student, Mary Elizabeth Cleary, as a better match. See *James Joyce: The Years of Growth 1882–1915* (London: Kyle Cathie, 1992), p.189.

6. Friends and contemporaries included John Francis Byrne (Cranly in *A Portrait*), Vincent Cosgrave (Lynch in *A Portrait* and *Ulysses*), George Clancy (Davin in *A Portrait*), Francis Skeffington (McCann in *A Portrait*) and Constantine Curran (Donovan in *A Portrait*). Joyce's brother Stanislaus appears as Maurice in one scene only and quite obliquely in *A Portrait* (P, 73) and anonymously as 'my whetstone' in *Ulysses* (9.977).

7. See C(onstantine) P. Curran, *James Joyce Remembered* (New York: Oxford University Press, 1968), pp.35–6.

8. Jacques Aubert, *Introduction a l'esthetique de James Joyce* (Paris: Didier, 1973), translated as *The Aesthetics of James Joyce* (Baltimore, MD: Johns Hopkins University Press, 1992).

9. Ellmann, *James Joyce*, p.87.

10. Stanislaus Joyce, *My Brother's Keeper*, edited and with an Introduction by Richard Ellmann (London: Faber and Faber, 1958), p.58.

11. Letter to C.P. Curran dated at early July 1904 by Ellmann (*SL*, 22).

12. Stephen says of the Ballast House clock: 'It has not epiphanised yet' (*SH*, 190).

13. Ellmann, *James Joyce*, p.69.

14. Ibid., p.103.

15. Ibid., p.141.

16. The French original was established by Jacques Aubert in *l'esthetique de James Joyce*. More recently, however, Fran O'Rourke has added Victor Cousins as a further source following Herbert Gorman's hint in *James Joyce* (New York: Farrar and Rhinehart, 1939), p.94. See O'Rourke, *'Allwisest Stagyrite: Joyce Quotations from Aristotle* (Joyce Studies, 21) (Dublin; National Library of Ireland, 2004), p.6.

17. Contents of the 'Paris Notebook' were transcribed by Herbert Gorman in *James Joyce* and others added in *The Critical Writings of James Joyce*, ed. Ellsworth Mason and Richard Ellmann (New York: Viking, 1959), though the Aristotelian sentences given in Gorman were unaccountably omitted. All available records of the contents were collated in Robert Scholes and Richard Kain (eds), *The Workshop of Daedalus* (Evanston, IL: Northwestern University Press, 1965). The editors of the *Critical Writings* were obliged to say in 1959 that the originals from which Gorman worked 'no longer exist', having presumably been lost in wartime Paris. In 2002 the 'Paris Notebook' appeared again and went on sale. It is now held in the National Library of Ireland.

18. Joyce, *My Brother's Keeper*, p.230.

19. The 1904 'Portrait' can also be found in Scholes and Kain (eds), *Workshop of Dedalus* and Hélène Cixous, *The Exile of James Joyce*, trans. Sally Purcell (London: Calder, 1976). The manuscript and typescript versions have been reproduced in Michael Groden (ed.), *The James Joyce Archive*, Vol. VII (New York: Garland Press, 1978).

20. John Eglinton, *Irish Literary Portraits* (London: Macmillan, 1935), p.136.

21. See Vivian Mercier, 'John Eglinton as Socrates: A Study of "Scylla and Charybdis"', in *James Joyce: An International Perspective*, ed. Suheil Bushrui and Bernard Benstock (Gerrards Cross: Colin Smythe, 1982), p.76.

22. See Richard Ellmann, A. Walton Litz and John Whittier-Ferguson (eds), *Poems and Shorter Writings, including 'Epiphanies', 'Giacomo Joyce' and 'A Portrait of the Artist'* (London: Faber and Faber, 1991), p.216 (hereafter referred to as *PSW*).

23. Ellmann, *James Joyce*, p.85. In *Stephen Hero*, Joyce makes Stephen quote whole sentences from it with an air of mystical conviction: 'Why do you fly from our torches which were made out of the wood of the trees under which Christ wept in the gardens of Gethsemene. Why do you fly from our torches which were made from the sweet wood after it had vanished from the world and come to us who made it of old tunes

with our breath?' (SH, 161). See W.B. Yeats, *Short Fiction*, ed. and intro. G.J. Watson (Harmondsworth: Penguin, 1995), p.211.

24. Forrest Read, *Pound/Joyce: The Letters of Ezra Pound to James Joyce, with Pound's Critical Essays and Articles about Joyce* (New York: New Directions, 1965), p.2.

25. Ellmann, *James Joyce*, p.327.

26. The case can be made that Joyce derived the name 'Daedalus' from an ode to intellectual freedom by Giordano Bruno, beginning '*Daedaleas vacuis plumas nectere humeris / Concupiant alii*' [Let others seek to weave the wings of Daedalus on their empty shoulders], which appeared in Samuel Taylor Coleridge's *Literary Remains* (1836).

27. Translated as 'Fenianism', 'Home Rule Comes of Age' and 'Ireland at the Bar' (*CW*, 187ff, 193ff and 197–200).

28. Translated as 'Ireland, Island of Saints and Sages' and 'James Clarence Mangan (2)' (*CW*, 153ff and 175–86).

29. Ellmann, *James Joyce*, p.274.

30. Joyce either misremembered or actively misled the editor of *Stephen Hero* when the latter wrote enquiring about the fragmentary state of the manuscript in 1938. See Theodore Spencer's introduction to *Stephen Hero* (11–12) and the 'Publisher's Note' appended to the 1958 edition (21).

31. Frank Budgen, *James Joyce and the Making of 'Ulysses'* (London: Oxford University Press, 1972), p.105.

32. See Charles Peake, *James Joyce: The Citizen and The Artist* (London: Edward Arnold, 1977).

33. 'Ulysses, Order and Myth', in Robert Deming (ed.), *James Joyce: The Critical Heritage* (London: Routledge & Kegan Paul, 1970), Vol.1, pp.268–71 (p.270).

34. Ellmann, *James Joyce*, p.490. Letter to Virginia Woolf, 26 September 1922; in *A Writer's Diary*, ed. Leonard Woolf (London: Hogarth Press, 1954), p.50.

35. T.S. Eliot, 'The Metaphysical Poets', in *Selected Essays* (New York: Harcourt, Brace and World, 1964), p.247.

36. Aaron Kelly, *Twentieth-Century Irish Literature* (London: Palgrave Macmillan, 2008), p.77.

37. See Thomas E. Connolly, ed., intro. and annot., *James Joyce's Scribbledehobble: The Ur-Workbook for 'Finnegans Wake'* (Evanston, IL: Northwestern University Press, 1961).

38. See Michael Groden (gen. ed.), *James Joyce Archive* (New York: Garland Press, 1978), Vols. XXVIII–XLIII ('*Finnegans Wake* Notebooks').

39. Ellmann, *James Joyce*, p.559.

40. See Frank Budgen, *Further Recollections of James Joyce* (London: Shenval, 1955 [1934]), p.8.

41. Mary and Padraic Colum, *Our Friend James Joyce* (New York: Doubleday, 1958), p.123.

42. S. Beckett, 'Dante ... Bruno. Vico.. Joyce', in *James Joyce/'Finnegans Wake': A Symposium. Our Exagmination Round His Factification For Incamination Of Work In Progress* (New York: New Directions, 1972 [1929]), p.16.

43. Bernard Benstock, *Joyce-Again's Wake: An Analysis of 'Finnegans Wake'* (Washington, DC: Washington University Press, 1965), p.vi.

44. *Finnegans Wake* (New York: Viking, 1939). The line and page are given here as in Clive Hart, *A Concordance to 'Finnegans Wake'* (New York: Paul Appel, 1976). In the present

writing I have avoided extensive quotation from or commentary on the text of that work.

45. Roland McHugh, *The Sigla of 'Finnegans Wake'* (London: Edward Arnold, 1976), p.6.

46. See David Hayman (ed.), *A First-Draft Version of 'Finnegan's Wake'* (London: Faber and Faber, 1963).

47. See Read (ed.), *Pound/Joyce*, p.228. Pound had just read 'Shaun the Post' (Bk. III, i).

48. See Carol Loeb Shloss, *Lucia Joyce: To Dance in the Wake* (New York: Farrar and Strauss, 2004).

49. Ellmann, *James Joyce*, p.725.

50. Ibid., p.710. Quoting an interview with Stanislaus in 1954.

51. Ibid., p.740.52. Ibid., p.753.

52. Ibid., p.753.

CHAPTER THREE

The Curious Language of *Dubliners*

DAVID G. WRIGHT

When George Russell wrote to Joyce in early July 1904, soliciting a short story for *The Irish Homestead*, he specified that any submission should be 'simple, rural?, livemaking? [and display or elicit] pathos' and asked that Joyce aim 'not to shock the readers' (LII, 43). This prescription served as a thinly veiled but precisely coded warning to Joyce that if he wanted the *Homestead* to publish his work he should curtail undesirable literary impulses which Russell may already have detected in him. While delineating the type of material which an agricultural journal like the *Homestead* would logically seek to publish, it aims to shape Joyce into a particular kind of writer, manifesting certain attitudes to readers and to Irish society. As such, the warning proved a failure. Indeed, Joyce seems to have embarked on a prompt and systematic evasion, or ironizing, of the entire prescription, an evolving strategy which in its later instances would lead him into conflict not only with George Russell himself but with two publishers whose names oddly echoed Russell's own: Grant Richards and George Roberts. It all began, we might suspect, with his pointed refusal to supply rural pathos to the *Homestead*, his intuition about what the literary opposite of (or antidote to) rural pathos might be, and his consequent assessment of how such contrasting material could be developed.

As Hans Walter Gabler has shown, when Joyce set about crafting his first piece for the *Homestead* he took as a model Berkeley Campbell's story called 'The Old Watchman'. This text had already appeared in the *Homestead* on 2 July 1904, and Russell apparently sent it to Joyce to illustrate the kind of work he wanted.[1] As he rapidly drafted his first version of 'The Sisters', within a mere two weeks of receiving Russell's invitation to contribute, he used aspects of Campbell's story as a partial basis for his own. Thus he adopted the technique of parodically rewriting an existing text, which was to serve him in the creation of so many later works. If Russell noticed how precisely yet perversely Joyce had drawn on Campbell's story, he may have regretted supplying the text, since Joyce's mode of rewriting allowed him to give the impression of following the *Homestead* pattern while surreptitiously inverting it.

But he also had another tempting verbal target even closer to home which remained available for parodic or ironic treatment: Russell's own letter inviting him to contribute. We can hardly doubt that Joyce kept this letter open beside him, figuratively at least, as he wrote his story, and that he systematically subverted Russell's requirements as encoded in the key words 'simple', 'rural', 'livemaking', 'pathos' and in the instruction 'not to shock'. While other stories which had appeared in the *Homestead* might inadvertently fail to manifest one or other of these qualities, Joyce deliberately set out to evade them all.

From its first version, for instance, 'The Sisters' studiously avoided simplicity, becoming complex, subtle and elusive in its implications. Far from operating as a 'rural' text, the story remained as stringently confined to the urban landscape of Dublin as any of Joyce's later works. Even an awareness of contrasts between urban and rural environments – as sometimes shown by Stephen Dedalus in the early chapters of *A Portrait of the Artist as a Young Man* – remains absent. As for 'livemaking', Joyce's story evaded that recommendation in several senses, most obviously through its focus on the death of a central character and the lack of positive or regenerative conclusions to be drawn from that death. ('The Old Watchman' also included a character who died, but the bleakness of Joyce's text seems a satirical response to Russell's letter more than a rewriting of content from the earlier tale.) And 'pathos' in the sense Russell presumably intended – material likely to elicit sentimentally sympathetic responses – is carefully avoided in Joyce's text as well. While we might overstate the case by claiming that Joyce's story sets out deliberately to 'shock' its readers, it could easily unsettle or upset them, as Joyce must have anticipated. It is certainly not the soothing tale Russell had requested: quite the reverse.

In subverting Russell's literary prescriptions as he wrote the first version of 'The Sisters', Joyce may also have kept in mind, and targeted, the readership of the *Homestead*. Presumably, they were accustomed to a literary diet featuring livemaking rural pathos and other such ingredients. Joyce seems to have decided that they might therefore benefit from an infusion of his clear-sighted urban astringency, and from his desire to satirize a flawed society which their usual reading might have encouraged them to regard with complacent contentment.

Curious nomenclature continued to envelop Joyce's stories as they accumulated and evolved. In fact, such terms began to proliferate and interbreed. Only two weeks after starting to draft 'The Sisters', Joyce had already formulated the idea of producing a number of such stories. He set out this plan in a crucial letter to his friend Constantine Curran in mid-July 1904, furnishing in the process an early artistic manifesto. At this stage he still imagined the stories appearing in the *Homestead* rather than in book form, but already he envisaged them somehow bearing the collective title 'Dubliners', so as 'to betray the soul of that hemiplegia or paralysis which many consider a city' (LI, 55). This formulation introduces to the discussion an esoteric term, 'hemiplegia', though Joyce helpfully supplies its more common synonym 'paralysis'. The formulation also confirms that, before the first story appeared in print, Joyce had definitively rejected Russell's prescription, even though he apparently expected the editor to continue publishing his stories. The aim at a systematic exposure of Dublin's moral and spiritual paralysis is as far from 'livemaking' fiction as it could well be. Who knows whether Russell's prim prospectus, and Joyce's predictably ironic and perverse response to it, may even have prompted those subsequent depictions of paralysis?

In the revised version of 'The Sisters', the word 'paralysis' appears directly within the text itself, on the story's first page (D, 9), forming a strong link to Joyce's earlier statements of intent outside the text, and making his programme seem still more insistent. As Tony Thwaites notes, the word 'paralysis', along with the terms 'gnomon' and 'simony' which appear on the same page of the revised text, adds a curious link between the story and its external contexts: these words all 'occupy a liminal position, neither fully inside the story nor simply outside it but a disturbance of its edges'.[2] The implications of 'gnomon' and 'simony' are never explained within the text of 'The Sisters', though simony (like paralysis) is invoked in an oblique but naturalistic way as the narrator imagines himself 'smiling feebly as if to absolve the simoniac of his sin' (D, 11). The word 'gnomon', moreover, seems exactly the kind of cryptic term Joyce tended to use when discussing the stories. It has been variously glossed, but most take it to denote a parallelogram with a similarly shaped parallelogram excised from one of its corners. This figure has been linked by critics to numerous specific items featured within the text of *Dubliners*, but it might also seem an apt imaginative analogy for each individual story, or for the whole collection. Each story, that is, and the collection as a whole, can be seen as drawing attention to forms of lack and inadequacy, delineated through parallel structures for which the gnomon supplies a useful visual correlative.

To take another example of Joyce's curious language: since the first volume of his correspondence as edited by Stuart Gilbert appeared in 1957, Joyce's readers have understood that in the same 1904 letter to Curran where 'hemiplegia or paralysis' was specified, he imagined his future stories forming 'a series of epicleti'. In a footnote to Joyce's letter, Gilbert explains the puzzling term 'epicleti' as 'derived from *epiclesis* (invocation)' (LI, 55). The same letter to Curran reappears in Joyce's *Selected Letters*, edited by Richard Ellmann, published in 1975, and still bearing exactly the same footnote (SL, 22). Innumerable critics have made assumptions about Joyce's implications in using the term 'epicleti'. Many have taken it as a more precise and refined designation of his intentions than the better-known term 'epiphany', which Joyce glossed at length, as for example in the manuscript novel *Stephen Hero* which he was drafting at the same time as his early *Dubliners* stories. The word 'epicleti' is so unusual that it would appear to be a unique coinage. But the presence of this apparent Greek neologism might seem unsurprising in a letter by Joyce, who would use the rare term 'hemiplegia' just two sentences later in the same letter to Curran. If we plan to analyze hemiplegia, we may well want to shape our texts on the topic into epicleti.

Yet it seems equally possible that Joyce never, in fact, envisaged calling his stories 'epicleti' at all. Even as early as 1904, his handwriting could be unclear. Recent inspection of his manuscript letter to Curran suggests that he may actually have written 'epiclets'. Gabler recapitulates and endorses this discovery,[3] and Wolfhard Steppe provides a further extended analysis.[4] Since Joyce glosses 'hemiplegia' as 'paralysis' elsewhere in the letter, we could expect him to gloss the even stranger term 'epicleti' as 'invocations', if 'epicleti' is what he actually meant to write. He includes no such gloss, which might imply that he thought his meaning was clear, a conclusion which supports the 'epiclets' reading. Thus it might seem that all the cherished theories about Joyce's epicleti must be abandoned.

However, it is doubtful whether Joyce's use of the term 'epiclets', if that is what he intended, would help his readers greatly, as those who made this apparent discovery understandably began by supposing. The term might encourage readers seeking affinities between *Dubliners* and the expansively epic *Ulysses*, or pondering Stephen Dedalus's claim that literature develops from lyrical forms (forms which Joyce had already deployed in his early poems, known to George Russell) to epic and then dramatic ones (P, 214–15). But as a description of the *Dubliners* stories, the term appears hardly apt or useful. Presumably, epiclets are little epics. Yet while Gabler cheerfully describes the word as constituting in its form 'an ordinary English diminutive',[5] in semantic terms it seems to begin deconstructing itself immediately, or to become a kind of quirky oxymoron at best. Epics are large and grand objects: typical dictionary definitions will emphasize features such as textual length, elevated diction and heroic content. Could all these qualities be removed, reversed or even drastically scaled down, as would obviously be necessary in the course of producing an epiclet, and still leave behind them any kind of epic at all? Even a mock-epic would presumably require more vestiges of grandeur than a typical *Dubliners* story displays.

On the other hand, Joyce's 1904 notes to Curran tend to be arch or facetious in their overt tone, even while remaining intensely serious about the imaginative writing itself. So the term 'epiclets' might suggest a degree of defensive self-mockery, and perhaps an attempt to offset the seriousness, even pomposity, occasionally visible elsewhere in the correspondence. Besides, at the time he wrote the crucial letter, Joyce had drafted only one of the stories, though he claims already to project a 'series' of ten such tales. Even if he had meant to convey something specific by the term 'epiclets', the concept which this word evoked for him at such an early stage was almost certain to change later as he worked on the construction of further stories. Such a caveat, of course, would remain equally applicable if the term he used had, in fact, been 'epicleti'. Later stories might well become less epic-like, or less like invocations, for that matter.

The vital fact is that, whichever word Joyce actually intended to write and whatever he meant by it, he never used it again in any document that has survived. Steppe's analysis suggests that Curran himself felt baffled by Joyce's term, though unfortunately he does not seem to have asked for clarification, at least not in a letter. In his own book about Joyce, published in 1968, Curran quotes the original letter in full, and gives the word in question as 'epicteti' (sic).[6] This error suggests that he recalled reading the word as 'epicleti' rather than 'epiclets', though he might also have been influenced by Gilbert's use of 'epicleti' in his edition of Joyce's letters. Curran's memory of a 1904 letter could easily have faded by the 1960s, but we know that he consulted Gilbert's edition, since he cites it on another occasion in his own book.[7] In any case, he says nothing about what Joyce's word may have conveyed to him when he first read the letter, and it seems reasonable for us to deduce that it had conveyed very little. Whether Joyce meant to write 'epicleti' or 'epiclets', the striking oddity of the term, its evidently marginal relevance to the stories as they now exist, and the fact that Joyce abandoned it after using it once, all suggest that readers should be wary of taking it to mean anything specific. More significant, in fact, may be Joyce's less conspicuous claim made in the letter to Curran that the epicleti or epiclets were to form a 'series'. The notion of a series was an even more vital step in the evolution of *Dubliners* than Joyce's idea about the structure of its individual components.

Russell himself may have inadvertently prompted the plan for a series in the first place. While his initial invitation spoke only of a single story, it evidently sounded welcoming enough that Joyce rapidly imagined himself writing several short narratives. Publication in a periodical like the *Homestead* would also make the notion of a series of stories seem an obvious option: the periodical existed as a series in its own right. The first three contributions Joyce sent to the *Homestead* already depict their protagonists at successive stages of life, a hint that the plan for a lengthier series arranged on this basis formed in his mind early in the process. The boy in 'The Sisters' appears to be aged about 12 or 13 (Joyce himself was 13 in July 1895, the date of the story, though admittedly the year remains unspecified in the story's first version, being added during later revisions). Eveline (in the second written story) is about 19, and Jimmy Doyle (in the third written story) is about 26.

It remains unclear, nevertheless, whether at any time Russell deliberately encouraged Joyce to embark on a 'series' of stories for the *Homestead*. He may have done so, or Joyce may simply have assumed that if he continued to write stories, the journal would continue to publish them. There were risks in adopting this approach. If the stories asserted strong affinities with each other from one issue to another, as Joyce's use of the term 'series' surely implies, they might begin to subvert the tone or rhythm of the journal itself – all the more so since Joyce seemed determined to avoid producing the kind of story which the *Homestead*, through Russell, had specifically requested. Besides, Joyce's radical reconstruction of Russell's prescription for *Homestead* stories meant that, while one quirky and rebellious story from him might be tolerated as a curiosity, a lengthy sequence of such tales would inevitably meet increasing resistance from editors and readers on the grounds of theme and tone. It was scarcely reasonable to imagine that the *Homestead* would ever accept ten such stories. In the event, Russell baulked after three, and refused to take any more.

For that and other reasons, Joyce soon began contemplating the notion of issuing *Dubliners* as a book. He produced several new stories during 1905, and the originally projected series of ten rapidly reached that number, then continued to expand. Joyce now began discussing the stories extensively in letters to potential publishers, a process which became increasingly urgent and necessary as his work encountered growing resistance. By contrast with his earlier remarks in private letters to people like Curran, these comments seem closer to public pronouncements. Publishers tend to keep copies of such letters for their records, and presumably Joyce realized that they would do so. The nature of such a correspondence, as he must have come to appreciate, might therefore require the construction of elaborate arguments over the course of successive letters. So the letters themselves inevitably became a kind of 'series', operating in parallel to the accumulating sequence of stories he was writing at about the same time. Like the stories, these letters can be cryptic – and curious – in their own way.

During 1906 Joyce generated as many pages in the course of corresponding with Grant Richards, a potential publisher, as he did in developing his 'creative' writing. He half-acknowledged this point himself to Richards on 5 May, observing ruefully that 'my letter is becoming nearly as long as my book' (LII, 135). Construction of the stories of *Dubliners*, and of the letters to the publisher, proceeded in parallel. Joyce may have seen more affinities between these two modes of textual production than his readers have noticed, and leaned on them in ways we have not fully detected.

The Richards correspondence often reads strangely. In the least surprising exchanges, Joyce reluctantly agrees to make minor alterations to the text if these will render the typescript more acceptable to the publisher. He also insists that there are certain other alterations he will not contemplate, rejecting them on the grounds that the stories would be seriously damaged if these particular changes were made. Even these relatively straightforward cases of negotiation occasionally disclose a degree of self-parody by Joyce – a tendency to explore and mock his own solemnity in the role, which he seems to have played quite consciously, of a young author earnestly corresponding with his potential publisher. More mysteriously, however, Joyce draws attention to possibly problematic passages in the *Dubliners* typescript which the publisher had so far overlooked, notably the entire story 'An Encounter'. He mentions this story pointedly several times, until eventually Richards responds to all the prompting by deciding: 'On consideration I should like to leave [it] out altogether' (D, 275).

Although Joyce may have inadvertently blurted out some of these self-critical comments in moments of irritation, and without much regard to possible consequences, he also wanted at least a tinge of martyrdom, as well as a sense that in bringing his collection to the public he had managed to overcome substantial difficulties. His writing of the stories themselves, as he complained to his brother Stanislaus, had failed to give him a sufficient sense of conquering obstacles. Thus his correspondence about the stories might supply some of the stress and conflict which the composition process had not generated. The rhetorical value of *Dubliners* would be greatly enhanced, at least in Joyce's own eyes, if he had completed it despite an obstructive publisher – even if, in some cases, that publisher had to be coaxed into suitable degrees and kinds of obstructiveness. Joyce seemingly wanted to control the manner in which Richards accepted and regarded the stories, not merely to have them appear in print. He hoped to goad the publisher, as an embodiment of conservative social opinion, into thinking out and clarifying his own standards of judgement, which do seem, as Joyce implies, to have been sometimes muddled. As a particular example, he wanted to ensure that the story 'An Encounter' was as troubling as he doubtless meant it to be. If the publisher had initially missed the sexual ambiguity of this story and found it entirely innocuous, might not Joyce's readers do likewise? Yet this seems a dangerous strategy, and the risk that Richards might decide to reject the story altogether was one which Joyce perhaps took too blithely.

In the course of these letters, Joyce carefully cultivated an ability to mimic and parody Richards's typical manner of expression, to write to him in publisher-speak. In fact, the 1906 correspondence gradually shapes itself into a text related to *Dubliners* and serving several analogous purposes. In a letter to Richards on 23 June, Joyce declares: 'I seriously believe that you will retard the course of civilisation in Ireland by preventing the Irish people from having one good look at themselves in my nicely polished looking-glass' (LI, 64). This 'looking-glass' is obviously the text of *Dubliners*, but by this stage Joyce was using much the same strategy in his letters to the publisher: prompting him to have a good look at himself, in a looking-glass of Joyce's own fabrication. Joyce was aware that the *Dubliners* typescript and the Richards correspondence had become parallel texts, each operating as a reflection or parody of the other. In these letters he may also have explored specific modes of address which could then be transferred to the stories – notably, and aptly, the story 'Counterparts', whose fussy office language closely echoes the tone of the letters, a further suggestion that Joyce may have seen the text of the stories and the Richards correspondence as 'counterparts' of one another.

Joyce claimed to have written his stories 'in a style of scrupulous meanness and with the conviction that he is a very bold man who dares to alter in the presentment, still more to deform, whatever he has seen and heard' (LII, 134). The phrase 'scrupulous meanness', while it may reflect a little harshly on the tone of the stories, seems broadly congruent with many of them. Yet the primary meaning of 'scrupulous', according to the Oxford English Dictionary, is 'troubled with doubts or scruples of conscience'. Joyce normally deploys the word in precisely this sense, often with a negative implication: the doubts or scruples mostly do damage, and we are not to sympathize with those who hold them. Otherwise, he uses the word in a parody of this sense. For example, the sister of Father Flynn, who dies during the first Dubliners story, remarks that the priest 'was too scrupulous always … The duties of the priesthood was too much for him' (D, 17). So Father Flynn has died, in part, of scrupulosity. Joyce's apparently solemn use of the word 'scrupulous' in writing to his publisher is countermanded by most of the other occasions where he uses the word during the ensuing few years. There, the word is normally employed negatively or facetiously or parodically.

The word 'meanness' in that same letter might seem to be employed with a more apparent tinge of self-directed irony, evoking by reflection a noble austerity on Joyce's part, rather than a reprehensible stinginess. Yet dictionary definitions of the word 'mean' equate it to 'common, base, or sordid', and it typically appears in Joyce's fiction with a critical emphasis. As Little Chandler contemplates his wife's face in a photograph, 'he found something mean in it'. He also 'found something mean in the … furniture which he had bought for his house on the hire system. Annie had chosen it herself and it reminded him of her … A dull resentment against his life awoke within him' (D, 83). Michael Brian points out, incidentally, that Skeat's Etymological Dictionary gives the original sense of 'little' as 'deceitful' or 'mean'.[8] That note seems an apt gloss on the more negative side of Little Chandler's personality. In a review of the poetry of William Rooney, Joyce remarked that 'little is achieved in these verses, because the writing is so careless, and yet so studiously mean … An ordinary carelessness is nothing but a false and mean expression of a false and mean idea' (CW, 85). Joyce ostensibly aligns himself with the 'scrupulous' and the 'mean', by contrast with the 'very bold man' who dares to judge, 'alter' or 'deform' things. Yet usually, and above all in the *Dubliners* years, he would think of himself as one of those 'bold' writers who seek to change their society by judiciously depicting its follies. Such writers may do so, indeed, by selectively emphasizing society's own scrupulosity and meanness, its own pointless fussiness and triviality. The letter implies that in the stories Joyce aims only at naturalistic authenticity, at transcribing what he knows; but he chose his material for particular effects and never hesitated to alter or deform portions of reality to suit his purposes.

In the letter Joyce also asserts that in his stories he depicts accurately 'whatever he has seen and heard'. Here he designates specifically two primary targets of his attention and his parodic impulses in the stories: the written and the spoken language of his fellow Dubliners. If he writes his text with 'scrupulous meanness', he does so chiefly in order to mimic and to catalogue the limited modes of expression which he perceived the Dublin population to employ. In short, they are the ones who are scrupulous and mean, and who betray these characteristics in their discourse. Implicitly, Joyce writes didactically to advocate a different stance. Richards may have been surprised, however, in turning from Joyce's letters to the manuscript stories themselves, to find so few apparent traces of such an impulse. In story after story, the narrators exhibit great restraint in judging characters and situations, offering no single vantage point from which the material can be assessed. Most early readers of 'A Mother' favoured the stance taken by the male concert organizers in opposition to Mrs Kearney. Several recent readings of the story have reacted by making a case for her position, and Margot Norris sums up such readings in her account of the story.[9] Yet for the reader, simply switching sides here should seem too simple a strategy. Rather, the revisionist readings of this story serve as a reminder that readers need to withhold judgements requiring people to take sides, especially in the kind of dispute which the story depicts. To label Mrs Kearney right or wrong in the dispute may be to adopt the very stance which the story carefully warns its readers to avoid.

How then to reconcile Joyce's insistence on the nicely polished looking-glass, the course of civilization in Ireland and similar weighty concerns, with the quiet reticence of these stories, their repeated reluctance to give advice on how to read them? As one obvious response to the puzzle, readers could choose to claim that Joyce's explicit statements of intent became not merely strategic but disingenuous. Yet the stories do incorporate materials which, reassembled and more explicitly labelled, could form an expressly satirical and didactic depiction of Dublin life, even though readers may feel that, in the stories as published, Joyce and his narrators have largely refrained from undertaking this construction themselves. And this, in turn, could be the real point of the looking-glass metaphor: what Joyce's audience may need to confront is a willingness to see the inadequacies of their society without taking action to correct them. A didactic text instructing them to pursue certain courses might not produce the necessary degree of self-recognition. It could always seem to be a case of Joyce's word against theirs.

Especially significant, in these terms, is Joyce's concept of a 'series' of seemingly autonomous stories. Each narrative operates as a snapshot of a portion of the city, apparently chosen at random. Each adds its contribution to the mosaic, insisting that the repeatedly invoked problems are pervasive, that they are everywhere much the same, and hence that they must be the product of a deeper and more widespread malaise or pathology. They are, therefore, everybody's present business, not matters to be shelved for someone else's attention at another time. More subtly, the series of stories suggests that such social inadequacies thrive in a situation where nobody looks outside immediate contexts for a solution. Though Bob Doran reflects in 'The Boarding House' that in a small city like Dublin everyone knows everyone else's business, the stories themselves nowhere demonstrate that such forms of knowledge, and such implicit interactions, are actually prevalent. Rather, the major characters in each story seem entirely dissociated from those in all the others. While they do form a series, as individual texts the stories also assert their separateness from each other.

Yet the relationships among individual stories do often seem to be hinted at through their titles, another mode of verbal mediation, sanctioned by Joyce, between his texts and the world outside. The book title *Dubliners* might itself seem initially to mark the historical high point of his normally limited enthusiasm for explicit naming. He claimed to Richards that this title, unlike other aspects of his work, ought to be entirely uncontroversial: 'What would remain of the book if I had to efface everything which might give offence? The title, perhaps?' (LII, 137). At one stage Joyce claimed he had chosen the title because of its semantic aptness. Writing to Richards on 15 October 1905, he observes that 'the expression "Dubliner" seems to me to have some meaning and I doubt whether the same can be said for such words as "Londoner" and "Parisian" both of which have been used by writers as titles' (LII, 122). It is possible, of course, that Joyce intended through his stories not merely to exploit but to change the connotations of the word. And he may, in fact, have succeeded in doing so: since the story collection appeared, many people thinking of 'Dubliners' as a group of citizens will have Joyce's depictions implicitly or explicitly in their minds.

Nevertheless, Joyce's wiliness operates even here, and his naming practices in Dubliners can seem quite as 'curious' as his discourse in describing the stories. It remains unclear precisely what kind of community Joyce thought his depicted citizens composed, or should compose. The concept of 'the Dubliner' remained for Joyce diffuse, ill-defined or problematic, an uncertainty which the stories reflect and which the collective title may have been designed to emphasize, for all Joyce's protestations about it. Given the heterogeneity and fragmentation evoked within the stories, the cohesiveness at which the overall title hints may even seem pointedly hollow or ironic. We recall Joyce's earlier claim to Curran that the collective title signalled the hemiplegia of Dublin society, an implication which no doubt remained present even after Joyce busied himself conveying more positive connotations to Richards.

Many of the titles of individual stories in the collection appear at first to be logical and appropriate, if occasionally cryptic. But none of Joyce's choices seems, on closer inspection, altogether straightforward or innocent. While the opening story 'The Sisters' does incorporate a pair of sisters, it would be difficult to interpret the text in a way which makes these characters seem as significant as the title suggests. This title, in fact, appears evasive and circumlocutory in reference, like the elliptical discourse of the characters within the story itself. An analogous displacement appears in the fact that Father Flynn – brother of the sisters in question and apparently more important in the scheme of things – is dead throughout the text so that, in effect, readers never meet him. The anonymity of the boy who narrates the story casts further doubt on the utility or clarity of acts of naming. The sisters remain mostly peripheral to the tale as told, especially since it records the perceptions of the narrator, who pays them little heed. Readers might even pause briefly to ponder whether the first-person narrator had selected his own title.

So the first story title in the collection warns readers at the outset to expect indirection, and perhaps veiled hints, from the other titles to follow. The title 'The Sisters' also draws attention to what might seem a minor or marginal phenomenon, implicitly arguing that it is more central than it first appears. The sisters, that is, deserve more attention from the people around them than they have so far received. The real key to the puzzle posed by the whole story may be the question: What has happened to the sisters? Valuable sociological, economic and political comments have been made by critics, especially about the ways in which Father Flynn might have inadvertently – or knowingly – exploited and marginalized his siblings. Readers also need to notice, and the title in its obliqueness may be meant to make them reflect, that the two women are sisters not only of one another but also of their brother. That is, there is a need to see people in the context of multiple kinds of familial, social, economic and other relationships. This emphasis remains important in many of the subsequent stories, creating uncertainties that become part of our experience of the text.

'Ivy Day in the Committee Room', for example, seems at first a reassuringly precise and denotative title, perhaps the most transparent in the collection. This is one of only two stories to take place in a single location – the only one, in fact, to be confined to a single room – and the title specifies this location clearly enough. It also, uncharacteristically for *Dubliners*, supplies the exact day of the year, 6 October, when the story's events occur. This level of specificity helps shape our responses to the text. Although the poetic tribute to Parnell recited at the close seems loyal and heartfelt, if poetically thin, it obviously clashes with the spirit expressed by the action through most of the story. This spirit tends to be mostly venal, pragmatic and entropic, evoking the strain and fraying of relationships rather than their strengthening. So a sad and even elegiac tinge colours the treatment of contemporary Dublin local politics: present political practices have not kept faith with the grander concerns which seemed accessible in Parnell's day, and the kind of infighting which contributed to his fall appears to be continuing, inconclusively, with no inspirational leader now present to take his place and counteract all the squabbling.

While the story does indeed unfold in a committee room, no kind of committee activity takes place. Instead of the orderly procedures and cooperative ventures which committees might ideally entail, especially in the ostensible present context of community, teamwork and election campaigns, there is a pronounced tendency to disorder and bickering. Once readers finish the story, they will feel that the apparently bald title hints at many of these nuances, which it will thus encapsulate when they see it in the future even if they do not reread the story at the time. It therefore seems, for all its apparent austerity, one of the richest titles in the collection, but also marked with touches of irony: committee rooms should encourage more communal forms of behaviour; Ivy Day should have greater significance for the people of Dublin; and Irish society generally should shake off some of its apathy and its self-defeating modes of behaviour.

The analogous title 'The Boarding House' also seems precise. In fact, these two titles operate in markedly different ways, quietly setting up a pattern of mild instability when compared. Whereas the title 'Ivy Day in the Committee Room' supplied several connotations appropriate to its text, and specified time as well as place, the title 'The Boarding House' conveys nothing beyond a location. The text never implies that the particular and rather peculiar moral atmosphere at Mrs Mooney's establishment characterizes all boarding-houses in Dublin. On the contrary, Bob Doran reflects that Mrs Mooney's 'boarding house was beginning to get a certain fame' (D, 66), so distinguishing it from others of its class, even though it never occurs to him to seek a less notorious or perilous place to live. The apparently generic nature of the title, then, carefully contrasts with the uniqueness of the setting.

Two other titles, 'Araby' and 'Eveline', seem equally specific and straightforward, but in each case there remains a disruptive degree of obliqueness. Moreover, these are neighbouring stories, so that such shared characteristics reinforce each other with particular clarity. The Araby bazaar appears only at the very end of the story named after it, but in association with Mangan's sister it preoccupies the narrator throughout most of the text: 'What innumerable follies laid waste my waking and sleeping thoughts after that evening [when the bazaar was first discussed]!' (D, 32). After reading the two previous stories 'The Sisters' and 'An Encounter', readers should be prepared for another text whose main focus, at least as evoked and defined by its title, appears towards the conclusion: the sisters and the encounter also feature at the end of these stories, and indeed remain largely unheralded earlier in the texts, except through the titles themselves. In the third story, the Araby bazaar proves disappointing, not the anticipated culmination of the boy's hopes but an occasion for his disillusionment and romanticized, though still painful, self-laceration. This title, applied to the last of these stories, designates failed escapism, loss and absence rather than satisfaction and fulfilment; it therefore projects some of the same sad irony as the title 'Ivy Day in the Committee Room'.

As a title, 'Eveline' appears at first to foreground subjective experience and the centrality of character as unambiguously as, say, the title of Jane Austen's *Emma*. Yet 'Eveline', which immediately follows 'Araby' in the collection, like that story reaches a sad conclusion involving, this time, a failure of self-fulfilment on the part of Eveline. Her fiancé Frank has represented Eveline's dream of escape to a better life, and as such, a more substantial focus of hope than the Araby bazaar, which never could have met the boy's wishes for it. Yet Eveline has seemed throughout the story to be at risk of losing her individuality in the face of expectations directed towards her by others. Frank's expectations, while she herself differentiates them emphatically from those imposed by other people, may actually work in quite a similar way. In any case, the title eventually becomes an expression not of subjectivity but of limitation. For readers, Eveline remains the girl who never boarded the ship with Frank, and the title 'Eveline' – denoting a story about a little Eve who resists temptation – labels forever her act of refusal and self-denial.

While the title 'Araby' delineated an entity only fully present at the end of its story, 'Eveline' denotes this story's central focus, a character who is present from the beginning of the text. In this way it resembles the two ensuing titles 'After the Race' and 'Two Gallants'. The first of these does indeed open at the end of a race, and in the second the gallants are present from the outset. Thus the transition from 'Araby' to 'Eveline' – two single-word, dactylic story titles, incidentally – declares itself in this further way to be structurally significant. The first three stories in the collection, concentrating on childhood experience, entail much anticipation, while the next three, concerned with adolescence, evoke present reality and even some limited retrospection. The titles of all six stories, considered as a group, quietly reinforce these emphases.

Further story titles in Dubliners seem considerably more slippery, ironic and multivalent, particularly when juxtaposed as part of a series. 'Two Gallants', for example, can be seen as an obviously ironic label for Lenehan and Corley, conveying precisely the contrast between their grandiose self-evaluations – especially in Corley's case – and the drab reality. It is, however, also a title which could easily designate a different story in the collection instead of its own, a tendency which will become increasingly pronounced as we move through the remaining text of Dubliners. The titles 'The Sisters' and 'The Dead' are in some respects interchangeable, as critics have often noted, though in fact 'The Sisters' seems oblique as a title for either of these stories.[10] The narrator and Mahony in 'An Encounter' begin their expedition in a mood of bravado which a title like 'Two Gallants' could have denoted with suitable irony. This latter title is also echoed by the opening words of 'Grace', 'two gentlemen', and in this story the word 'gentlemen' works in a consistently ironic manner, like the word 'gallants' in the case of the earlier one. That is, nobody in 'Two Gallants' is really a gallant, and nobody in 'Grace' is much of a gentleman.

The titles 'After the Race', 'Clay', 'Grace' and 'A Mother' all operate initially by evoking specific matters treated within the stories. But these titles also ramify further, and seem applicable to other stories besides their own. 'After the Race' offers not merely a parable of Dublin life after rich Continentals have ravished the city, but also a portrait 'after' the Irish race, evoking a shared national willingness to capitulate to such pressures. In doing so, the title obviously hints that similar processes will operate in other stories in the collection – the behaviour of the men in 'Ivy Day in the Committee Room' comes immediately to mind – and in Dublin society more generally.

The cryptic title 'Clay' may be understood to allude to death and therefore associates this text with the collection's finale 'The Dead', once *Dubliners* becomes a complete book. Initially Joyce titled the story 'Hallow Eve', and he had completed a preliminary version of it by January 1905 (D, 483). He changed the title to 'The Clay' by September 1905, and further revised the text in November 1906, presumably choosing the definitive title at this time. These stages in the evolution of the title point, simultaneously and therefore oddly, to both increasing specificity and increasingly broad reference. The title moves from serving as a general label for the day of the story's events to denoting a particular motif within the narrative. The clay, however, also operates as a reminder of mortality, or of the danger of leading an empty life until the moment of death, not only on Hallow Eve but all year. The subsequent title change from 'The Clay' to 'Clay' then moves the emphasis further from a single depicted incident to the kind of inclusiveness invoked at the end of the whole collection in the mention of 'all the living and the dead' (D, 224). 'The' clay remains a part of the game depicted in the story, but in more general terms clay represents the destiny awaiting everybody. Yet the final, published title 'Clay' also remains gently euphemistic, cryptic and evasive. The word never appears within the story itself, even though most readers learn to associate clay with the 'soft wet substance' featured in the fortune-telling game.[11] Maria wears a blindfold during this sequence and so never catches a glimpse of the clay, which to protect her sensitivities is then discarded before she has a chance to see it. Therefore, readers never see it either, leaving a gap between title and text.

The title 'Grace' operates in much the same way as 'Two Gallants': the word 'grace' inevitably becomes debased, like the term 'gentleman', in Tom Kernan's vicinity. Interpretations of 'Grace' seem richer once the various spiritual and profane connotations of the term are explored. The title embodies the duality which underlies the story and Tom Kernan seems in need of its sanctifying power, even if he is unlikely to receive it given the realities of his character and environment. Yet grace also signifies the (sometimes flexible) time available before a financial debt falls due – and this is the only form Kernan can hope to encounter. The word receives further qualification in an account of his faith in the dignity of his calling: 'He had never been seen in the city without a silk hat of some decency and a pair of gaiters. By grace of these two articles of clothing, he said, a man could always pass muster' (D, 154). The conversation in Kernan's room, despite its ostensible spiritual focus, becomes largely worldly, and even Father Purdon's retreat sermon is also tainted with materialism. Like Kernan himself, the other men in his group tend to be defined by their financial debts, and Purdon's congregation includes both a moneylender and a pawnbroker.

The generic-sounding title 'A Mother' implies that this story explores the role of the mother in Dublin. As John Wyse Jackson and Bernard McGinley suggest, 'she is A Mother: there are many others like her, scattered like confetti near the Kingstown and Dalkey line'.[12] Parental conduct is, in fact, scrutinized not only in this story but also in several others: 'The Boarding House' immediately suggests itself as a closely parallel case. Emphasis falls on the social and financial pressures which might require a Dublin mother to behave in the ways depicted in both these stories. The title 'A Mother' also asserts an evident if oblique link to 'The Sisters', and some of the dysfunctional aspects of family relationships evoked in both stories become mutually reinforcing, suggesting broader patterns operational within the larger society.

The remaining titles in the collection, while most have plausible attachments to their particular stories, also combine the cryptic, general and archetypal. These titles could easily be applied to other stories in the collection as well as to their own. The title 'A Little Cloud' remains especially enigmatic, its connection to its story apparently amorphous. John Gordon suggests that the title chiefly denotes Little Chandler himself, but it still appears to call for a key, and seems on the surface so oblique that it could as well designate a different story, within *Dubliners* or elsewhere.[13] No clouds in the literal, meteorological sense actually appear in 'A Little Cloud', as they do in both the opening stories of the collection, 'The Sisters' and 'An Encounter'. All we see are the 'clouds of [cigar] smoke' in which Gallaher takes refuge (D, 78). These may seem an echo of the 'little clouds of smoke' produced by the priest's snuff in 'The Sisters' (D, 12).

The title 'The Dead', besides seeming a suitable label for 'The Sisters', has varying relevance to most of the rest of the collection as well. It is apt that the story serving as the collection's coda should bear such a title, since so many of the stories illustrate the power of the dead over the living, or depict characters who are so socially entrapped as to seem only half alive themselves. Maria in 'Clay' serves as an obvious example.

The remaining three story titles denote situations, syndromes or modes of analysis which seem applicable to almost every part of the collection: 'A Painful Case', 'An Encounter' and 'Counterparts'. 'A Painful Case' might serve as a title for almost any of the stories, as Ulrich Schneider has pointed out.[14]

For that matter, it would suffice as a title for the whole collection, especially if we recall Joyce's comments about his theme of pervasive hemiplegia. Nearly all the stories depict some kind of encounter and many of them, notably 'Ivy Day', 'The Boarding House' and 'The Dead', are organized around a series of encounters. 'An Encounter' especially resembles 'The Dead' in that its depicted encounter, like Gabriel's confrontations with Lily, Molly Ivors and Gretta, does not evolve along expected lines and serves chiefly to admonish the story's central character. The title 'Counterparts' might similarly serve as a paradigm for the whole collection, since story after story prompts readers to find and to develop associations among characters, creating links which the characters themselves would not notice or acknowledge. It may be meant as a deliberate hint that readers should seek such resemblances between stories as well as within them. Moreover, the verbally echoic titles 'An Encounter' and 'Counterparts' also seem particular counterparts of one another, like the stories they designate. These titles offer an invitation to exchange them, in much the same manner as 'The Sisters' and 'The Dead'. The story 'Counterparts' depicts a series of encounters, while the story 'An Encounter' brings together two characters, the narrator and the josser, who turn out in certain respects to be counterparts.

Eventually, then, *Dubliners* would take on proportions and degrees of complexity which Joyce himself could not have envisaged in detail when he first set about responding to Russell's invitation to write a simple story of rural livemaking pathos, calculated not to shock the reader. From his initial impulse to subvert Russell's programme, through his developing concern with a satirical treatment of Dublin hemiplegia in a series of autonomous stories, and his refinement of tone into a scrupulous meanness parodying the meanness of the society under examination, he would eventually conceive the grand notion of providing a chapter in the moral history of Ireland. Yet, even though he did revise some of the early stories to fit them better into the collection as it evolved, he also seems to have envisaged the contours of the whole enterprise remarkably quickly. The end of the collection not only offsets the beginning, but also harmonizes with it. 'The Dead', still more than 'The Sisters', is richly complex, entrenched in urban settings and preoccupations, much concerned with the influence of the dead on the living, and coolly aloof from any tendency to sentimentalize its subject matter. In its radical exploration of issues of hospitality, gender and national identity, moreover, it might well shock, or at least provoke, a thoughtful reader. In other words, Joyce may indeed have kept some of the limitations of Russell's initial prescription in mind as a satirical target throughout the project. Ironically, his fullest reply to Russell may have come in 'The Dead', a text which not only provides a capstone to *Dubliners*, but marks the moment when Joyce abandoned the short story form altogether.

NOTES

1. See H.W. Gabler and W. Hettche (eds), *Dubliners* (New York: Garland, 1993), p.2.
2. T. Thwaites, *Joycean Temporalities: Debts, Promises, and Countersignatures* (Gainesville, FL: University of Florida Press, 2001), p.40.
3. Gabler and Hettche (eds), *Dubliners*, p.3, n.5.
4. W. Steppe, 'The Merry Greeks (With a Farewell to epicleti)', *James Joyce Quarterly*, 41 (1995), pp.597–617.
5. Gabler and Hettche (eds), *Dubliners*, p.3, n.5.
6. C.P. Curran, *James Joyce Remembered* (New York: Oxford University Press, 1968), p.49.
7. Ibid., p.80.
8. M. Brian, '"A Very Fine Piece of Writing": An Etymological, Dantean, and Gnostic Reading of Joyce's "Ivy Day in the Committee Room"', in R. Bosinelli and Harold F. Mosher Jr (eds), *ReJoycing: New Readings of 'Dubliners'* (Lexington, KY: University Press of Kentucky, 1998), p.218.
9. M. Norris, *Suspicious Readings of Joyce's 'Dubliners'* (Philadelphia, PA: University of Pennsylvania Press, 2003), pp.185–96.

10. See, for example, J.W. Jackson and B. McGinley (eds), *James Joyce's 'Dubliners': An Annotated Edition* (London: Reed, 1993), p.11.

11. See also the discussion of the role of clay in Norris, *Suspicious Readings of Joyce's 'Dubliners'*, pp.151–3.

12. Jackson and McGinley (eds), *James Joyce's 'Dubliners'*, p.134.

13. J. Gordon, *Joyce and Reality: The Empirical Strikes Back* (Syracuse, NY: Syracuse University Press, 2004), pp.33–9.

14. U. Schneider, 'Titles in *Dubliners*', in Bosinelli and Mosher, *ReJoycing*, p.203.

CHAPTER FOUR

The Materiality and Historicity of Language in
A Portrait of the Artist as a Young Man

KEVIN J.H. DETTMAR

Now that the dust of the previous century has settled, there seems little doubt that James Joyce was the most significant, the most influential English-language prose writer of the twentieth century. His one short-story collection, three novels, one play and two volumes of poetry have won him the devoted attention of students, scholars and general readers alike; in scholarly terms alone, Joyce is now the second most densely explicated of English-language authors, after only Shakespeare. He has become, in both the public and scholarly imagination, the bespectacled (or sometimes eye-patched) public face of modern literature, in all its difficulty and hard-won pleasures.

Such a fate was far from evident in the early reaction to his writing: both his collection of fifteen short stories, *Dubliners* (1914), and his auto-biographically based first novel, *A Portrait of the Artist as a Young Man* (1916), very nearly never saw the light of day. The eventual publisher of *Dubliners*, London-based Grant Richards, first issued Joyce a contract for the book in February 1906; the collection itself wasn't published until more than eight years later, however, and after a running battle with a series of publishers and printers that Joyce described in an open letter, 'A Curious History', which he later proposed Richards publish as a preface to the book. At issue, first and foremost, were questions of obscenity and libel – epiphe-nomena of the realism of Joyce's stories – for which publishers believed they would be prosecuted. Joyce's indiscretions are, by contemporary standards, quite tame: A man conducting an adulterous affair is described as having 'two establishments to keep up'; King Edward VII is called by one character 'a bit of a rake'; and the obscene colloquialism 'bloody' pops up with uncomfortable frequency in the second half of the collection (D, 92, 132). At the same time, as Joyce peevishly pointed out in a 1906 letter to Richards, the much grosser obscenity of stories like 'An Encounter' and 'The Boarding House' had been completely overlooked. Richards replied, by return mail, that 'On consideration, I should like to leave out altogether "The [sic] Encounter".'[1] Censors very rarely have a sense of humour.

In 'A Curious History', Joyce throws in the towel:

> I wrote this book seven years ago and, as I cannot see in any quarter a chance that my rights will be protected, I hereby give Messrs Maunsel publicly permission to publish this story ['Ivy Day in the Committee Room'] with what changes or deletions they may please to make and shall hope that what they may publish may resemble that to the writing of which I gave thought and time ... I, as a writer, protest against the systems (legal, social and cere-monious) which have brought me to this pass. (SL, 199)

The pre-publication difficulties of Dubliners mark a minor episode in the larger struggle over censorship that was waged by early twentieth-century writers such as D.H. Lawrence and Radclyffe Hall, and was fought most memorably over Joyce's own 1922 masterpiece Ulysses. As it turns out, Joyce's 'A Curious History' was curiously proleptic: it was written in August 1911, when the book's strange odyssey was barely half done. A Dublin edition of the stories, having been set in type by Maunsel & Co., was summarily destroyed by a scrupulous printer in September 1912. On the back of the annulled contract Joyce wrote a broadside poem, 'Gas from a Burner'; it opens with these lines, spoken by a figure compounded of Maunsel's manager, George Roberts, and the scandalized printer, John Falconer:

> Ladies and gents, you are here assembled
> To hear why earth and heaven trembled
> Because of the black and sinister arts
> Of an Irish writer in foreign parts.

He sent me a book ten years ago.
I read it a hundred times or so,
Backwards and forwards, down and up,
Through both ends of a telescope.
I printed it all to the very last word
But by the mercy of the Lord
The darkness of my mind was rent
And I saw the writer's foul intent. (*CW*, 242–3)

As Joyce's poem closes, the heretical work goes up in flames, as all heretics must: 'I'll burn the book, so help me devil. / I'll sing a psalm as I watch it burn' (245). While Joyce's martyr imagination believed his book to have been burned, in fact the print run was probably just cut and pulped; having come this close to fruition, however, the book's publication was thus delayed by another twenty-one months, until Grant Richards stepped back into the fray and brought the book out in June 1914.

Even while *Dubliners* was fitfully slouching toward London to be born, Joyce was at work on his first novel, *A Portrait of the Artist as a Young Man* (as well as his first volume of poems, *Chamber Music*, published in 1907). Conceptually, *Portrait* is the earlier book: its germ is to be found in a 2,500-word essay that Joyce wrote on 7 January 1904, 'A Portrait of the Artist', whereas the earliest of the *Dubliners* stories, 'The Sisters', was not begun until six months later. Like *Dubliners*, *Portrait* nearly went up in flames before it found its readership. In a famous story, the unfinished manuscript was snatched from the fireplace by Joyce's sister Eileen in 1911, after Joyce had thrown it on the flames in a fit of despair.

This rescued manuscript had already gone through an intermediate stage, in which the short essay 'A Portrait' was expanded into an unfinished novel of twenty-six chapters; the remaining portions of that earlier version were published after Joyce's death as *Stephen Hero*, though the manuscript is said to have been rejected by twenty different publishers before Joyce began its wholesale revision as *Portrait*. Even with the novel in its final form, however, and with both *Chamber Music* and *Dubliners* already in print, Joyce had a great deal of difficulty finding a home for *Portrait*. In what is surely a characteristic opinion, the reader's report prepared for the publisher Duckworth & Co. in June 1916 found both

Joyce's social realism and his narrative experimentation a bit too much to contend with:

> James Joyce's 'Portrait of the Artist as a Young Man' wants going through carefully from start to finish. There are many 'longueurs' [boring passages]. Passages which, though the publisher's reader may find them entertaining, will be tedious to the ordinary man among the reading public ... It is too discursive, formless, unrestrained, and ugly things, ugly words, are too prominent; indeed at times they seem to be shoved in one's face, on purpose, unnecessarily ...
>
> The author shows us he has art, strength and originality, but this MS. wants time and trouble spent on it, to make it a more finished piece of work, to shape it more carefully as the product of the craftsmanship, mind and imagination of the artist. (P, 320)

Having worked on the novel by turns for more than twelve years, Joyce cannot have been pleased to read that the manuscript was in need of 'time and trouble spent on it'. Although the author of the report acknowledged that some of 'the old conventions' concerning fiction were then falling away, he could not yet discern the larger outlines of Joyce's narrative experiment, in which great 'time and trouble' were spent precisely in honing the novel's continually evolving prose – blurring his protagonist's ultimate fate and the novel's plot trajectory, as Joseph Conrad had done in *Heart of Darkness*, in a healthy dose of narrative fog (P, 320).

While Joyce struggled against what, in 'A Curious History', he called 'legal, social and ceremonious' systems in order to get *Dubliners* published, his vision for the stories seems not to have changed significantly from his earliest conception: it was from the beginning to be a collection written 'to betray the soul of that hemiplegia [partial paralysis] or paralysis which many consider a city', written 'for the most part in a style of scrupulous meanness' (SL, 22). In writing *Portrait*, on the other hand – his troubles with publishers notwithstanding – Joyce's main hurdles were personal and artistic, not public. In the 1904 essay he writes with dissatisfaction about the conventions of autobiography, in which the 'features of infancy' are presented only in their 'iron, memorial aspect': youth is narrated only from the hindsight of maturity, and with a false confidence that betrays the real uncertainty of those early years (P, 257). Joyce states as a goal – though one he is unable satisfactorily to accomplish in the early essay – an autobiographical style that would present the past as 'a fluid succession of presents, the development of an entity of which our actual present is a phase only' (P, 257–8). The essay's opening, manifesto-like paragraph concludes with the statement that for those exceptional individuals for whom an autobiography is a worthwhile undertaking, 'a portrait is not an identificative paper but rather the curve of an emotion' (P, 258).

Joyce thus sought to forge (a word that plays an interesting role in Portrait, as we'll see) a style of shifting emphases and perspectives, drawing its imagery and vocabulary from different sources during different periods of his protagonist's life – a technique we might today, in light of the nearly simultaneous work in narrative technique being carried out in England by writers like Conrad and Ford Madox Ford, call 'impressionism'. Joyce's 'Portrait' essay is certainly impressionistic – nearly to the point of incomprehensibility; his impressionism in presentation is combined with a preciosity of style, rendering the resultant text narrowly self-involved. Over the years of its genesis, however – and because of, not merely in spite of, its trials and persecutions – this first 'Portrait' became *A Portrait of the Artist as a Young Man*, achieving a nearly perfect accommodation of style to mood and thought – 'the curve of an emotion', precisely. In the much discussed 1997 Random House poll that named Joyce's *Ulysses* the number-one novel of the twentieth century, *Portrait* came in a close third, behind F. Scott Fitzgerald's *The Great Gatsby*; this novel that nearly arrived stillborn has now been confirmed as a twentieth-century classic and has been installed as a mainstay of high-school and college curricula in English-speaking countries around the world.

* * *

Though written very nearly in tandem, *Dubliners* and *A Portrait of the Artist as a Young Man* have very different agendas and represent very different reading experiences. We might, for purposes of illustration, think of Joyce's first two works of fiction as representing critiques of two rather different literary genres: *Dubliners*, a critique of the short story as Joyce had inherited it, in which complicated psychological struggles are simplified and resolved in the course of three thousand words; and *Portrait*, a critique of the deeply romantic legacy of the *Bildungsroman* (novel of education and maturation) and its close relative the *Künstlerroman* (which focuses on the development of the artist), forms that perpetuated a notion of heroism wholly unsuited to the realities of life and art in the twentieth century.

In *Dubliners* a handful of writers and would-be writers make up a supporting cast: The protagonist-narrators in the first three stories clearly have literary pretensions, as do Little Chandler ('A Little Cloud'), Mr Duffy ('A Painful Case'), Joe Hynes ('Ivy Day in the Committee Room'), and Gabriel Conroy. In *A Portrait of the Artist as a Young Man*, of course, a would-be artist is at the absolute centre of the novel's action and narration: a presence so central that, in ways that were being fleshed out in physics and astrophysics at the very time Joyce was writing *Portrait*, all other objects are more or less deformed in his field. In the novel, the competing claims of religion and art are laid out, and in Chapters 3 and 4, especially, we see them at war. One thing not often remarked upon in the criticism of *Portrait*, however, is that within the novel's pages, it is far from clear that art comes out on top. In the sermons of Chapter 3 a poetic and rhetorical inventiveness is brought to bear that dwarfs anything our young artist himself musters; the mystic, scholar and writer Thomas Merton, for instance, converted to Catholicism as a result of reading them. By comparison, the writing that Stephen himself produces during the course of the novel is pale and bloodless; we read *about* a poem rehearsing romantic platitudes on 'the maiden lustre of the moon', for instance, and his artistic production for the period covered in the novel culminates in his 'Villanelle of the Temptress', which represents an advance only in that Stephen is parroting *fin de siècle* rather than earlier-century clichés (P, 70).

The scene describing the writing of Stephen's first poem, in the second 'scene' of Chapter 2, is instructive. In a passage recalling the discussion of epiphany in *Stephen Hero*, Joyce describes Stephen Dedalus's habits of attention: 'He chronicled with patience what he saw, detaching himself from it and testing its mortifying flavour in secret' (P, 67). What follows, though not labelled as such in the text, are precisely three epiphanies. A full description of the epiphany is one of the elements that Joyce stripped out of *Stephen Hero* in making *Portrait*; if we turn back to that earlier text, however, we discover the following explanation of its place in Stephen Dedalus's evolving aesthetic philosophy:

> This triviality [of a banal conversation he has overheard] made him think of collecting many such moments together in a book of epiphanies. By an epiphany he meant a sudden spiritual manifestation, whether in the vulgarity of speech or of gesture or in a memorable phase of the mind itself. He believed that it was for the man of letters to record these epiphanies with extreme care, seeing that they themselves are the most delicate and evanescent of moments. (SH, 211)

Two of these revelatory moments in *Portrait*, in fact, are based on incidents recorded in Joyce's own epiphany notebook. Like the *Dubliners* stories, these vignettes are spare, closely observed and slightly mysterious. The third, describing the tram ride back from Harold's Cross in which Stephen's initials-only love interest E – C – seems eminently embraceable but remains unembraced, is the provocation for the poem Stephen then attempts to write. These three brief prose sketches – based on what we see in *Dubliners*, for instance, as well as the mature prose sections of *Portrait* – represent something similar to what Joyce thought twentieth-century literature ought to be accomplishing, that 'style of scrupulous meanness' he saw as a kind of moral ideal (SL, 83).

In explicit contrast, Stephen's poem is ... well, strictly speaking, it's just not there at all. We watch Stephen write; but we're shown no writing. Just when it seems that his attempts to write the poem will fail, even by Stephen's standards, he pushes forward by 'brooding' on the tram incident, and in the process of writing the poem,

> all those elements which he deemed common and insignificant fell out of the scene. There remained no trace of the tram itself nor of the trammen nor of the horses: nor did he and she appear vividly. The verses told only of the night and the balmy breeze and the maiden lustre of the moon. Some undefined sorrow was hidden in the hearts of the protagonists as they stood in silence beneath the leafless trees and when the moment of farewell had come the kiss,

which had been withheld by one, was given by both. (P, 70–1)

Whereas Joyce's own practice insists on focusing on the actual details of a scene until they come starkly into view – chronicling with patience what one sees – his artist 'as a young man' instead 'broods' (never a good sign, in Joyce) until everything real falls away and all that's left is a sodden lump of romantic clichés. A sharply observant prose like that of the Dubliners stories is written about Stephen's experience, but he himself can write only a vaporous and derivative poetry. (Joyce emphasizes the schoolboy quality of the poem by having Stephen write it in a school exercise-book, with the motto Ad Majoram Dei Gloriam ['to the greater glory of God'] at the head and Laus Deo Semper ['praise to God always'] at its close, the obligatory topoi of his classroom writing exercises under the Jesuits.) As if the point were not yet clear, the paragraph concludes: 'having hidden the book, he went into his mother's bedroom and gazed at his face for a long time in the mirror of her dressing table' (P, 71). A very Narcissus in Dublin.

In the course of this scene, and others beside (compare, for instance, the prose describing the 'bird girl' in Chapter 5 with the jejune villanelle he makes out of the same episode), Joyce seems to be suggesting that if poetry had been the leading edge of literary innovation in the nineteenth century, it would be prose that would lead the way in the twentieth. (On the far side of the twentieth century now, we cannot help but be impressed by Joyce's prescience.) As long as Stephen fetishizes writers like George Gordon, Lord Byron, Percy Bysshe Shelley and Algernon Charles Swinburne, the authentic literary voice of the twentieth century, the modern world, will remain gagged. As a young writer Joyce first thought of himself as a poet, though had his reputation depended on his poems, his name would now be forgotten: a perusal of Joyce's own first volume of poems, Chamber Music, quickly confirms that his prose was as avant-garde as his poetry was derrière-garde. Thus the move from poet to prose writer was one that Joyce knew something about, for it was a move he himself had already made by the time he wrote Portrait. As the example of Stephen's first poem makes clear, Portrait supports a very complicated narrative structure: it is an autobiographical novel about a former self – a self about whom the author now has some misgivings, even feels some embarrassment. But in strict accordance with what critic Maud Ellmann has called modernism's 'poetics of impersonality',[2] Joyce forbids himself anything like explicit, third-person commentary on Stephen's beliefs, positions and actions. The novel contains only dramatic 'showing', no authorial 'telling', and the aesthetically calculated juxtaposition (the prose and poetic versions of Stephen's tram ride, for instance) is the most explicit commentary Joyce will allow himself. This stealthy mode of criticizing his protagonist, providing a kind of ironic counterpoint, differentiates *Portrait* from the abortive draft *Stephen Hero*, in which Joyce did indulge, in small doses at least, in commentary on the callowness of his protagonist. In *Stephen Hero*, when Stephen flies a bit too high, for instance, the narrative calls him a 'fantastic idealist'; in *Portrait*, this kind of criticism must remain always unspoken, merely implied, so that, for example, Stephen believes the most sublime and transcendent moment of *The Count of Monte Cristo* to be Dantes' 'sadly proud gesture of refusal': ' – Madam, I never eat muscatel grapes' (SH, 34; P, 63).

Hence the overarching structural irony of *Portrait*, which has made the tone of the book so very hard for so very many readers over the years to discern. It's a novel about a devotee of an anachronistic literary cult, written by a writer who has himself outgrown his infatuation with that same cult but who writes with a conviction that the only legitimate form of critique is precisely the patient and detached description found in Stephen's epiphanies. Joyce's reluctance to 'weigh in' has made for an interesting reception history; as in *Dubliners*, in *Portrait* Joyce seeks to hold up his finely polished looking-glass to us for our inspection. But since we readers tend to identify with, rather than criticize, the aspirations and idealism of Stephen Dedalus – because his foibles are so nearly our own – we have tended not to see Joyce's understated criticism. This, finally, is what makes Joyce's writing in *Dubliners* and *Portrait* so powerful for so many readers: we're never allowed simply to sit in judgement of their characters, but must instead recognize that their follies are our own. We are drawn, propulsively, into an imaginative identification with these characters and their plights. The reader whose heart doesn't respond to Stephen Dedalus's high-flown aspirations ('I go to encounter for the millionth time the reality of experience') hasn't truly engaged these texts in the spirit with which they were written (P, 252–3). Regarding his most famous protagonist, the nineteenth-century French novelist Gustave Flaubert wrote, 'Madame Bovary, c'est moi': Flaubert held himself neither superior to, nor different in kind from, his deeply flawed character. And like Flaubert, the reader of *Dubliners* and *Portrait* must be able to say, when she has come to the end: 'Gabriel Conroy, c'est moi', and 'Stephen Dedalus, c'est moi'. For in the letter quoted above, Joyce promises (as Shakespeare does in *Hamlet*) not to 'hold ... the mirror up to nature' – but instead, much more menacingly, he holds the mirror up before his readers, that they might '[have] one good look at themselves in [his] nicely polished looking-glass' (*SL*, 90).

Portrait, in other words, moves the *Bildungsroman* and the *Künstlerroman* into the twentieth century, although in the process it drags along with it a resolutely nineteenth-century protagonist. In one of his last diary entries Stephen attempts to outdo his fellow countryman and poet William Butler Yeats. Yeats, who had referred to himself as one of Ireland's 'last romantics', expresses the desire through his character Michael Robartes to 'press / My heart upon the loveliness / That has long faded from the world'.[3] With even more romantic hunger than Robartes' nostalgic longing betrays, Stephen expresses his desire 'to press in my arms the loveliness which has not yet come into the world' (*P*, 251). While Joyce does not allow the narrative of *Portrait* to level any explicit criticism at Stephen, other characters are free to do so, and seeing the great gulf opened up between Joyce's prose and Stephen's poetry, we might sympathize with Lynch's closing comment on Stephen's discourse on aesthetic philosophy: ' – What do you mean, Lynch asked surlily, by prating about beauty and the imagination in this miserable God forsaken island?' (*P*, 215). What, indeed?

* * *

One point upon which Joyce insists in *Portrait* is the absolutely fundamental role that language plays in our being-in-the-world; throughout the novel, he forces us to pay careful attention to the language in which we cast our dreams, and to which we perforce bend our realities. Here again Joyce anticipates new discoveries made in the sciences, in this case the human science of linguistics. The idea, called in one of its early formulations the 'Whorfian hypothesis', is that we never use language

without language at the same time using us: language is not merely
descriptive of, but in fact constitutive of, what we know as 'reality'.
Words, Joyce realized early on, always drag along with them the history
of their prior associations and usages; words, in one sense, are never
purely aesthetic objects, 'certain good' in Yeats's phrase,[4] but are always
already political objects. Stephen recognizes this, if inchoately, when he
muses on the English-born dean of studies' condescending attention to
Stephen's use of the word 'tundish':

> — The language in which we are speaking is his before it is mine. How
> different are the words home, Christ, ale, master, on his lips and on mine!
> I cannot speak or write these words without unrest of spirit. His
> language, so familiar and so foreign, will always be for me an acquired
> speech. I have not made or accepted its words. My voice holds them
> at bay. My soul frets in the shadow of his language. (P, 189)

While Stephen may desire to press in his arms 'the loveliness which has
not yet come into the world', there is an awareness at the textual level,
if not perhaps at a conscious level, for Stephen, that he has not 'made or
accepted' the words of any human tongue, but must instead receive
them at second hand. And this hand-me-down language, Stephen can't
help but notice from the very earliest pages of the novel, is always somewhat shop-worn. Stephen's vision of pure artistic creation from nothing
(ex nihilo), something completely fresh and new, requires a pristine and
univocal language: And yet everywhere, language equivocates. In the
same conversation with the dean of studies, Stephen calls attention to
this problem, using as his example the various connotations of the word
'detain'; and confirming his worst fears, the dean misunderstands
Stephen's point initially because his own usage is loose and sloppy. In
Through the Looking-Glass (a text that enthralled Joyce, as Finnegans Wake
clearly evidences), Humpty Dumpty insists to Alice that, 'When I use a
word ... it means just what I choose it to mean';[5] like Humpty Dumpty,
Stephen would like to exert complete mastery over language and meaning, but his experience consistently brings home the fact that none of us
has such power. He may complain, in Ulysses, that 'history ... is a nightmare from which I am trying to awake', but he realizes that he must do
so in a language conditioned by that very history (U, 2.377).

The inherently equivocal structure of language (and to be clear, this is the structure of all human languages, not just English) – language's consistent difference from itself – has both this historical dimension and another, ahistorical component. The words upon which Stephen muses while talking with the dean of studies, 'home', 'Christ', 'ale' and 'master', all resonate differently for Stephen owing to the history of colonial subjection of Ireland by Great Britain; for the ambiguity of these words, to quote the Englishman Haines in *Ulysses*, 'it seems history is to blame' (U, 1.649). But even if this history could be factored out, language is always at odds with itself. The French philosopher Jacques Derrida has termed this frustrating and elusive structure of language *différance*; it means that the momentum of writing is always centrifugal, always toward what Derrida calls the 'dissemination' of meaning, rather than its consolidation, as the idealized will of its author, in a text. In his best-known example, Derrida examines the way that the word 'supplement' (which he comes across in a passage from Jean-Jacques Rousseau) means both 'surplus' and 'remedy for a deficit': the supplement is the surplus that (inadvertently) betrays a lack. Such, according to Derrida, is the fundamental structure of all human language.[6]

Though no linguist, Joyce seems intuitively to have had a sense of this dynamic; this principle is observable on both the level of the individual word and on the larger level of phrases, sentences and narrative units, in all of Joyce's writing. (In an early example, Joyce punningly titled his first volume of poems *Chamber Music*, betraying both the poems' delicate beauty and invoking the sound of urine in a chamberpot.) The truth of language's inherent slipperiness is first made manifest to Stephen Dedalus just a couple of pages into *Portrait*. Stephen, cold while playing football in the fall air,

> kept his hands in the side pockets of his belted grey suit. That was a belt round his pocket. And belt was also to give a fellow a belt. One day a fellow had said to Cantwell:
> – I'd give you such a belt in a second. (P, 9)

Belt as security, belt as violence: 'belt', it would seem, is an especially paradoxical word, something like its own antonym. In truth, however, as Stephen soon discovers, language is full of similarly slippery terms: in quick succession he is given to contemplating the mystery of words like 'suck', 'queer' and most famously of all, 'smugging'. Indeed at the very close of the novel, which the diary-entry form suggests that Stephen himself has written, the final formulation of his artistic credo is undermined by just such a slippage: 'Welcome, O life! I go to encounter for the millionth time the reality of experience and to forge in the smithy of my soul the uncreated conscience of my race' (P, 252–3). 'Forge', like the good old English word 'cleave', is its own antonym. Using the metaphor of a blacksmith working metal, Stephen promises to 'forge ... the uncreated conscience of his race' by heating and hammering the red-hot metal of the English language, bending it to his will. But to forge is also, of course, to counterfeit: forgery, whether in one's smithy or in one's basement, is an act of criminal deception, an attempt to pass off the ersatz as the genuine article. Is Stephen aware of the equivocation in his declaration, the *différance* between intention and utterance, the dissemination of his meaning every which way? We cannot know the answer to this question; the next sentence is the text's last, as Stephen invokes the protection and aid of his mythic forebear, the Dædalus of the novel's epigraph. But there may be, too, a meaningful difference between Stephen's own awareness of his writing's betrayal, or lack thereof, and our understanding as readers. Perhaps, even if Stephen has not, we are able to enjoy a kind of hard-won epiphany; and while our 'artist as a young man' wrestles to make an intractable language conform to his meaning, his author instead focuses our attention on the stubborn materiality and historicity of language. A wiser writer – like Joyce, perhaps – would learn to work in accord with language's stubborn resistances, rather than trying in vain to master them.

As suggested earlier, it's not simply individual words that slip – as if that weren't bad enough. But phrases, too, sometimes carry with them untoward baggage, refusing to mean simply what they appear to say. On an early page of the novel, for instance, the affluence of one of Stephen's classmates at Clongowes Wood School is invoked: 'Rody Kickham had greaves in his number and a hamper in the refectory' (P, 8). A hamper in the refectory means simply that Rody Kickham has a private supply of food available to him in the dining hall – a luxury that Stephen's family certainly cannot afford for him. The phrase 'greaves in his number', however, is a bit more layered. The standard annotations will tell us that it means 'shin-guards in his locker', suggesting the possibility that shin-guards are not issued to all the boys at Clongowes as standard equipment: again, the Kickham family's wealth buys young Rody a degree of luxury that Stephen cannot afford, and when playing football Rody gets kicked in the greaves, while Stephen takes it in the shins. However, a look into the historical *Oxford English Dictionary* suggests a further dimension. The word 'greaves' is quite rare, out of use since the late nineteenth century, and the OED gives as its literary exemplars passages from an obscure poem of Lord Byron, 'The Bride of Abydos', as well as a passage from a far more familiar poem of Alfred, Lord Tennyson, 'The Lady of Shallot': 'The sun came dazzling thro' the leaves, / And flamed upon the brazen greaves / Of bold Sir Lancelot.'[7] Hence 'greaves' isn't just any old word for shin-guards, but a particularly literary one (the OED also tells us that the word 'shin-guards' was in use back in the 1880s); further, it's not just literary language, but language retaining the flavour of its earlier usage in Tennyson: an identifiably Tennysonian affectation on Stephen's part (if, as is common in the criticism, we assume Stephen's consciousness to be shaping, if not exactly writing, the prose of this section). With this Tennyson connection unearthed, it's easy to look back to a sentence earlier in the paragraph and find Tennyson's fingerprints there, too: 'The evening air was pale and chilly and after every charge and thud of the foot-ballers the greasy leather orb flew like a heavy bird through the grey light' sounds a lot more like something from *Idylls of the King*, or even 'The Lady of Shallot', once we're alerted to Tennyson's lurking presence in the passage (P, 8). Further, the early flirtation with Tennyson that lingers around these images and archaisms sheds an interesting light on a later episode in the novel, when Stephen is beaten up by his classmate Heron and his goons for suggesting that Byron is a better poet than the 'rhymster' Tennyson. Stephen's Tennysonianism suggests he had not always thought so (P, 80).

Moving up one level, we witness Stephen's growing attraction to the story of the 'dark avenger' of *The Count of Monte Cristo* throughout the first two chapters of the novel. Stephen's grasp on the specifics of the plot seem somewhat shaky, but one thing he knows for certain:

> He wanted to meet in the real world the unsubstantial image [of the love interest in *Monte Cristo*, Mercedes] which his soul so

constantly beheld. He did not know where to seek it or how but a premonition which led him on told him that this image would, without any overt act of his, encounter him. They would meet quietly as if they had known each other and had made their tryst, perhaps at one of the gates or in some more secret place. They would be alone, surrounded by darkness and silence: and in that moment of supreme tenderness he would be transfigured. He would fade into something impalpable under her eyes and then in a moment, he would be transfigured. Weakness and timidity and inexperience would fall from him in that magic moment. (P, 65)

While Stephen seems to be imagining some sort of amorous tryst, his imagination has not yet been fed any of the stark details of actual, physical sex: like his poem about riding the tram home with E – C – just a few pages later, his inexperience leads him here to the brink of a scene that he is unable to imagine. *The Count of Monte Cristo*, too, is evasive on these questions; and precisely because the story he wishes to act out has skirted the issue, Stephen's imagination runs into a kind of wall when the actual moment of his 'fall' is to take place.

Stephen's fall from sexual innocence into experience takes place in the closing pages of Chapter 2; and when he wanders into the red-light Nighttown district of Dublin, and ends up in the bed of a prostitute, every feature of his earlier fantasy centring on Mercedes is ironically fulfilled. Not knowing where to look for Mercedes, his feet seemingly of their own accord take him 'into a maze of narrow and dirty streets' (P, 100). He knows that his role in his encounter with his Mercedes will be entirely passive, and in his transaction with the prostitute, Stephen 'would not bend to kiss her', and later 'swoons' or perhaps, less poetically, passes out (P, 101). He does indeed 'fade into something impalpable under her eyes'; but this is *Monte Cristo* with an ironic difference (P, 65). With the veil of a romantic fantasy interposing itself between Stephen and the prostitute, it's almost as if he's not present at his own deflowering. The narrative, in this case, both trumps and dictates the real.

One lesson, then, that we might take away from this exquisitely well-written book is that narrative in particular, and language in general, is in a sense the 'prison-house' that German philosopher Friedrich Nietzsche, another near contemporary of Joyce's, claimed that it was:

reality, or 'the reality of experience', is unavailable to human vessels excepting through the somewhat distorting vehicle of human language.[8] Some, like young Stephen Dedalus, might expend their energies wishing for, working for, a language that would escape all such limitations: a sort of pre-Babel super-language, infinitely adaptable to the infinitely shifting shapes of the real. Another response suggests itself, however – one that Joyce was to work out in greater detail, and with greater care, in his next novel, *Ulysses*: that if stories are the only means we have to 'encounter reality', it matters very much which stories we carry around in our heads. *A Portrait of the Artist as a Young Man*, a novel that, on one level, counsels caution about the stories with which we furnish our imaginations, makes a very good start.

NOTES

1. See Robert Scholes, 'Grant Richards to James Joyce', *Studies in Bibliography*, 16 (1963), p.147.
2. See Maud Ellmann, *The Poetics of Impersonality: T.S Eliot and Ezra Pound* (Cambridge, MA: Harvard University Press, 1988).
3. See W.B. Yeats, 'He Remembers Forgotten Beauty', in *The Collected Works of W.B. Yeats*, ed. Richard J. Finneran (New York: Scriber's, 1996), p.62.
4. See Yeats, 'The Song of the Happy Shepherd', in Finneran (ed.), *The Collected Works of W.B. Yeats*, p.7.
5. Lewis Carol, *Through the Looking-Glass*, in *Alice's Adventures in Wonderland and Through the Looking-Glass*, ed. Hugh Haughton (Harmondsworth: Penguin, 1998), p.186.
6. See Jacques Derrida, *Of Grammatology*, trans. Gayatri Chakravorty Spivak (Baltimore, MD: Johns Hopkins University Press, 1997), pp.141–64.
7. Alfred Lord Tennyson, 'The Lady of Shallot', in *Alfred Loyd Tennyson: Selected Poems*, ed. Michael Barron (London: Everyman, 2004), pp.6–10.
8. See Friedrich Nietzsche, *Beyond Good and Evil: Prelude to a Philosophy of the Future*, trans. Walter Kaufmann in *Basic Writings of Nietzsche* (New York: Modern Library, 2000), pp.179–436.

CHAPTER FIVE

'Not ... love-verses at all, I perceive': Joyce's Minor Works

MIRANDA HICKMAN

Addressing Joyce's so-called 'minor works' involves entering an area of critical unease about how to reckon with such early texts as the lyric poems of *Chamber Music* (first published as a volume in 1907), *Giacomo Joyce*, the notebook of erotic meditations from Joyce's Trieste days as a language teacher (published posthumously in 1968), and Joyce's one play, *Exiles* (published 1918). These texts are all decidedly exiles from the centre of the Joycean canon – and critical responses to them have contributed to the demarcation of the canon's centre from its edges. The tenuous position of these texts within Joyce's œuvre, the dismissiveness with which they are often treated, the critical gallantry with which their value has sometimes been asserted: all these point to an opportunity to reassess both the texts themselves and the critical standards by which they have been marginalized.

The three minor works on which this chapter focuses all date from the early stages of Joyce's career, and all had come to fruition before Joyce established a major reputation. The brief, delicate poems eventually collected as *Chamber Music* comprise some of his very first writing, developed between 1901 and 1904 while Joyce was still in Dublin, the time of their composition overlapping with the period during which he began work on the stories of *Dubliners*. *Giacomo Joyce*, emerging from Joyce's 1907–15 experiences in Trieste as a private language teacher, was committed to paper in final form in the summer of 1914. *Exiles* was begun in late 1913, also in Trieste, just before Joyce started work on *Ulysses* in the spring of 1914. Thus all three works were essentially finished by Joyce's breakthrough year in 1914 when Dubliners finally appeared in book form and Portrait of the Artist as a Young Man was serialized in The Egoist.

All three of these minor works often occasion disquiet and even dismay. Richard Brown invokes the notion of the 'ugly duckling' to capture the reputation of Exiles and Giacomo Joyce,[1] and Louis Armand figures the latter through a trope appropriate to the text's transgressive eroticism: that of the bastard child.[2] As Henriette Power notes of Giacomo Joyce in particular, it prevents critics from feeling 'comfortable or intimate' with it, and 'can complicate … attempts to produce a unified reading' of Joyce's corpus.[3] Indeed both the poems and Exiles might be said to provoke critical anxiety, creating troubling anomalies within the Joyce canon. Power even asks whether Giacomo Joyce should be considered part of the Joycean corpus at all; and Herbert Howarth argues that the place of Chamber Music 'is at once first, last, and nowhere. Chronologically it is first. It is last for most critics. It is nowhere for most readers, who ignore it or read it too rapidly to gather what it can give.'[4]

That these works tend to be placed together in accounts of Joyce's œuvre as his 'minor' or 'shorter' works, collapsed into one category, indicates that for most readers it is the marginalized status they share that overrides their considerable differences: what appears paramount in many critical assessments is that they are not Dubliners, A Portrait of the Artist as a Young Man, Ulysses or Finnegans Wake, and that they read as remote from all of these. And this, in turn, is because they are widely regarded as suffering from a lack of the aesthetic, philosophical and attitudinal sophistication associated with Joyce's most celebrated works – as well as an absence of humour – which makes us miss the wit as we do when reading Wilde's Salomé and lamenting the absence of Wilde's incisive dandies.[5]

As Wallace Stevens once said of T.S. Eliot, it is the 'prodigiousness' of Joyce's reputation that conditions responses to these texts, arousing expectations that are usually disappointed: as Bernard Benstock notes of the reaction to Harold Pinter's successful 1970 production of Exiles, 'It was magnificent, but it was not quite Joyce'.[6] The way these works have been treated reveals much about the standards of judgement that have come to prevail in critical conversations about Joyce. In view of the criteria developed for, and from, Joyce's major works, these minor texts have also often been read as merely derivative, failing to appropriate and transmute source material as adroitly as do their major counterparts. And although, strictly speaking, only the poems of *Chamber Music* could be considered juvenilia, the sensibility they convey, reading to many as unleavened by the humour that enlivens Joyce's major works, has often been taken to indicate an immaturity or *naïveté* that the later, grander works transcend.

Even when these minor works are appreciated, their worth is often regarded as deriving from the light they can shed on the major works. At their most beneficent, critics try, as Robert Spoo puts it, to 'redeem...' these works 'from the margins' by suggesting that, if not successful works in their own right, they are nonetheless valuable for their ability to illuminate the sources of many of Joyce's later, most widely circulating ideas and formulations.[7] Filaments from *Chamber Music* and *Giacomo Joyce* reappear, permuted, in both *Portrait* and *Ulysses*: the poems of *Chamber Music* enhance understanding of the villanelle that plays a pivotal role in Stephen's imaginative life in *Portrait* (P, 210) and look forward to the musical playfulness of the Sirens episode of *Ulysses*; a paragraph from *Giacomo Joyce* provides material for a central moment in *Portrait* (P, 225); the voyeuristic perspective of *Giacomo Joyce* anticipates that of the Nausicaa episode of *Ulysses*; and the topic of adulterous desire on which *Exiles* meditates reappears in *Ulysses*. All three texts can be regarded, then, as seedbeds or quarries for later work, awareness of whose resources can benefit scholarship. The critical narrative implicit in such an approach, however, problematically treats these texts as raw, comparatively unfinished material that was later recycled – even redeemed – by its later reincarnations.[8]

As signalled by such recent cues as Louis Armand and Clare Wallace's recent edition of *Giacomo Joyce*, however, the moment seems ripe for a new perspective on these minor works. As Djuna Barnes puts it in *Nightwood* (which Joseph Frank in 1947 compared to *Ulysses*), when we find something we do not like in a person we know and like, we engage in 'convulsions of the spirit, analogous to the displacement in the fluids of the oyster, that must cover its itch with pearl' – 'by which what we must love is made into what we can love'.[9] I would suggest that the critical manoeuvres in response to these texts, though valuable for scholarship, have sometimes attempted to produce comforting pearls in response to irritants, when it might be well to let the irritants stand as they are in all their instructiveness. Here I turn again to Bernard

Benstock's response to Pinter's successful 1970 stage production of *Exiles*: that 'it was not quite Joyce'. At this juncture, these 'minor works' allow us to discern what, at the centenary of Joyce's first publication, we consider, and want to consider, 'quite Joyce' – what qualifies as eligible for inclusion within that imaginative construct.

Chamber Music, *Giacomo Joyce* and *Exiles* offer opportunity for troubling, or at least reconsidering more thoughtfully, the standards according to which we define the 'Joycean', Joycean success, and by extension, modernist success. As Louis Armand suggests of *Giacomo Joyce*, insofar as these minor works haunt the Joycean canon as supplementary, we can enlist them to deconstruct the assumptions on which our dominant notions of the Joycean rely.[10] When Eliot published *The Waste Land* in 1922, poets publishing work at the same time – William Carlos Williams and Wallace Stevens – both suffered from Eliot's ascent to success and the consequent enshrinement of his aesthetic as the best that 'our modern experiment', as Pound put it, had to offer.[11] Williams was vociferous in his laments, suggesting that poets seeking to accomplish different poetic objectives according to different poetic values would suffer by comparison to the man being touted as a titan of modernist experiment. Stevens, too, publishing *Harmonium* in 1923, was left out in the cold by the blaze of Eliot's triumph. Retrospective accounts of this jockeying for ascendancy among the writers of this period underscore that what was considered dominant at that point is not necessarily how we wish to hierarchize matters now; time has brought both Williams's and Stevens's verse to a prominence and respect it never enjoyed in the 1920s. I am thinking here of the way that *The Waste Land* and *Ulysses* have widely come to be read as, to use a Joycean term, 'counterparts' in verse and prose, the two signal achievements of that modernist *annus mirabilis* of 1922. If the dominance of the standards implied by *The Waste Land* has been interrogated in years since, then perhaps the dominance of those implied by *Ulysses* deserve re-examination as well. And in this instance, what has been frozen out by *Ulysses* is not the work of other writers besides Joyce, but rather, to use Armand's metaphor, Joyce's own illegitimate children. What the outlier status of Joyce's minor works might beneficially prompt is a reassessment – though not necessarily an overturning – of the judgements according to which they have been relegated to 'minor' status to begin with.

It is above all the passion for Joycean irony that has shunted these works to the margins. The earnestness of *Chamber Music* and *Exiles*, the unredeemed self-involvement of the voyeur figure in *Giacomo Joyce*: these leave these minor works out in most discussions of Joyce's chief contributions. And Joyce himself had much to do with how we valorize that irony, as he often indicated progress toward maturity in his work by an increase in irony, accomplished through a characteristic narrative strategy that lifts a textual element evocative of a certain perspective or sensibility, initially treated with seriousness in one context, and transfers it to another context, where it is newly embedded in such a way as to receive satirical mockery that shows up its foibles and limitations. Thus, in many ways throughout his corpus, Joyce invites us to equate a growth in ironic detachment with a rise in sophistication. The poems of *Chamber Music* have been likened to the 'Villanelle of the Temptress' that Stephen composes in *Portrait* ('Are you not weary of ardent ways?'), for instance, a poem Joyce actually wrote seriously at an earlier period but ironized in *Portrait*, where he uses it to evidence Stephen's naïveté.[12] Richard Rowan's gloomy musings on fidelity and liberty in *Exiles*, if read against the highjinks of *Ulysses*, come across as a first-stage emotional response that is later transcended by the Nietzschean gaiety of *Ulysses'* mischievous meditations on adultery as a fact of life. The force field of the Joycean canon, along with the pressures of the postmodern climate, have convinced us that irony is the road to maturity, and that texts devoid of the ironic wink lack sophistication. Through contrasts like the one between the Stephen of *Ulysses*, framed by the complex environment of *Ulysses* that involves Bloom's narrative, and the younger Stephen of *Portrait*, Joyce trains us to be alert for moments of supersession when a more detached perspective trumps a naïve one, usually marked by Romantic longing, humourlessness and self-engrossment.

At this moment, however, it would be well to resist the tendency to regret the lack of signature Joycean irony in these so-called minor texts and attempt, as Armand suggests with respect to *Giacomo Joyce*, to accept these texts on their own terms, as worthy of critical treatment in their own right. Their placement in the framework of Joyce criticism has often distorted them, pulled them ellipsoid in efforts to make them in some way serve or match the terms of other works. In general, evaluation of these texts according to the criteria of judgement derived from the 'major' works has occluded other dimensions of them that deserve consideration. As Padraic Colum notes in his introduction to *Exiles*, 'Among Joyce's works his single play has never been given a fair show. *Exiles* comes after *Portrait of the Artist* and before *Ulysses*, and critics have recorded their feeling that it has not the enchantment of the first nor the richness of the second, and they have neglected to assess what quality it actually has' (E, 7). Colum's remark captures the methodology of this chapter — to leave to the side claims emphasizing the failure of these texts to live up to the example of their grander siblings — in fact, for purposes of discovery, to bracket off temporarily that they have siblings at all — and consider what these minor works 'actually have'.

* * *

Chamber Music comprises a suite of thirty-six lyric poems whose sequence, as finally chosen by Joyce's brother Stanislaus,[13] traces a time-honoured trajectory: a narrative catalyzed by the speaker's love for a young woman, entailing the rise of desire, seduction and love's eventual diminution and loss.[14] The poems are highly stylized, conventional and even mannered, displaying the influences of Elizabethan lyric poetry, Romantic verse and Irish folk songs.[15] Unlike the famous poetic sequences to which their genre points, such as the Shakespearean sonnets or Petrarch's *Rime Sparse*, these brief poems do not register the harsher vicissitudes associated with love — its agonies of spirit, fears of betrayal and lack of mutual feeling — nor to any great extent even describe the beloved's beauty; as Spoo notes, the speaker's attention tends to 'bend upon the self rather than the other', such that 'the beloved's reality and body' are all but 'expunged'.[16] The many adroit manoeuvres of these gossamer creations, however, call attention to Joyce's skill itself; Yeats persuasively noted that these poems read as the work of 'a young man who is practising his instrument, taking pleasure in the mere handling of the stops' (PSW, 6). Especially through his deft repetitions of words and phrases with slight variations, Joyce creates effects of intensity and elegance. By virtue of their conspicuously graceful phrases and participation in long-established topoi, the poems of *Chamber Music* create a world in which 'all's accustomed, ceremonious' ('Prayer', 74). Joyce himself noted to Nora that the beloved in *Chamber Music* was made of received ideas: 'a girl fashioned into a curious grave beauty by the culture of generations before her' (LII, 237).

The verbs featured in the poems evoke varieties of light, gentle, graceful motion, velleities and slight tropisms rather than forceful physical gestures: in the first poem, 'Love', personified, 'wanders', 'softly playing' the '[s]trings in the earth and air'; his 'fingers' are 'straying', his 'head' 'bent' 'to the music' (13). In II, the speaker's beloved, as though in gestural rhyme of Love's movements in Poem I, similarly '*bends*' her head 'upon the yellow keys' of the piano while her hands '*wander* as they list'. Chief among the adjectives with which Joyce conjures the atmosphere here are, predictably, 'sweet' (III, 7) and 'soft' (13), and then, in a precise gesture that heightens their effect, he joins the two in the penultimate line: 'Soft sweet music' (14).

The lover's effort at seduction emerges in Poems IV and V, the speaker offering himself as a 'visitant' (IV, 12) compelled by the beloved's bewitching visual beauty ('Lean out of the window / Goldenhair', V, 1–2) and singing ('I heard you singing / A merry air', 3–4) to leave his studies and his room: 'My book was closed; / I read no more ... I have left my book, / I have left my room' (V, 5–6; 9–10). These statements offer some of the most emphatic motion in the sequence, reminiscent not only of the discarded book evoking Paolo and Francesca's sudden passion, but also, as Spoo notes, of the critical moment at which Tennyson's Lady of Shalott breaks from her enclosed chamber: the 'room' (10) and 'gloom' (12) of Joyce's Poem V recall the 'loom' (109) on which the Lady weaves.[17] But if the Lady of Shalott finally responds to the gleaming vision of Lancelot with a violent rupture and flight from her sanctuary-become-prison ('the mirror cracked from side to side', 115), the gestures of Joyce's poems after this moment of crisis involve no such ensuing turbulence or escape. The poems that follow return to the now familiar words 'soft' and 'sweet' in various roles and positions – 'I would in that sweet bosom be / (O sweet and fair it is!)'; '(O soft I knock and soft entreat her!)' (VI, 1–2; 7) – and to the light motions evoked at the outset: in VII, we hear that 'My love is in a light attire'; 'My love goes lightly' (VII, 1, 11).[18] With the exception of the very last poem in the sequence, 'I Hear an Army', which was to become one of Pound's favourites and appear in the 1914 *Des Imagistes*, these poems never, as it were, move beyond the initial 'chamber' of lightness, softness and sweetness.

If *Chamber Music* maintains the gallant, gentle gestures appropriate to the seductions of courtly love ('Go seek her out all courteously', XIII, 1), *Giacomo Joyce* showcases the kind of bitter and brutal feelings involved in erotic desire that are banished from the sweet and soft imagination of *Chamber Music*. Juxtaposed against the earlier poems, *Giacomo Joyce* reads as enacting a return of what is repressed in the world of 'good courtesy' (XIII, 9). Even when the lover of *Chamber Music* must accept the cooling and passing of love, and feels some pain ('Dear heart, why will you use me so?' XXIX, 1), we find nothing particularly candid or raw. *Giacomo Joyce*, however, features aspects of desire not permitted by courtly custom. According to Richard Ellmann, who first broke the news of the existence of this notebook of erotic sketches in 1959, '*Giacomo Joyce* displays its hero's erotic commotion over a girl pupil to whom he was teaching English' (GJ, xii), whom Ellmann identified as Amalia Popper, a young Jewish Italian girl of a well-to-do family in Trieste.[19] Later work has suggested that the 'young person of quality' featured in *Giacomo Joyce* is, in fact, a composite of several students with whom Joyce worked in Trieste.[20] There is no evidence that Joyce ever intended to publish this sixteen-page sequence of impressions. He copied it into a notebook, as Ellmann notes, in his 'best calligraphic hand' (GJ, xi), leaving conspicuously wide spaces of varying sizes among the fifty segments that compose the text, emphasizing their status as separate, isolated fragments. The text seems constructed as a private erotic journal designed to capture fleeting snapshots of the object of the speaker's desire. If, taking a cue from Nancy Vickers, we often read the psychological moves of the lover in Petrarchan love poetry, epitomized in the convention of the blazon, as effecting an objectification and fragmentation of the beloved, here, there is no question that such operations are in play, uncloaked and often merciless.[21] In the first segments, a full vision of the woman under the eroticized gaze is markedly denied as we are introduced to her through slight fragmentary glimpses: 'a pale face surrounded by heavy odorous furs', then as 'quizzing glasses'; then 'long eyelids' that 'beat and lift' (1). The pattern of attention displayed throughout these sketches continues to register the object of desire in brief, fetishistic impressions, both visual and auditory: 'High heels clack hollow'; 'A skirt caught back by her sudden moving knee' (9). The motion of the objectifying gaze here bespeaks an observer involved in erotic obsession, notably not tender, respectful or courteous, but rather plainly caught up in the play of sheer lust. We might think here of the moment in 'The Dead' when Gabriel's admixture of 'tenderness' and physical desire for Gretta after the Christmas party becomes suddenly aggressive: 'the dull fires of his lust began to glow angrily in his veins' (D, 219). Giacomo's position as the social inferior of this young 'person of quality' appears to fuel his *ressentiment*, which in turn both engenders and colours his lust; in another moment of fetishization, as Giacomo admires the 'Great bows' on the woman's 'slim bronze shoes', he calls them 'spurs of a pampered fowl' (8). Such cues of her social station, which makes her unreachable and therefore even more desirable, indeed seem to 'spur' Giacomo's desire.

Read together, *Chamber Music* and *Giacomo Joyce* appear as two sides of the same coin of desire – one showing the bright face of tenderness, the other the darker face of lust, capable of describing its erotic object as having '[l]ong lewdly leering lips: dark blooded molluscs' (5). As Richard Ellmann notes, Joyce copied these voyeuristic jottings into a notebook on sheets 'faintly reminiscent of those parchment sheets on which in 1909 Joyce wrote out the poems of *Chamber-Music*' for Nora (PSW, xi–xii). But more importantly, Joyce himself invites comparison of the two works through a prominent textual cue in *Giacomo Joyce*, for after several meditations on sightings of his object of desire out in the city, her Jewishness and her opinions, he includes a segment that seems out of place: 'I play lightly, softly singing, John Dowland's languid song. *Loth to depart*: I too am loth to go.' This assertion is clearly evocative of the mood in the poems, and Joyce focuses our attention on the way such a mood cannot be maintained in this new, darker, baser context: within the paragraph, that brief impulse toward 'light' and 'soft' song is overmastered by other forces more characteristic of *Giacomo Joyce*. The gesture whereby it is overwhelmed occurs in the space of one sentence: 'Here, opening from the darkness of desire, are eyes that dim the breaking East, their shimmer the shimmer of the scum that mantles the cesspool of the court of slobbering James.' Nearly the same passage will appear in *Portrait* (P, 225), but as it is situated here, we cannot miss the 'turn' in feeling precipitated by the 'dark desire': it occurs just as one kind of 'shimmer' turns into another. To reinforce this, a congruent turn is inscribed in the next sentence, moving us away from what are clearly the moods and lights of the world of *Chamber Music* to a different world: 'Here are wines all ambered, dying fallings of sweet airs' (we are made to think of Orsino in Shakespeare's *Twelfth Night*),[22] 'the proud pavan, kind gentlewomen wooing from their balconies with sucking mouths, the pox-fouled wenches ...' (9). The cues of 'sweet', 'gentle' and 'woo', evocative of *Chamber Music*, give way here to images equally Elizabethan but now conspicuously corrupt: 'sucking mouths' and 'pox-fouled wenches'. Joyce also points back to *Chamber Music* as an intertext for *Giacomo Joyce* with other subtle cues, such as the 'Who' at the beginning of *Giacomo Joyce* which indicates Giacomo's process of coming to know more about the object of his desire, notable to him first as an attractive object (a 'What') and only then later as 'Who' – as a human woman with a social role and station. But the interrogative pronoun also recalls the lilting queries of *Chamber Music*'s Poem VIII: 'Who goes amid the green wood ... Who goes amid the merry green wood ...?' (1, 3). And that Joyce forcefully separates, with conspicuous untidiness and wayward spacing, his different sketches in this notebook, suggests a darkly parodic relationship to the separate poems of *Chamber Music*: with the spaces, he invokes a sequence, but one whose elements have been pulled askew, unceremoniously scattered, distorted and misshapen by the forces of rough desire.

Joyce demonstrates the power of the erotic condition limned in *Giacomo Joyce* to overcome the delicate sentiments associated with customs of courtly wooing that pervade *Chamber Music*, and in this exhibitionist text, showcases the circuits of lust. Ellmann, seeking to win an audience for *Giacomo Joyce* in 1968, called the text a 'love poem which is never recited' (GJ, xi); Harry Levin likewise calls it a 'love letter'.[23] But Joyce clearly marks off the zone of *Giacomo Joyce* as different from that 'love', at least of the kind associated with 'true love' in the earlier poems. Anthony Burgess called *Giacomo Joyce* an 'essay in private onanism',[24] and as Mahaffey and others point out, it anticipates Bloom's condition of mind in the Nausicaa episode of *Ulysses*, though with even darker tones: Giacomo here, after all, is far more willing than Bloom to rake the erotic object over the coals of his lust and resentment. Indeed the woman in *Giacomo Joyce* 'listens: virgin most prudent' (9), sounding much like Gerty MacDowell, but in this different climate, such 'prudence' is subjected to Giacomo's sardonic mockery. Joyce is even willing for Giacomo to engage in sadistic fantasy, equating his desired entrance of the woman with the cut of a knife: when Giacomo learns that the woman has undergone surgery, though he indicates a twist of pity for her, he also expresses jealousy that the surgeon has gone where he wishes to go: 'The surgeon's knife has probed in her entrails and withdrawn, leaving the raw jagged gash of its passage on her belly ... O cruel wound! Libidinous God!' (11) The surgeon's actions, marked as 'libidinous', are thus linked to Giacomo's own desire.

As Fritz Senn notes, *Giacomo Joyce* inscribes an 'urge toward confessional exhibitionism' – but what's 'confessed' and 'exhibited' here are not only Joyce's desires as registered through Giacomo's, but, as the cues pointing back to *Chamber Music* indicate, the way that desire can turn most foul. Joyce engages in a process of candid exposure, an effort to document honestly the winding, shifting, callous, often cruel attitudes associated with the 'dull fires of ... lust'. And through the signals that direct us back to *Chamber Music*, Joyce himself couples these texts to exhibit twin faces of desire, the light and the dark.[25]

*　*　*

At just the point that he was recording *Giacomo Joyce* in his notebook (July–August 1914), Joyce also began composing the first notes for *Exiles*,[26] thus significantly linking these two works. That the completion of one and the beginning of the other fall within the same temporal window, I would offer, is significant. To elaborate the case: *Giacomo Joyce* replies to *Chamber Music*, I would argue, in a way that recalls a comment on the latter Joyce made when dedicating the volume to Nora in 1909. In a letter, Joyce tells Nora that her entrance into his life showed up his fantasies of love in *Chamber Music* as products of culture rather than actual experience. When he had written the poems of the collection, he noted,

I was a strange lonely boy, walking about by myself at night and thinking that some day a girl would love me ... Then you came to me. You were not in a sense the girl for whom I had dreamed and written the verses you find now so enchanting. She was perhaps (as I saw her in my imagination) a girl fashioned into a curious grave beauty by the culture of generations before her, the woman for whom I wrote poems like 'Gentle lady' or 'Thou leanest to the shell of night'. But then I saw that the beauty of your soul outshone that of my verses. There was something in you higher than anything I had put into them. And so for this reason the book of verses is for you. It holds the desire of my youth and you, darling, were the fulfilment of that desire. (LII, 236–7)

Here, then, Joyce acknowledges transcending the liminal perspective associated with *Chamber Music* through Nora to find greater fulfilment in reality. In *Giacomo Joyce* his pointed gestures to the poems similarly indicate that he had likewise moved perspectivally beyond a narrow emotional and psychological 'chamber' – not in this case toward 'the beauty' of Nora's 'soul', but rather toward the kind of erotic experience that the cultural frame of the love lyric, as he had inhabited it, did not admit. Like the experience inscribed by the poems, that of *Giacomo Joyce*, too, is positioned in his imagination in relation to Nora and what she stands for, as signalled by the way that Giacomo responds when he feels himself attacked by the desired woman, now suddenly and uncharacteristically aggressive in her erotic advances. At that point, there is an intrusion of the line: ' – Jim, love! – ' (usually taken to evoke Nora, as she called Joyce 'Jim'), and then, a few lines later, similarly indented and flanked by dashes, a parallel line that confirms this as Nora's voice breaking into the scene: ' – Nora! (GJ, 15) – '. Joyce thus positions 'Nora' here not only as signifying the limit under threat during this erotic encounter, but also as the protective force that may save him from temptation.

Notable also, in this text so evidently featuring lust, is the introduction of the word 'love', along with its clear link to Nora. 'Love' is a word that churned through Joyce's imagination during the Trieste period, in part because he at first refused to use it to describe his feelings for Nora in the letters he sent her as they planned their escape to the Continent.[27] Later, Joyce does use the word 'love' in his letters, though it is not clear whether out of his own lexicon or in deference to hers. Whatever the case, it is used at strategic moments in Joyce's writing in ways that indicate his continued scrupulousness – perhaps even 'scrupulous meanness' (D, 269) – about how to use it, when it pertains, and when what is being addressed qualifies as love. And when the word is used, it leads in his imagination to Nora.

Indeed, through omission both *Chamber Music* and *Giacomo Joyce* bring into focus what Theo Dombrowski calls the 'problem of love'.[28] In a 1907 letter to Stanislaus, written as the poems of *Chamber Music* were being published, Joyce noted, 'I don't like the book but wish it were published and be damned to it. However, it is a young man's book. I felt like that. It is not a book of love-verses at all, I perceive' (LII, 219). The collection of poems thus comes in his imagination to gesture toward 'love', as Joyce comes to understand the concept, not through what it does but rather through what it fails to do. In *Giacomo Joyce*, meanwhile, Joyce is careful to place the call to 'love' (' – Jim, love! – ') as a boundary, a check, on the renegade currents of lust; the implication here, too, is that the invocation of love points to a universe of feeling that is conspicuously absent in *Giacomo Joyce*. Joyce's dismissive remarks about *Chamber Music* ('It is not a book of love-verses at all, I perceive') are glossed in the same August 1909 letter to Nora, suggesting that she has shown him the love which *Chamber Music*, for all its talk of 'true love', does not reach and cannot compass.

It seems obvious that Nora is at the centre of Joyce's thoughts as he begins *Exiles* in 1913, as she was central to his thoughts during much of their life together. But in late 1913 and early 1914, as he began *Exiles* and was ruminating on both *Giacomo Joyce* and the poems of *Chamber Music* (he quotes *Chamber Music* in the notes to *Exiles*, 169, indicating its continued place in his ken), Nora was connected especially in his imagination with this condition of love. Yet this imaginative linkage between Nora and love presented him with a problem, given the way that she was providing him with what neither the conventionally ceremonious nor the riots of lust could. And this problem arose from his unconventional union with Nora, the common-law marriage on which Joyce insisted – a crux that he pursues through the partially autobiographical narrative of *Exiles*. Was the social arrangement on which he had decided for himself and Nora, one that had emerged from his principled refusal of conventional marriage, a viable one?

Joyce undertook the union with Nora, which involved their eloping to the Continent in October 1904, to defy social convention and arrive at an arrangement that could accommodate more realistically what he believed to be the actual currents of human desire. As Richard Brown notes, with his decision, Joyce was participating in the era's wider debate about the institution of marriage.[29] He sought to quarrel with social conventions, especially within Ireland, that manacled the free play of erotic desire – above all the prohibitions of the Catholic Church against extramarital sex. When he left Ireland with Nora, refusing to marry, he was playing out his refusal of what he regarded as constraints that would suffocate life, attempting instead to establish a social practice in 'conformity', as he put it to his brother Stanislaus, with his own 'moral nature' (LII, 99). The problem with which he was wrestling, then, was how to respond morally to desire, with an honest rather than sham morality. But, under Nora's influence, and especially as the notion of love associated with her becomes more forcibly present to him during these years, he wonders if this social arrangement is the best answer to how to remain, in his defiant Romantic commitment, honest to human feeling and responsive to its needs.

This is the question driving Exiles, a play in which Richard Rowan, a writer, and his common-law wife, Bertha, have just returned to Ireland after a long absence on the Continent. Like Joyce and Nora, they have eloped without formal marriage. Joyce's signature concept of 'exile' – principled, ironic and critical distance from an idea or context once called home – is related to Richard's having left Ireland, as his friend Robert Hand puts it, in its 'hour of need' (E, 142), but as the play opens, it is most readily applicable to Richard's and Bertha's state in the eyes of many associates because of their choice to enter into an illicit union. We learn that Richard's mother never forgave the decision (26), such that she and Richard remained estranged at her death; and that the stigma attached to it has kept him from certain jobs. That he now has a chance at a university post is thanks to Robert's careful management of Richard's image so as to lighten some of its stains (55–6).

In the course of the play the terms of the union between Richard and

Bertha and its consequences are placed under pressure and critique: we become vividly aware of the cost of both what Richard decided then – to allow both of them 'complete liberty' (73–4) – and of the principled code to which he still adheres. But somewhat surprisingly, it is not the social cost of their decision that the play foregrounds. Instead, we learn that the heterodox union has sacrificed sensitivity to the human needs of Bertha, diminishing the intimacy between them. Although meant to draw them together, it has left them exiled from each other, prompting Bertha to cry out at one point, 'I am living with a stranger!' (149).

Joyce constructs a situation inspired by fears he experienced during the early years of his union with Nora that she was being pursued by another man: here, figured by Robert, Richard Rowan's old friend who has played a large part in coaxing him back to Ireland. Robert was also Richard's disciple in their salad days, inspired by the latter's philosophy of free love and lofty disregard for social convention whenever it conflicted with the dictates of passion. Robert now desires Bertha, and the text presents his pursuit of her as a set of actions emerging from the philosophy he and Richard had once shared: that if strongly felt, desire for a woman should be pursued, regardless of social prohibition. The confusion that Robert's efforts to seduce Bertha produce, both in Bertha and Richard, show up the inadequacy of their arrangement. If playing out an affair with Robert would enable adherence to the principles of freedom to which Richard has committed, and to which Bertha has agreed, these principles are shown to do real damage to the hearts concerned here.

Brought into focus again by the play are impulses associated with the desires of *Chamber Music*, and *Giacomo Joyce*. Richard's feelings for the ethereal character of Beatrice Justice, Robert's cousin, are akin to the sentiments played out in *Chamber Music*, and Beatrice resembles the delicate and wraith-like beloved of *Chamber Music*, gone wan without having bloomed. Robert's impetuous desire, meanwhile, is comparable to Giacomo's hectic lust, though certainly more considerate (Robert brings Bertha overblown roses) and susceptible to the cultural clichés of amorous play (Robert sprays perfume in the cottage to which he invites Bertha). Neither of these forms of desire is presented as sustainable or valuable: both the options Beatrice and Robert represent here are presented as unripe, as is Richard's unrelenting adherence to his code of 'complete liberty'. The beating and complex heart of the situation here, surfaced by the mercilessness of the terms of Richard's and Bertha's union that scrape against it, is the bond between Bertha and Richard, which we feel has been hurt into a 'wound' (E, 162) by a social arrangement that does it too little kindness.

Exiles thus scrutinizes the kind of experiment Joyce made in life: to pursue this free play of desire without forcing it into a shape it would not, of its own natural accord, take. When Robert returns to Richard and confronts him with a philosophy which was once his, the creed is presented as something Richard has left behind, which now brings only emptiness. In weary response to Robert's cry that 'All life is a conquest, the victory of human passion over the commandments of cowardice', he says only, 'Yes. It is the language of my youth' (99). What has become apparent in the interim, we glean from the cues here, is a feeling that was not known before – love – which Richard foregrounds by defining it in a way that counters Robert's definition:

Robert: Those are moments of sheer madness when we feel an intense passion for a woman. We see nothing. We think of nothing. Only to possess her. Call it brutal, bestial, what you will.

Richard: [A little timidly.] I am afraid that that longing to possess a woman is not love.

....

Robert: But if you love .... What else is it?

Richard: [Hesitatingly.] To wish her well. (88)

In the first lines of his notes for Exiles, Joyce foregrounds this concept of love, observing, 'Love (understood as the desire of good for another) is in fact so unnatural a phenomenon that it can scarcely repeat itself' (E, 163). That this comment appears so early in the notes to Exiles, together with the fact that it is placed at such a pivotal moment in the play and that other indications suggest Joyce's focus on the topic of love at this juncture, suggests that the concept forms the kernel of Exiles.

Taken together, then, these three texts trace a progression of Joyce's thought over the multiple facets of a single problem – about forms of desire and love, how they should be defined and how differentiated from each other, and how they are best served by social arrangements. The pairing of *Chamber Music* and *Giacomo Joyce*, again, not only showcases two faces of a Janus-like desire, but also brings into view, through Joyce's comments within and on them, that which neither of the two faces can represent – the concept of love. And love – pointed to as that which neither of these early texts can touch – is significantly on Joyce's mind in 1913–14, when he begins *Exiles*. The pressure of this concept, again introduced at a crucial moment in both *Exiles* and in *Giacomo Joyce*, drives Joyce to consider the rightness of an unorthodox marriage – rightness not in the eyes of external society, but rather rightness with respect to the emotional needs and hungers of those involved. Marking this topic as a problem for serious philosophical consideration is Joyce's decision to develop *Exiles* conspicuously in the style of the dramatist whom he had long admired, Ibsen, whose genius for constructing philosophically substantive problem plays Joyce celebrated and, here, sought to emulate.[30]

Joyce begins *Exiles* at the same time that *Ulysses* begins to take shape, and the latter, too, along with many other topics, takes up the question of what social arrangements best accommodate the vicissitudes of love and desire. What *Exiles* does that *Ulysses* does not, however, is follow to its logical conclusion a single trajectory of misgiving about the effectiveness of defiant social arrangements like the one that holds Richard and Bertha together, like that which governed Nora's and Joyce's lives. *Exiles*, as Hugh Kenner and R.B. Kershner suggest, shows up the commitment to a non-traditional union as arid, naïve and immature in its extremist idealism, much like Gregers's philosophy in Ibsen's *The Wild Duck*: together, Richard Rowan and Robert Hand illuminate a Joycean comment about the errors of a philosophy that celebrates the expression of passion before all else by allowing one's partner 'complete liberty'.[31] While we remain not altogether sure at the end of the play what might provide the road to truer liberty and connection, we are given a glimmer of what this might be through the faith toward each other that Richard and Bertha display.

Exiles arrives at this judgement in a way that, for instance, given its idiom, *Ulysses* could not. Playing out his questions about love in different genres – that of the lyric sequence, the erotic journal and the Ibsenesque drama – Joyce is led in different directions by the generic pressures, patterns, the pull of each; each permits him some roads and forecloses others. *Ulysses*, as a great comic novel, allows him neither the agony nor stringency of moral judgement that *Exiles* does. In the current climate of Joyce scholarship, we are inclined to read the irony of *Ulysses* – its flights of wit, its ribaldry, its aloof detachment, its exaggerations – as far more sophisticated than the lugubrious exchanges of *Exiles*. Certainly *Ulysses* is more virtuosic, and I would not want to claim that *Exiles*, and not *Ulysses*, should reach the top when we compile inventories of the greatest literary achievements of the twentieth century. But *Exiles* accomplishes something that *Ulysses* does not: the play makes an effort at sober judgement on an issue with which Joyce himself was reckoning soberly, particularly during the Triestine period as he was developing *Giacomo Joyce*, and thinking, through this text, about the implications of his first published poems.

Reading these lyrics in 1920, Pound suggested, 'I got the impression that the real man is the author of *Chamber Music*, the sensitive. The rest is the genius: the registration of realities on the temperament, the delicate temperament of the early poems.'[32] Cued by Pound's remarks, we might parse Joyce's writerly temperament into two parts: one plainly visible in the arcs of ironic virtuosity in *Ulysses* and another revealed to us through these three 'minor' texts. I have suggested that *Giacomo Joyce* shows the obverse of *Chamber Music*, so in that sense, it certainly reveals a different aspect of Joyce's 'temperament' than do the early lyric poems. But all three texts could be said to emerge from, and register, a non-ironic awareness, placing an 'importance' on being 'earnest' – and I use the Wildean terms deliberately.

Having cordoned off the minor works up to this point to facilitate illumination, I would like to turn back to their implications for the Joycean canon as a whole. Several commentators have suggested the possibility of an 'other' Joyce – the term is Armand's – as distinct from the cool, ironic modernist. These 'two Joyces' are visible in texts that feature different temperamental inclinations in conflict. Herbert Howarth, for instance, argues that 'There were two Joyces: the lyrical and the satirical, the singer and the clown.'[33] Robert Spoo likewise identifies in *Chamber*

Music Poem XII two attitudinal currents, monkish and ribald, that map on to two tendencies at work more generally in Joyce's œuvre. Given their tonal incongruity with the major works, the minor works thus likewise spell out 'two Joyces' – and distil out an attitudinal cluster that constitute a non-ironic 'other' Joyce, a kind of alterity, perhaps even a kind of 'minor literature', within the Joycean canon.

This 'other Joyce' is similar to the 'other Wilde' that becomes apparent in Wilde's corpus if one takes into account not only the famous wit of the plays and essays, but also the meditations of Salomé, De Profundis and even The Picture of Dorian Gray – all of which Joyce was reading, as his letters and a 1909 lecture attest. As we do Wilde, perhaps we owe Joyce a serious look at 'the other side' of 'the garden',[34] in an attempt to assess the dimensions of his work that show more earnestness and shadow, and that resort less to the armour of irony. There is of course a courage in irony, but as Wilde suggests in De Profundis, it can also function as a strategy of moral evasion. If we are to come to terms with Joyce the moralist of scrupulous meanness – and there is no question at this late date, certainly, that this forms a crucial dimension of his work – then we need to take the so-called 'minor works' as other than minor, take them in their own right, for the serious matters they display.

If we do decide that the minor works map out an 'other Joyce', we need to be careful, too, of how we classify and judge this 'other'. It is too easy to use Pound's terms, to read Chamber Music, Giacomo Joyce and Exiles as the products of the 'real man', the raw, the unburnished, when the sparkling wit and agility of the 'genius' was not yet fully in play. Through the minor works, then, we might even re-evaluate not only what we mean by 'Joyce', not only standards for 'Joycean' success, not only how we value modernist irony and the criteria that have often governed judgements of success in modernist literature, but perhaps even what we understand by modernist 'genius'.

NOTES

1. R. Brown, 'Eros and Apposition: Giacomo Joyce', Joyce Studies Annual, 1 (1990), p.132.
2. L. Armand, 'Introduction', in Giacomo Joyce: Envoys of the Other, ed. L. Armand and C. Wallace (Bethesda, MD: Academica Press, 2002), p.1.
3. H. Power, 'Incorporating Giacomo Joyce', James Joyce Quarterly 28, 3 (1991), p.623.

4. H. Howarth, 'Chamber Music and its Place in the Joyce Canon', in *James Joyce Today: Essays on the Major Works*, ed. Thomas F. Staley (Bloomington, IN: Indiana University Press, 1966), p.11.

5. For a concise account of the basis on which Joyce's minor works are usually regarded as differing from his major works, see V. Mahaffey, 'Joyce's Shorter Works', in *The Cambridge Companion to James Joyce*, 2nd edn, ed. Derek Attridge (Cambridge: Cambridge University Press, 2004), p.172.

6. B. Benstock, 'Exiles', in *A Companion to Joyce Studies*, ed. Z. Bowen and J. Carens (Westport, CT: Greenwood Press, 1984), p.362.

7. R. Spoo, 'Rival Confessors in "Chamber Music"': Meaning and Narrative in Joyce's Lyric Mode', *James Joyce Quarterly*, 26, 4 (1989), p.496.

8. Mahaffey, 'Joyce's Shorter Works', argues that *Chamber Music* and *Giacomo Joyce* especially build larger units through an aggregate of smaller, self-contained units and thereby anticipate Joyce's signature principles for structural development in the major works. If Joyce's early works achieve copia through an aggregation of distinct units, then Joyce's principle of structural development points not only to Imagism, which was taking shape as he was finishing *Giacomo Joyce* and beginning *Exiles*, but also to the strategy for developing a long poem with which Pound was experimenting as he began his *Cantos*, initially conceptualizing the project as a 'Vorticist long poem' and imagining it as building toward epic scale through a concatenation of smaller, intensely focused, concentrated units. This was also the strategy that Eliot would employ, encouraged by the collaborative work with Pound on revisions, in *The Waste Land*.

9. D. Barnes, *Nightwood* (New York: New Directions, 1961), p.36.

10. Armand, 'Introduction', p.2.

11. Ezra Pound, *Selected Letters 1907–1941*, ed. D.D. Paige (New York: New Directions, 1971), p.180.

12. R. Ellmann, *James Joyce* (New York: Oxford University Press, 1966), p.86.

13. In a mid-twentieth-century reading which has become a mainstay commentary on *Chamber Music*, William Tindall reads the sequence thus: 'The thirty-six poems tell a story of young love and failure. At the beginning the lover is alone. He meets a girl and their love, after suitable fooling, is almost successful. Then a rival intrudes. The hero's devotion gives way to irony and, at last, despair. Alone again at the end, the lover goes off into exile' – W. Tindall, Introduction to *Chamber Music* (New York: Columbia University Press, 1954), p.41. While I would not put such a fine point on the narrative's episodes – it is not clear that the lover is 'alone' at the outset, for instance, nor that the intrusion of a rival *per se* interrupts the lovers – there is a progression implied here by the sequence as decided on by Stanislaus, which was arrived at after three other possible arrangements. Stanislaus noted to Tindall in letters of 1953 that he had ordered the poems as 'approximately allegretto, andante cantabile, mosso – to suggest a closed episode of youth and love' – quoted in C. Anderson, 'Joyce's Verses', in Bowen and Carens (eds), *Companion to Joyce Studies*, p.130. Joyce evidently surrendered responsibility for the poems' arrangement after wearying of them. In a letter to Stanislaus written at a point just before publication of

Chamber Music, Joyce notes that he does not 'know' if the order of the poems is 'correct', but he suggests that he is beyond caring (LII, 219).

14. Spoo rightly notes that much about these lyrics, including their 'introverted rhetoric', the ambiguity of whom they address and their static qualities, complicates efforts to 'narrativize' them, but as he points out, such troubles beset efforts to narrativize Shakespeare's sonnets as well, given the 'deep tendency of lyrics to be self-referential and static' – Spoo, 'Rival Confessors in "Chamber Music"', p.495. Here, I will accept William Tyndall's reading of the sequences as implying a narrative arc, even if it is slender and sometimes difficult to trace.

15. See *Poems and Shorter Writings*, ed. Richard Ellmann, A. Walton Litz and John Whittier-Ferguson (London: Faber and Faber, 1991), pp.3, 6. Anderson, 'Joyce's Verses', p.123 notes that influences on Joyce's early poetry, composed between 1900 and 1904, include Dante, Shakespeare, Dowland, Jonson, Byron, Shelley, Blake, Verlaine, Symons, Dowson, Russell and Yeats.

16. Spoo, 'Rival Confessors in "Chamber Music"', pp.495, 493.

17. As intertext for Joyce's lines in V, see especially: 'She left the web, she left the loom / She made three paces through the room' ('The Lady of Shalott', 109–10).

18. The notion of the 'true love' surges up in VIII and IV, and so too does the lover's effort to persuade the beloved to transition from one state into another, from the liminal hovering of desire into a state of love. In X, as in V, there again arises a stress and emphasis unusual for the sequence, here issuing from forceful rhetoric attempting to persuade. The speaker enjoins the beloved to leave dreams and enter reality: 'Leave dreams to the dreamers ... [T]he time of dreaming / Dreams is over.' Then, with a plain and bold declarative statement anomalous in this universe of soft lights and gentle tendencies and therefore affectingly keen: 'As lover to lover, / Sweetheart, I come' (PSW, 5, 13–16). The 'I come' will be chimed again in the poem that points toward marriage (XIII), invoking an 'Epithalamium'. The clearest seduction scene is staged in XI, in which the speaker seeks to 'woo' the beloved, enjoining her to bid 'adieu' to 'girlish days', 'girlish ways' and 'maidenhood' and move to mature love, marking the passage from one state to another, bidding her begin the gestures that will facilitate this passage: 'Begin thou softly to unzone / Thy girlish bosom unto him / And softly to undo the snood / That is the sign of maidenhood' (XI, 9–12). The 'softness' we have come to recognize as a signature of this atmosphere is now relocated and reintroduced adverbially into an archetypical gesture of surrender. The climactic moment of the sequence occurs in XIV which repeats and emphasis the word 'arise', which is then also used to begin poem XV. From there, we pass through the stages of love's ripening, growing peaceful, and falling away: but this speaker bids his beloved not to be sad; his reigning philosophy is that love passes, and its transience must be accepted: 'Gentle lady, do not sing / Sad songs about the end of love; / Lay aside sadness and sing / How love that passes is enough' (XXVIII, 1–4).

19. Summarizing how Ellmann introduced *Giacomo Joyce* to the public, Mahaffey notes that Ellmann's biography of Joyce, 'when it appeared in 1959, contained an interesting section on *Giacomo Joyce* in which Ellmann identified Amalia Popper as the pupil who

had inspired it ... Virtually nothing more is heard of *Giacomo Joyce* until September 28, 1967, when the front page of the *New York Times* reported, "MS. of Joyce Autobiographical Love Story Found". This front-page news item ... marked the beginning of a remarkable sales campaign by Viking Press to promote the forthcoming publication of *Giacomo Joyce* in its entirety, to be edited by Ellmann. From comparative obscurity, these sixteen pages were suddenly illuminated by international attention. On January 1, 1968, the limited first edition appeared, complete with introduction, notes, and facsimile pages, all handsomely boxed and highly priced at ten dollars. It was reset and reissued for a regular trade edition that appeared in May ... The book was extensively publicised and widely reviewed throughout 1968' V. Mahaffey, 'Giacomo Joyce', in Bowen and Carens (eds), *Companion to Joyce Studies*, pp.387–420 (p.388).

20. See F. Senn, 'On Not Coming to Terms with *Giacomo Joyce*', in Armand and Wallace (eds), *Giacomo Joyce*, p.18; Senn credits the work of John McCourt especially for the awareness that the 'She' of *Giacomo Joyce* is likely a composite.

21. See N. Vickers, 'Diana Described: Scattered Women and Scattered Rhyme', *Critical Inquiry*, 8 (1981), pp.265–79.

22. William Shakespeare, *Twelfth Night*, I, I, 4–5.

23. Cited in Mahaffey, 'Giacomo Joyce', p.390.

24. Ibid.

25. In a letter to Nora of 1909, he notes, 'Love is a cursed nuisance especially when coupled with lust also' (*LII*, 251).

26. In November 1913, March 1914, August 1914; see R. Norburn, *A James Joyce Chronology* (New York: Palgrave, 2004), p.62.

27. Richard Brown, *James Joyce and Sexuality* (Cambridge: Cambridge University Press, 1985), p.14; *LII*, 55.

28. T. Dombrowski, 'Joyce's *Exiles*: the Problem of Love', *James Joyce Quarterly*, 15 (1978), pp.118–27.

29. Brown, *James Joyce and Sexuality*, esp. Ch. 1, 'Love and Marriage', pp.12–49.

30. See J. Joyce, 'Ibsen's New Drama', *Fortnightly Review*, 67 (1 April 1900), pp.575–90.

31. See R.B. Kershner, *Joyce, Bakhtin, and Popular Culture* (Chapel Hill, NC: University of North Carolina Press, 1989), esp. pp.286–96.

32. E. Pound, *Pound/Joyce: The Letters of Ezra Pound to James Joyce, with Pound's Essays on Joyce*, ed. Herbert Read (New York: New Directions, 1970), p.178.

33. Howarth, 'Chamber Music and its Place in the Joyce Canon', p.19.

34. Oscar Wilde, *The Oscar Wilde Reader* (Ann Arbor, MI: Tally Hall Press, 1997), p.518.

CHAPTER SIX

The Complex Simplicity of Ulysses

MICHAEL GRODEN

The summer 2006 host of 'Sounds Like Canada', a national mid-morning radio programme on the Canadian Broadcasting Corporation, announced on his first show in mid-June that he was determined to read Ulysses by the end of the season and would document his progress on the air. Echoing a popular CBC-Radio book feature called 'Canada Reads', Jian Ghomeshi called his project 'Canada Intends to Read'. He armed himself with an array of on-air experts and fellow readers to help and encourage him, asking listeners to email the programme if they made any great discoveries about the book or felt completely undone by it. Ghomeshi needed to stay up all night before his last show in September, but he did succeed in reading Ulysses through to the end.

Most readers do not resort to exposing their page-count publicly on national media in order to get themselves through a book. But ever since it was published in 1922 Ulysses has provoked strong and unusual responses. To some of its first readers it seemed brilliantly important and innovative. Ezra Pound, for example, proclaimed that 'All men should "Unite and give praise to Ulysses"; those who will not, may content themselves with a place in the lower intellectual orders'. For T.S. Eliot, Joyce's method in Ulysses had 'the importance of a scientific discovery' and was 'a step toward making the modern world possible for art'. Edmund Wilson saw Ulysses as 'a work of high genius' that '[set] the standard of the novel so high that it need not be ashamed to take its place beside poetry and drama'. And Virginia Woolf, reading early versions of some episodes in the American literary magazine The Little Review, enthused that 'If we want life itself here, surely we have it'.[1] More recently, in a poll from 1998, *Ulysses* was named the English-language novel of the century, and celebrations occurred throughout the world on 16 June 2004, one hundred years after the day on which *Ulysses* takes place, reported by one newspaper under the headline, 'One Day Turns 100'. 'Bloomsday', the name by which that day is now known (Joyce mentioned the name in a June 1924 letter, spelling it 'Bloom's day' [LI, 216], and Herbert Gorman used it in his 1939 biography of Joyce), has entered the language to the extent that in March 2006 it became an entry in the *Oxford English Dictionary*.[2]

From the start, though, for some readers *Ulysses* was boring, vulgar, meaningless, obscene (any or all of the above). Alfred Noyes found 'no foulness conceivable to the mind of madman or ape that has not been poured into its imbecile pages'. A pseudonymous Irish reviewer considered Joyce 'a perverted lunatic who has made a specialty of the literature of the latrine', and *Ulysses* 'incoherent' and a 'stupid glorification of mere filth'. For George Moore, '*Ulysses* is hopeless; it is absurd to imagine that any good end can be served by trying to record every single thought and sensation of any human being. That's not art, it's like trying to copy the London Directory.' And Virginia Woolf, less impressed by the finished book than by the earlier periodical episodes, wrote in her diary that she was, 'puzzled, bored, irritated, and disillusioned by a queasy undergraduate scratching his pimples' whose 'book is diffuse. It is brackish. It is pretentious. It is underbred.'[3] As the new millennium began, *Ulysses* found itself on a list of works currently considered 'timeless' that would be forgotten a century in the future, and the 2004 centenary celebrations prompted such headlines as 'The Bloomsday Philistines Arrive' and 'Bloomsday, Bloody Bloomsday'.[4]

Paralleling this exuberant praise countered by equally energetic condemnation was *Ulysses*' incredibly fast journey into 'classic' status accompanied by an instant and seemingly permanent reputation as a difficult, even unreadable, book. Because a United States court in early 1921 ruled that a section of Joyce's novel that appeared in the *Little Review* was obscene, the finished book version could not be published in the US, and, fearing prosecution for printing an obscene work, no British printer would touch it. To Joyce's rescue came Sylvia Beach, an American bookseller in Paris, who set up a publishing venture named after her bookshop, Shakespeare & Co., to publish *Ulysses*, which she did on

Joyce's 40th birthday, 2 February 1922. During the years in which the book was unavailable in English-speaking countries,[5] Joyce encouraged friends to write articles and even books about it, and, along with other writers working independently, they did this. For example, Herbert Gorman's *James Joyce: His First Forty Years* (1924), Stuart Gilbert's *James Joyce's 'Ulysses'* (1930), Frank Budgen's *James Joyce and the Making of 'Ulysses'* (1934), and Edmund Wilson's chapter in *Axel's Castle: A Study of the Imaginative Literature of 1870–1930* (1931) established *Ulysses* as a book worthy of serious analysis and debate.[6] When a second US court case in 1933 tested the 1921 obscenity charge, Joyce's lawyers filed a 'Petition for Release and Admission of Book into the United States on the Ground that it is a Classic' and in this and other documents repeatedly called the eleven-year-old *Ulysses* 'a modern classic' that had 'endured the test of time'.[7] Within ten years of its legal introduction into the US in 1934 (the UK followed two years later) *Ulysses* was the topic of a Ph.D. dissertation,[8] and it quickly became a staple of university English department courses. By now, only Shakespeare's works are written about more than Joyce's, with *Ulysses* as the subject of a substantial portion of the writings on Joyce.

But as *Ulysses* became a classic, it was also branded as difficult to read. Condemning it in 1922, Shane Leslie charged that 'as a whole, the book must remain impossible to read'. Praising it, Mary Colum acknowledged that 'the difficulties in the way are very real' and listed some of those road-blocks as Joyce's use of details from Roman Catholicism, recent Irish struggles for independence, the city of Dublin and its inhabitants, many different literatures and 'odd bits and forms of knowledge'. The claims have persisted. Just after it published *Ulysses* in the US in early 1934, Random House ran a two-page advertisement in the *Saturday Review of Literature*, headed 'How to Enjoy James Joyce's Great Novel *Ulysses*', which began,

> For those who are already engrossed in the reading of *Ulysses* as well as for those who hesitate to begin it because they fear that it is obscure, the publishers offer this simple clue to what the critical fuss is all about. *Ulysses* is no harder to 'understand' than any other great classic. It is essentially a story and can be enjoyed as such.

And in 1998, a cartoon responding to the naming of *Ulysses* as novel of the century shows a young woman taking the book to the beach to read, trying a few pages, and then putting it down in favour of a novel called *Flaming Hot Winds of Desire*. If *Ulysses* is a classic, for some people it is also entrenched in that special subgroup, the 'unread masterpiece'.[9]

Colum's remarks point to one reason why *Ulysses* seems so difficult: the prevalence in it of detailed knowledge that many readers do not share. This includes *The Odyssey*: Joyce based the episodes of *Ulysses* on incidents from Homer's poem, even giving each episode a Homeric name (although he did not include these names in the book itself).[10] *Ulysses* also introduces an unfamiliar technique – presenting the thoughts of its main characters as if a tape-recorder has preserved them without editing them for either significance or taste – and then, when the technique begins to seem familiar, replaces it with a wild series of experiments in telling a story. And Joyce plunges his readers into the action, such as it is, with no accompanying details as to who the characters are, what their backgrounds might be, or what kind of story he is about to tell – without, that is, those bits of information that a traditional novel might be expected to offer its reader at the start. These details do exist in *Ulysses*: some of them occur piecemeal along the way, but many appear only in the last two episodes.[11] For example, we know from the start that Stephen Dedalus is in mourning for his mother but learn only near the end that she died nearly a year before (U, 17.951–3). We also learn only at the end about Leopold Bloom's Hungarian father's move to Dublin and conversion to Catholicism, about his own three baptisms, and, significantly, about the ten-year period before 16 June 1904 during which Leopold and Molly Bloom did not enjoy 'complete carnal intercourse' (17.532–47, 1634–40, 2278). A major effect of this backloading of information is that many readers on their way through the book keep losing, finding, relosing, and (maybe) refinding their bearings – often feeling confused and bewildered in the process – whereas a second time through *Ulysses* can be a very different experience because of the information that a first-time reader learns in the novel's last two episodes.

Joyce also creates a very close connection between his third-person narrator and the main character whose story is being told. The traditional terms for third-person narrators – omniscient (knows everything), limited (knows only a few things) – do not really apply to Joyce's narrators, since they reveal only what is necessary to place the characters, even if they may seem to know more than they say, as in 'Mr Bloom entered and sat in the vacant place. He pulled the door to after him and slammed it twice till it shut tight. He passed an arm through the armstrap and looked seriously from the open carriagewindow at the lowered blinds of the avenue' (6.9–12). The narrators often mimic the kind of language the characters use. In *Dubliners* and *A Portrait of the Artist as a Young Man*, this means that the narrators' vocabulary and sentence structure mirrors the character's age, education level or social class, and in *Ulysses* it can also indicate the character's mood at the particular time of day. For example, as Bloom, newly awake and fresh in the morning, looks at his cat, he 'watched curiously, kindly the lithe black form' (4.21), but later in the day when he is depressed from hunger, 'His smile faded as he walked, a heavy cloud hiding the sun slowly, shadowing Trinity's surly front' (8.475–6). And as Bloom sits in a church, apparently unaware of the word 'ciborum', the narrator says that 'The priest went along by them, murmuring, holding the thing in his hands' (5.344–5), allowing Bloom's word 'thing' to replace the correct name.[12] Through this method Joyce provides a detailed depiction of what the characters do and think without giving the reader much guidance as to how to interpret the character and the events.[13] Such an absence of direction is one of the hallmarks of Joyce's writing, and it causes one of *Ulysses*' primary difficulties: even if you know enough about Homer, Latin, Catholicism, Aristotle or Aquinas to follow Joyce's allusions in the text, you still receive no guidance as to what to do with the information. If you don't know the details, you can feel stupid and ignorant, and if you do know them, you can still feel lost and dangling. As a result, a reader of *Ulysses* can easily sympathize with the man in a *New Yorker* cartoon lamenting to his companion as they leave a theatre, 'Like all great art, it made me feel hopelessly inadequate'.[14]

Given these daunting complexities, Random House's claim that *Ulysses* is 'essentially a story' might seem like a mere marketing ploy. But Joyce made a similar remark to his friend Frank Budgen. Contrasting himself with an unnamed European writer, Joyce said that 'In my case the thought is always simple'.[15] He didn't elaborate on what he meant by simple thought, although there are various possibilities. He might have been referring to the plot. Joyce didn't feel that he was a good inventor of stories, and so he used existing ones, whether from his own experiences, from stories that people he knew told him or events that happened to them, or from earlier written texts. In *Ulysses* he used Homer's *Odyssey* as what he called a 'ground plan' and what Pound referred to as a 'scaffold'. Both Homer's poem and its hero Ulysses (Odysseus in Greek) made a strong impression on him when he read Charles Lamb's *Adventures of Ulysses* as a schoolboy. Lamb's 1808 prose retelling of parts of *The Odyssey* prompted Joyce to write about Ulysses in an assigned essay on 'My Favorite Hero', and he later told Budgen that the Greek adventurer was his example of 'a complete all-round character'.[16] The story he constructed using *The Odyssey* as a grid is a surprisingly simple one, covering one day in the lives of three Dubliners: Leopold and Molly Bloom, a man in his late 30s and his 33-year-old wife, and Stephen Dedalus, an unrelated younger man in his early 20s. Leopold Bloom, a canvasser for advertisements, goes about his ordinary business, which does not seem to be particularly pressing, and attends a funeral of an acquaintance who died from alcohol-related causes. Molly Bloom, a singer, stays at home all day and prepares for a rehearsal in the afternoon with Blazes Boylan, the manager of her upcoming short concert tour. The day would be completely ordinary except that Bloom strongly suspects that Molly will make love with Boylan when he arrives. Stephen, a poet who has recently returned to Dublin after a stay in Paris, is adrift, having determined that he won't live with his father and family and also that he will no longer stay with his friend Buck Mulligan in a rented tower. He wanders through the city, expounds a theory of *Hamlet* to reluctant listeners, drinks all day without eating, gets knocked down by an irate soldier late in the evening, and is rescued by Leopold Bloom, who has also been away from his home the entire day.

In *The Odyssey*, 20-year-old Telemachus awaits the return of Odysseus, his father and the king of his island Ithaca, who left to fight in the Trojan War when Telemachus was an infant. Odysseus experiences various adventures and ordeals during his ten-year struggle to get home, be reunited with his faithful wife Penelope and son, and reclaim his kingdom. Joyce's use of *The Odyssey* sets certain plot trajectories in motion. As a modern Telemachus, Stephen, whose biological father is still alive and is a secondary character in *Ulysses*, is in some way a son searching for a father, and Leopold Bloom, whose infant son died ten years previously, is a father searching for a son. Molly Bloom, waiting at home more for her soon-to-be lover Blazes Boylan to arrive than for her husband to return, is a version of faithful Penelope. Joyce's use of *The Odyssey* sets up a tension between what Arnold Goldman calls 'form' and 'freedom'[17] as it sets limits on the characters' freedom to act. They are completely ignorant of it, but in certain important ways their stories follow and echo their models in *The Odyssey*.

* * *

The first three episodes of *Ulysses* focus on Stephen Dedalus, the young would-be poet who was the main character of *A Portrait of the Artist as a Young Man*. Some of his experiences and personality traits duplicate Joyce's own, although two of Joyce's remarks to Frank Budgen − 'I haven't let this young man off very lightly, have I?' and Stephen 'has a shape that can't be changed'[18] − indicate the degree to which Joyce saw Stephen more as a character than as a version of himself. The episodes place Stephen in three different settings: in a Martello tower outside of Dublin with his friend Malachi ('Buck') Mulligan and their English guest Haines ('Telemachus', which takes place starting at 8:00 a.m.); at a private school in Dalkey where he works as a teacher ('Nestor', 10:00 a.m.); and then along the Sandymount Strand, where he walks alone and thinks ('Proteus', 11:00 a.m.). We see Stephen in small groups (Mulligan, Haines, and briefly a milkwoman in 'Telemachus'); teaching students and then conversing with the school's headmaster, his employer, in 'Nestor'; and then entirely alone in 'Proteus'. Stephen is moody and gloomy throughout, with the bleakness lightened occasionally by a corrosive irony which he directs back at himself as much as at others. At the end of *Portrait* he was about to leave Dublin determined to 'forge in the smithy of my soul the uncreated conscience of my race' (P, 253), but, as these episodes of *Ulysses* indicate, he accomplished very little in Paris before a telegram containing an odd mistake, 'Nother dying come home father' (U, 3.199), summoned him back to Dublin. He declared in *Portrait* that he was willing to make 'a lifelong mistake and perhaps as long as eternity' (P, 247) to ensure his intellectual and artistic freedom, but his refusal to grant his mother's dying wish that he pray for her at her bedside has left him consumed with guilt. His bitterness stems from more than his mother's death, though: to Haines he calls himself a 'servant of two masters', meaning 'The imperial British state ... and the holy Roman catholic and apostolic church' (U, 1.638, 643–4). He feels unable to hold his own against Mulligan's seemingly unending mocking wit (his last thought in 'Telemachus', encapsulating his resentment against Mulligan, England and the Church, is 'Usurper' [1.744]), but he does counter the foolish prattle of the headmaster, Garrett Deasy. When Deasy makes an anti-Semitic remark that Jewish merchants are ruining England, Stephen responds that a merchant 'is one who buys cheap and sells dear, jew or gentile, is he not?' and goes on to say that 'History ... is a nightmare from which I am trying to awake'. When Deasy retorts teleologically that 'All human history moves towards one great goal, the manifestation of God', and, coincidentally, at the same time one of the teams of schoolboys playing field hockey outside his office scores a goal and the boys start to cheer, Stephen responds that God is 'A shout in the street' (2.359–60, 377, 380–1, 386).

Stephen's problems inspire him to meditate on questions of history, including possible relationships between events that actually happened in the past and those that at some point in time seemed possible but never did take place (see, for example, 2.48–52, 67). These questions resonate with his particular situation – did he have the option of kneeling down and praying for his mother given that he didn't actually do it? – and with the situation Joyce has put him in as a Telemachus figure re-enacting the plot of Homer's character. When he is alone in 'Proteus', he also wrestles with complex philosophical and theological questions, such as Aristotelian questions regarding whether the aspects of the objects we perceive are inherent in the objects themselves, or might be modified or even partly come into being through our senses. Stephen's first thought in 'Proteus' – 'Ineluctable modality of the visible: at least that if no more, thought through my eyes' (3.1–2) – seems so impenetrable that many readers attempting to get through the novel on their own stop reading here. But in some ways the impenetrability of Stephen's meditations is the point. Stunned by his feelings of guilt over his mother's death, back in Dublin after a largely failed flight to Europe and very uncertain about his future, his philosophical questions directly relate to his predicament. They also reveal a great deal about his personality: faced with an overwhelming emotional crisis, he takes refuge in abstract philosophy. In a sense, Stephen's philosophizing is most important in its inadequacy as a strategy to help him with his dilemma.

Homer's Telemachus is a young man filled with worries about his absent father and with fears that one of the hundred suitors for his mother's hand will get his way and usurp Odysseus' (and his own) kingdom. We hear little about Stephen's father in the first three episodes; it is his mother who is present to him in her absence. Stephen also has been thinking abstractly about fathers, though. He has worked up an interpretation of Hamlet, a play about an absent (murdered) father that is also about a young man's troubled relationship with his mother; it is a theory in which, Mulligan tells Haines, 'He proves by algebra that Hamlet's grandson is Shakespeare's grandfather and that he himself is the ghost of his own father' (1.555–7). But his mother obsesses him. As he teaches his class in 'Nestor', he poses a cryptic riddle to the students, and the answer that he gives the class, 'The fox burying his grandmother under a hollybush' (2.115), displaces the original 'mother' in what must be an unconscious attempt to push any thought of his mother's death out of his mind.[19] She won't stay away, however: in 'Proteus' a sequence of thoughts leads him to wonder whether, as Mulligan did, he would be able to save a drowning man: 'His human eyes scream to me out of horror of his death. I ... With him together down.' Then the pronoun changes: 'I could not save her. Waters: bitter death: lost' (3.329–30). His mother has slipped unbidden back into Stephen's guilty mind.

In Joyce's schema for Ulysses he listed an organ of the body for each episode but left the column blank for each of Stephen's three episodes;[20] even with his intelligence and education, existing almost entirely in his head renders Stephen an incomplete human being. Episode 4 ('Calypso'), however, begins surprisingly with not just a completely new character but one who 'ate with relish the inner organs of beasts and fowls' and who 'Most of all ... liked grilled mutton kidneys which gave to his palate a fine tang of faintly scented urine' (4.1–5). Just as The Odyssey, after a few books focused on Telemachus, shifts to Odysseus on

Calypso's island, we move to the Odysseus figure here. But what an unexpected figure: this man moves about the kitchen of his home at 7 Eccles Street preparing breakfast for his wife and feeding milk and talking to his cat. The first three episodes dealing with Leopold Bloom – 'Calypso' (8:00 a.m.), 'Lotus Eaters' (10:00) and 'Hades' (11:00) – overlap Stephen's episodes in time, but, as David Hayman has noted, they move in an opposite direction: Stephen's episodes take him progressively more inward, so that in 'Proteus' he is entirely alone, whereas in his first three Bloom goes more and more out into the world of Dublin.[21] If Stephen is preoccupied with his private concerns, Bloom constantly responds to the world around him, whether to his cat ('Wonder what I look like to her. Height of a tower? No, she can jump me'), to the proprietor of a pub he passes in his neighbourhood ('Baldhead over the blind. Cute old codger. No use canvassing him for an ad. Still he knows his own business best'), or to the attractive backside of the woman who works in the house next to his ('catch up and walk behind her if she went slowly, behind her moving hams. Pleasant to see first thing in the morning' [4.28–9, 111–12, 171–3]). Bloom is comfortable in his body. He buys a kidney and savours it for breakfast, and then enjoys both a successful bowel movement ('Hope it's not too big bring on piles again. No, just right. So. Ah!' [4.467, 502–3, 509–10]) and the edifying experience of Philip Beaufoy's 'Matcham's Masterstroke', a *Titbits*-magazine story which he reads and then rips out to use as toilet paper. From his first appearance in *Ulysses*, Bloom lives moment by moment through his senses and his body.

Leopold Bloom is no intellectual like Stephen Dedalus, but he lives actively in his mind. Molly asks him to define a word from the novel *Ruby: The Pride of the Ring*. He struggles to explain 'metempsychosis', first describing it as 'the transmigration of souls'. When Molly responds in exasperation, 'O, rocks! ... Tell us in plain words', he tries again: 'Some people believe, he said, that we go on living in another body after death, that we lived before. They call it reincarnation ... Metempsychosis, he said, is what the ancient Greeks called it' (4.339–43, 362–75). Here is a character modelled after an ancient Greek one, with no awareness that he is re-enacting an old plot in a modern context, talking about souls from earlier centuries living on in new bodies. Bloom knows a little bit about a lot of things, much only half understood or half correct ('Because the weight of the water, no, the weight of the body in the water is equal to the weight of the what? Or is it the volume is equal to the weight? It's a law something like that' [5.39–42]). But his half-knowledge does not bother him, and he remains alive to, and curious about, almost everything he encounters. He lives for – and in a sense is himself – a shout in the street.

This modern Odysseus has a 15-year-old daughter Milly, who has recently moved away from home to work as a photographer's assistant. (A son, we gradually learn, died ten years earlier after living for only eleven days.) Bloom gets a letter from Milly this morning, and it causes him to think about her developing sexuality, but he is most strongly aware of the past and present sexual attractions and desires of Molly, Ulysses' Penelope. The mail brings her a letter from Blazes Boylan. She tells Bloom that Boylan will be visiting the house that afternoon to bring her the music for the two songs she will be singing on her tour – 'Là ci darem', a duet from Mozart's opera Don Giovanni, and the popular ballad 'Love's Old Sweet Song' – alerting Bloom to the likelihood that she will be unfaithful to him when Boylan is with her. When Bloom begins his Odyssean wanderings around Dublin starting in his second episode, 'Lotus Eaters', he spends half the day wondering if he should go home before 4:00 to thwart the assignation and the other half wondering what it will be like when, after long delays, he finally does return home. His bed about to be occupied by another man, his son taken from him by death, Bloom could easily, like Stephen, think 'Usurper', but instead his last thought in his first episode goes outward to his acquaintance who has died: 'Poor Dignam!' (4.551).

Bloom spends 16 June 1904 – 'the dailiest day possible', Arnold Bennett remarked in an early review[22] – wandering around Dublin. He busies himself during the day with picking up, reading and thinking about a letter he receives from Martha Clifford, a woman with whom he seems to be flirting via letters (in 'Lotus Eaters'); attending Paddy Dignam's funeral ('Hades'); trying to place an ad in Dublin newspapers for Alexander Keyes, Tea, Wine, and Spirit Merchant ('Aeolus'); eating lunch ('Lestrygonians'); buying a new soft-core porn book for Molly to read ('Wandering Rocks'); listening to songs in a pub ('Sirens');

arranging to contribute to an insurance fund for Paddy Dignam's widow and children ('Cyclops'); resting on the strand (near where Stephen walks in 'Proteus') and masturbating to the sight of a young woman's exposed underwear ('Nausicaa'); visiting a maternity hospital to see whether a pregnant acquaintance has given birth to her child yet ('Oxen of the Sun'); and following Stephen Dedalus into Nighttown, Dublin's red-light district ('Circe') and then inviting him home for a late evening cup of cocoa ('Eumaeus' and 'Ithaca'). Except for his preoccupations with Boylan and Molly (a huge preoccupation, of course), the day is quite ordinary. Bloom, too, seems unexceptional, but he also is an outsider in the city in which he was born and has always lived. His early episodes make the reason for this clear: Bloom is a Jew, and, even though he is a native Dubliner, no one seems to consider him one of them. Eventually we learn that Bloom has been baptized three times, including when he married the Catholic Molly Tweedy, and his mother wasn't Jewish, meaning that, according to Jewish law, he himself is not Jewish. But everyone in Dublin, including Bloom himself, considers him a Jew and reacts to him as one. If he is an Everyman, he is an Everyman as outsider.

As Bloom goes on his journey through Dublin, the episodes of Ulysses present modern versions of Odysseus' adventures: for example, avoiding eating the lotus flower and losing all will to go on ('Lotus Eaters', which focuses on the various narcotic elements in a modern city); a visit to the underworld ('Hades', the journey to the cemetery for Paddy Dignam's funeral); the island of the god of the winds ('Aeolus', which takes place in a newspaper office); the land of the human-eating Lestrygonians (lunch time, with an emphasis in the episode on the human digestive system); the alluring Sirens (Bloom sits in a side room of a pub listening to songs being sung and to two women flirting with various men, including Blazes Boylan); and the cannibalistic one-eyed Cyclopes (Bloom is in another pub, this one dominated by a ferocious Irish nationalist and vicious anti-Semite who taunts and threatens him). Bloom gets buffeted about, suffering large and small slights all day. Most significantly, he keeps seeing and almost running into Boylan, and people regularly mention Boylan's name to him. But he is resilient and comes out of each episode mostly unharmed.

Bloom seems like an ordinary man from the outside, and his conversations are startlingly unremarkable. But his inner life is extraordinarily rich, as is evident both in his responses to people and objects and in his ideas, preoccupations and memories. From his thoughts about what he looks like from his cat's perspective (4.28–9), to observations about a newspaper advertisement for potted meat that he sees as he looks down in an effort to distract himself during an unwelcome conversation (5.143–7), to ideas about how cemeteries might save space by burying people vertically (6.764–6), to an erotic memory of lying on Howth Hill with Molly on the day he proposed to her (8.897–916), his thoughts are lively, varied and always active. Whatever he is doing or thinking, his mind repeatedly takes him back to Molly. On this day when he suspects that she will be unfaithful to him, he thinks about her constantly, wondering whether she pronounces the Italian words in Mozart's duet correctly (4.327–8); recalling her clever remarks, such as describing Ben Dollard, a singer who has fallen on hard times because of drinking, as having a 'bass barreltone voice' (8.117–19); and remembering events from their lives together, including the time she saw two dogs mating outside a window and asked him to make love to her: 'Give us a touch, Poldy. God, I'm dying for it' (6.80–1). Bloom stays away all day, but he constantly returns home to Molly in his thoughts.

We build up a picture of an ordinary, humane, decent man, snubbed and derided by almost everyone. (A repeated question among the Dublin men is why a desirable young woman like Molly chose Leopold Bloom to marry.) He has his quirks – a sketchy fund of knowledge that leads to mistakes about things he only partly knows (the Catholic Church at 5.318–458, poetry at 6.940–1); a tendency towards masochism (the 'sting of disregard glowed to weak pleasure within his breast' when he misses the chance to walk behind the next-door servant girl and Martha Clifford's threat in her letter to 'punish you' thrills him all day [4.176–7, 5.244, 252]); and an inability, unwillingness, or refusal (it is never clear what the reason is) to go home before Boylan arrives in the late afternoon. But he also responds with sympathy and kindness when he meets an old friend whose husband has become mentally ill (8.202–314); feels compassion for a person desperate enough to commit suicide when one of the men he is with says that a suicide disgraces a family (despondent over the death of his wife, Bloom's father took his life eighteen years earlier [6.335–48, 17.623–32]); responds to a belligerent drunk who taunts him about his nationality with a claim that he believes in 'Love ... the opposite of hatred' (12.1485); and, a sonless father, follows and tries to take care of Stephen Dedalus, a fatherless son (his father is a hopeless alcoholic), when he realizes how much trouble this young man is in (14.264–76; 15.635–42).

The first eleven episodes feature a basically similar technique, a combination of narration, dialogue and interior monologue that Joyce, after he had moved away from it, called the novel's 'initial style' (LI, 129). These eleven episodes are far from identical to each other, though. The narrator in the first episode, for example, applies a series of adverbs to Buck Mulligan, who speaks 'sternly', 'briskly' and 'gaily' (U, 1.19, 28, 34); for a character who seems to have no interior, these adverbs describe what an observer might hear in Mulligan's voice and see on his face without implying any interior reality. In 'Lestrygonians', Bloom's lunchtime episode, the narration takes on the technique Joyce named as 'peristaltic movement':[23] 'Perched on high stools by the bar, hats shoved back, at the tables calling for more bread no charge, swilling, wolfing gobfuls of sloppy food, their eyes bulging, wiping wetted moustaches' (8.654–6). In 'Scylla and Charybdis' the narration incorporates and plays with the words the characters speak: 'A shrew, John Eglinton said shrewdly, is not a useful portal of discovery, one should imagine' (9.232). Most dramatically, in 'Sirens', the episode built around music, the narration assumes musical qualities: 'Bloowho went by by Moulang's pipes bearing in his breast the sweets of sin, by Wine's antiques, in memory bearing sweet sinful words, by Carroll's dusky battered plate, for Raoul' (11.86–8). Bloom's interior monologue remains relatively intact through these changes, but it takes on various inflections, such as flower imagery in 'Lotus Eaters', wind in 'Aeolus' and food in 'Lestrygonians', where it also picks up some of the peristaltic movement: 'Things go on same, day after day: squads of police marching out, back: trams in, out' and 'Look at the woebegone walk of him. Eaten a bad egg. Poached eyes on ghost' (8.477–8, 507–8).

None of these variations prepare a reader for the changes that occur in each episode starting with the twelfth, 'Cyclops'. Joyce gives the reader some advance warning when the seventh episode, 'Aeolus', which takes place in and around a newspaper's offices, includes lines of upper-case text that resemble newspaper headlines or subheads: 'IN THE HEART OF THE HIBERNIAN METROPOLIS', 'THE WEARER OF THE CROWN', 'GENTLEMEN OF THE PRESS' (7.1–2, 14, 20). Starting with 'Cyclops', each episode seems to be written as if it is the start of a new novel; in 'Ulysses' in Progress I argue that Joyce did not start working on Ulysses with a plan to use a new technique in each episode in the last half of the book, but rather eventually felt that he had exhausted the possibilities of his original method and began experimenting with other ways of telling his story. (Originally, 'Aeolus' didn't include the heads. Joyce added them as he was reading the proofs for the episode in August 1921 while he was writing the novel's last episodes, probably to make one of the early episodes look somewhat like the later ones.[24]) 'Cyclops' features a first-person narrator – a debt collector and barfly who has something negative (and very funny) to say about almost everyone – and the narration is interrupted by hilarious long parodies of newspaper articles and other kinds of writing that are as wide-eyed in their optimism as the narration is negative and brutal. Bloom's interior monologue disappears completely in the episode. 'Nausicaa' is split between an account of a young woman on the strand, told in a style that imitates and parodies a nineteenth-century romance novel (to Gerty MacDowell, Bloom has 'wonderful eyes ... superbly expressive' and a 'pale intellectual face' that is also 'the saddest she had ever seen' [13.414, 415–16, 370]), and a one-time return to the 'initial style' featuring Bloom's monologue. When Gerty leans back to look at fireworks that are going off behind her and exposes her underwear to Bloom, he masturbates, a scene (13.715–40) that provoked the New York court in early 1921 to declare Ulysses obscene. The main part of 'Oxen of the Sun', in which Bloom visits a maternity hospital, is told in forty paragraphs, representing the forty weeks of a human pregnancy, each one imitating an English prose writer from medieval times to the late nineteenth century. 'Circe', the visit to Nighttown (and by far the longest episode in the novel), is written as a script for a stage play, with Bloom's and Stephen's unconscious minds dramatized as fully as their conscious, waking lives. 'Eumaeus', the first of the three episodes Joyce called the 'Nostos', or return, in which Bloom takes Stephen to a cabman's shelter to rest before they begin their walk to 7 Eccles Street, is told in a windy, flabby style by a narrator who cannot resist using ten words when two would do and who has trouble keeping his pronouns straight: 'Preparatory to anything else Mr Bloom brushed off the greater bulk of the shavings and handed Stephen the hat and ashplant and bucked him generally in orthodox Samaritan fashion which he very badly needed. His (Stephen's) mind was not exactly what you would call wandering but a bit unsteady' (16.1–5). Joyce called 'Ithaca', where Bloom takes Stephen home, talks with him, offers him a room for the night (Stephen declines and leaves for an unspecified future), and then returns to his bed and to Molly, the novel's 'ugly duckling':[25] it is told in a question-and-answer style that, he said, would let 'the reader know everything and know it in the baldest coldest way' (LI, 159–60). And finally 'Penelope', Molly Bloom's thoughts as she falls asleep about her early life, many of the men she has known, her new lover Boylan, and her past and future with Leopold Bloom, closes the book in forty pages of almost totally unpunctuated interior monologue.

Not much happens in terms of plot. Joyce transforms even the big Homeric events into personal, domestic incidents. Leopold Bloom and Stephen Dedalus talk briefly as they drink cocoa in Bloom's kitchen, but after they urinate together in the back yard, Stephen leaves. As Bloom then joins Molly in bed, he accomplishes his own version of Odysseus' act of slaying the hundred suitors for Penelope's hand when he responds with 'more abnegation than jealousy, less envy than equanimity' (17.2195) to Molly and her infidelity and 'kisse[s] the plump mellow yellow smellow melons of her rump, on each plump melonous hemisphere, in their mellow yellow furrow, with obscure prolonged provocative melonsmellonous osculation' (17.2241–3). For Bloom, being home and next to Molly's body ultimately outweighs any outrage or betrayal. Molly's thoughts as she lies in bed next to Bloom culminate in a memory of the day sixteen years ago when he proposed to her (Bloom remembers the same scene earlier in the day as he eats lunch), ending with the famous words: 'then he asked me would I yes to say yes my mountain flower and first I put my arms around him yes and drew him down to me so he could feel my breasts all perfume yes and his heart was going like mad and yes I said yes I will Yes' (18.1605–9). In 'Cyclops', Bloom gets into trouble when the men in the pub think, mistakenly, that he has won a great deal of money on a horse named Throwaway, a 20-to-1 outsider who beats the favoured Sceptre in the afternoon's Gold Cup Race in England. (This race actually happened that day with these results[26]). Bloom ultimately wins the competition for Molly, too, as her thoughts gradually leave Sceptre/Boylan and return to Throwaway/Bloom. Stephen has departed for an unspecified future, and Leopold and Molly Bloom face a complicated new domestic reality, but in her own way Molly shows herself to be a faithful Penelope to Bloom.[27]

* * *

With this story and using these techniques Joyce crafted a novel that, over eighty years after its publication and over a hundred years after the day on which it is set, continues to strike readers as original and innovative, and as speaking about and to our own society and culture. As a result, Ulysses has proved amenable to almost every critical and theoretical approach to literature that has come along since the 1920s. (Terry Eagleton has quipped that the test of any theory is how well it would work with Finnegans Wake; he could just as easily have said this about Ulysses[28]). Echoing Joyce's remark that his thought was simple, Richard Ellmann writes that 'Joyce's theme in Ulysses was simple. He invoked the most elaborate means to present it',[29] and in one sense it is the elaborate means – the parade of techniques Joyce uses to tell his story, especially in Ulysses' second half – that makes the novel adaptable to many different approaches. But it isn't only the elaborate techniques. For example, Bloom's status as a Jew is much discussed both within Ulysses and in the criticism and analysis surrounding it. Technically, because his mother was Christian, he is not Jewish at all, as he is aware (16.1083–85). But he thinks and acts as a Jew, continuously feels that he is different from the other people around him, and other people react to him as someone who looks and is different from them. It is probably the precise balance between the recognizably Jewish aspects of Bloom's character and the ambiguities surrounding his identity that make him such a compelling outsider figure.[30]

Similarly, the Blooms' marriage is depicted with a combination of specific detail and rich understatement. Readers tend to puzzle over why Bloom will not go home to thwart Boylan's assignation with Molly, but his character is built on a conception of masculinity that does not involve aggression or, as Stephen sardonically puts it in his Shakespeare discussion, 'hold[ing] tightly also to what he calls his rights over her whom he calls his wife' (9.789–90). We learn relatively early on that Leopold and Molly stopped enjoying sex after their baby son died. Bloom thinks, 'Could never like it again after Rudy' (8.610), and the absence of a pronoun significantly leaves unclear whether he is talking about himself, Molly or both. In her monologue Molly thinks about Rudy's death, too, but in terms of 'we' – 'our 1st death too it was we were never the same since' (18.1450) – and the detailed information in 'Ithaca' reveals that 'complete carnal intercourse, with ejaculation of semen within the natural female organ, having last taken place 5 weeks previous, viz. 27 November 1893, to the birth on 29 December 1893 of second (and only male) issue, deceased 9 January 1894, aged 11 days, there remained a period of 10 years, 5 months and 18 days during which carnal intercourse had been incomplete, without ejaculation of semen within the natural female organ' (17.2278–84). Ulysses presents a picture of a couple traumatized by a tragic event, with no ability to talk about it with each other or anyone else. Significantly, the period during which the Blooms have not enjoyed full intercourse corresponds to the amount of time Odysseus spent trying to get home after the Trojan War. The sexual problem surely contributes in a major way to Bloom's fatalistic attitude towards Molly's affair with Boylan ('Useless to go back. Had to be' [8.633]) and also to his willingness to accept it as 'natural', 'not more abnormal than all other parallel processes of adaptation to altered conditions of existence', and as 'more than inevitable, irreparable' (17.2178, 2190–1, 2194). Within all of the verbiage of 'Ithaca', the repeated use of the word 'natural' in the paragraph depicting Bloom's acceptance of the adultery indicates just how hard he is struggling to convince himself: he accepts the event 'As as natural as any and every natural act of a nature expressed or understood executed in natured nature by natural creatures in accordance with his, her and their natured natures' (17.2178–80). Under all the technical virtuosity in these and countless other passages in Ulysses, there remains at its heart the poignant story of a couple still very much in love with each other after almost sixteen years of marriage, still unsteady after an event they could not control and cannot understand, trying to live their lives with each other and also fulfil their individual needs.

Joyce's vision is decidedly male, and most of Ulysses focuses on its male characters and their world, but his treatment of his male characters in the book and his portrayal of Molly Bloom and the secondary female characters, as well as its emphases on the plight of women in the novel's Irish society, have prompted much feminist criticism and scholarship. Ulysses presents its male characters as attractive in their garrulousness and sociability, but it condemns their shiftlessness and irresponsibility, and especially their alcoholism, and it graphically depicts the kind of man that many of the women are forced to marry and the huge families that many of them have.[31] The attention to Ireland's troubled relationship with Britain has led to much criticism and analysis of Joyce and politics, in recent years especially from the perspectives of post-colonial criticism and Irish studies, and it is interesting to speculate on how the years during and after the First World War, when Joyce was writing Ulysses, affected this supposedly apolitical writer who set his work ten years before the start of the war.[32] Critics have paid increasing attention recently to the prevalence of popular culture within Ulysses, including Joyce's use of popular songs, music hall and other theatre, and advertising.[33]

Likewise, the story of how Joyce wrote Ulysses and its various encounters with legal issues of obscenity and copyright are also fascinating aspects of the discourse surrounding Ulysses. Joyce started working on Ulysses in 1914, interrupted it later that year and into 1915 to write Exiles, and then returned to Ulysses. By March 1918 the Little Review in New York was serializing the novel; between then and the end of 1920 it published thirteen episodes (through 'Nausicaa') and the first part of 'Oxen of the Sun'. As he worked Joyce talked about finishing the novel in 1920 and then in 1921, but he kept writing and revising until 31 January 1922, when he finally stopped so that it could be published on his 40th birthday two days later. The many notes, drafts, manuscripts, typescripts and proofs that have survived offer fascinating evidence of Joyce writing *Ulysses* during its various stages of composition.[34]

While the *Little Review* was serializing *Ulysses*, Joyce worked quite consistently and submitted the new episodes with impressive regularity. As time went on, however, various forces – several severe eye attacks, his constant moves from apartment to apartment and from city to city, his always precarious financial situation – complicated and interrupted his progress and in some cases seriously delayed it. *Ulysses'* brushes with the law also affected the novel significantly. The United States Post Office prohibited the *Little Review* from mailing three different issues containing episodes of *Ulysses*, and then in February 1921 a three-judge panel declared the last part of the 'Nausicaa' episode in the July–August 1920 number to be obscene and prevented the *Little Review* from publishing further episodes. The trial effectively ended any chance for *Ulysses* to be published in an English-speaking country. Significantly, as I wrote in *'Ulysses' in Progress*, once Joyce was freed from *Little Review* deadlines, the episodes started taking him more and more time to write, and they grew increasingly elaborate. More recently, scholars have argued that Joyce reacted to the declaration of obscenity by emphasizing the schematic elements as a way of evading the censor and by encouraging critics such as Valery Larbaud and Stuart Gilbert to interpret *Ulysses* through the schema rather than through the possibly obscene thoughts and actions of its characters (Paul Vanderham) and that Joyce added courtroom scenes and legal terminology and even the 'legal interrogation' question-and-answer technique of 'Ithaca' (David Weir) in response to the *Little Review* trial. Joyce's main reaction to the suppression of the magazine and the declaration of obscenity was concern bordering on despair over whether *Ulysses* would ever be published, a worry that ended when Sylvia Beach and her newly created Shakespeare & Co. imprint became his publisher in Paris. (The publication in Paris opened up another legal complication, however, because it effectively eliminated the chance for the full *Ulysses* to obtain copyright in the United States.[35])

When Stephen decides not to return to the Martello Tower at the end of 'Telemachus', he leaves his key for Buck Mulligan (1.721–2), and Bloom, because he wears a black suit rather than his usual clothes to attend Paddy Dignam's funeral, forgets to take his house key as he leaves

7 Eccles Street in the morning (4.72–3; 5.468; 17.71–9). So both men walk around Dublin all day without keys, and they are described at the end of Ulysses as 'the, premeditatedly (respectively) and inadvertently, keyless couple' and Bloom as a 'competent keyless citizen' (17.80–1, 1019). Readers sometimes assume that if they could only find or discover a key, or the key, to Ulysses, they could unlock the book's complications and mysteries. But it is significant that Bloom is 'competent' without his key, and perhaps this is what Ulysses at its best trains its readers to be. We do not lack the key to interpretation or understanding; rather, there is no magic key. A reader gains some understanding of Ulysses during a first experience of the book and more and more during second and subsequent readings (if they happen), but Ulysses cannot be controlled or mastered. This is not because it is impenetrable or beyond human understanding but because it is based on rich ambiguities that cannot be reduced to clear answers. Ulysses would be immeasurably diminished if there were a key to mastering it. (Joyce recognized his readers' desire for mastery, however, when he told a friend that 'I've put in so many enigmas and puzzles that it will keep the professors busy for centuries arguing over what I meant, and that's the only way of insuring one's immortality' [JJ, 521].) A typically multilayered footnote in Finnegans Wake says, 'Wipe your glosses with what you know' (FW, 304 n.3), and this remark can apply to Ulysses as much as to the Wake. Each reader brings what he or she knows to Ulysses and glosses the book's details with this knowledge. The note also says to 'Wipe your glasses', a nod to the near-sighted author with his many eye problems and to the need to see Ulysses with clear vision, as well as 'Wipe your asses' with 'you know what', a recognition that, as Leopold Bloom demonstrates throughout the day, knowledge is not only in the mind but also in the body. Joyce's note points to the notorious lack of guide posts in Ulysses, since if you have to produce your glosses you are to a large extent on your own both in terms of what you understand and how you respond. For many readers, this is a major part of Ulysses' ultimate triumph.

Some readers will sympathize with George Moore's contention that Ulysses involves little more than 'trying to copy the London Directory' and will not respond positively to Joyce's book. To these readers, it might seem to contain too much arcane information, Joyce might seem to be showing off his virtuosity too much, Leopold Bloom might not be sufficiently compelling as a character, the world of Ulysses and the sensibility behind it might seem too male, etc. These complaints are genuine, and such readers do not need to feel confined to Ezra Pound's 'lower intellectual orders'. But in contrast to Moore, Joyce told Frank Budgen that he wanted 'to give a picture of Dublin so complete that if the city one day suddenly disappeared from the earth it could be reconstructed out of my book'.[36] Much of his city has indeed disappeared, as redevelopment in the prosperous Dublin of the Celtic Tiger years transformed many of its neighbourhoods, in the process destroying numerous buildings that Joyce names and describes. But, at the same time, Ulysses has become part of Dublin: a series of plaques are now embedded in the sidewalks to indicate places where Bloom walks along the streets, stops and looks in shop windows, and enters pubs during the 'Lestrygonians' episode, and a historical marker on a building indicates, 'Here in Joyce's imagination / was born in May 1866 / Leopold Bloom / Citizen, Husband, Father, Wanderer / Reincarnation of Ulysses'.[37] More important, though, as he welcomed participants to the Seventeenth International James Joyce Symposium in London in June 2000, Edward Barrington, the Irish Ambassador to the UK, declared that 'in many ways Joyce invented Dublin, and those of us living there now have to live in it according to his myopic lens'. Joyce's vision, like anyone's, is skewed, partial and biased, but by focusing on three specific people in Dublin, he showed how lives can be lived and how stories can be told about them in ways that have resonated and reverberated throughout the twentieth century and into the twenty-first and that not only continue to reflect but also to shape us.

NOTES

1. Ezra Pound, 'Paris Letter', The Dial, 72 (June 1922), reprinted in Forrest Read (ed.), Pound/Joyce: The Letters of Ezra Pound to James Joyce (New York: New Directions, 1967), p.194; T.S. Eliot, 'Ulysses, Order and Myth', The Dial, 75 (November 1923), reprinted in Frank Kermode (ed.), Selected Prose of T.S. Eliot (London: Faber and Faber, 1975), pp.177, 178; Edmund Wilson, review of Ulysses, The New Republic (5 July 1922), reprinted in Robert H. Deming (ed.), James Joyce: The Critical Heritage, 2 vols (London: Routledge and Kegan Paul, 1970), Vol. I, p.230; Virginia Woolf, 'Modern Fiction', The Common Reader: First Series (New York: Harcourt, Brace and World, 1953 [1925]), p.155.
2. Paul Lewis, 'Ulysses at Top As Panel Picks 100 Best Novels', New York Times, 20 July

1998, B1 (National Edition); Rebecca Caldwell, 'One Day Turns 100', *Globe and Mail*, (Toronto), 12 June 2004, R7; Herbert Gorman, *James Joyce* (New York: Rinehart and Co., 1939), p.118; *Oxford English Dictionary Online*, 'Bloomsday' Draft Entry, March 2006 <http://dictionary.oed.com/cgi/display/20002143?keytype=ref&ijkey=VTzv6zas djZ8I>.

3. Alfred Noyes, 'Rottenness in Literature', *Sunday Chronicle*, 29 October 1922, reprinted in Deming, *James Joyce: The Critical Heritage*, Vol.I, p.274; Aramis, 'The Scandal of *Ulysses*', *Sporting Times*, 1 April 1922, reprinted in Deming, *James Joyce: Critical Heritage*, Vol.I, p.192; George Moore, cited in *JJ*, 529; Virginia Woolf, *A Writer's Diary: Being Extracts from the Diary of Virginia Woolf*, ed. Leonard Woolf (Frogmore, Herts: Triad Panther, 1978 [1953]), pp.54, 56 (entries for 16 August and 6 September 1922).

4. Richard Bernstein, '*Ulysses*: Revered But Unreadable', in 'Great Hits Headed for the Attic', *New York Times*, 1 January 2000, p.3 (National Edition); Michael O'Laughlin, 'The Bloomsday Philistines Arrive', *Sunday Independent*, 'Living Section', 13 June 2004, p.14; John Banville, 'Bloomsday, Bloody Bloomsday', *New York Times Book Review*, 13 June 2004, p.31.

5. According to Paul Vanderham, because it had been judged obscene in the US and con-fiscated and destroyed in the UK, Canada and Ireland, 'by 1923 *Ulysses* was largely banned from the English-speaking world'. Vanderham, *James Joyce and Censorship: The Trials of 'Ulysses'* (New York: New York University Press, 1998), pp.82–3.

6. Herbert S. Gorman, *James Joyce: His First Forty Years* (New York: B.W. Huebsch, 1924); Stuart Gilbert, *James Joyce's 'Ulysses': A Study* (1930; rpt. with new preface, New York: Vintage, 1952); Frank Budgen, *James Joyce and the Making of 'Ulysses'* (1934; rpt. with introduction by Clive Hart, Oxford: Oxford University Press, 1972); Edmund Wilson, *Axel's Castle: A Study of the Imaginative Literature of 1870–1930* (New York: Scribner, 1931).

7. Alexander Lindey, 'Petition for Release and Admission of Book into the United States on the Ground that it is a Classic' (2 June 1933), reprinted in Michael Moscato and Leslie Le Blanc (eds), *The United States of America v. One Book Entitled 'Ulysses' by James Joyce: Documents and Commentary: A 50-Year Retrospective* (Frederick, MD: University Publications of America, 1984), p.189, also pp.186–9, 256, 267, discussed in Kevin Dettmar, 'James Joyce and the Great Books' *Common Review*, 2, 1 (Winter 2002), paragraphs 6–7. <http://web.archive.org/web/ 200304131505 32/http://www.greatbooks. org/tcr/dettmar21.shtml>.

8. Joseph Prescott, 'James Joyce's *Ulysses* as a Work in Progress'. Ph.D. dissertation, Harvard University, 1944. For further discussion of Joyce's early reputation, see Joseph Kelly, *Our Joyce: From Outcast to Icon* (Austin, TX: University of Texas Press, 1998) and Joseph Brooker, *Joyce's Critics: Transitions in Reading and Culture* (Madison, WI: University of Wisconsin Press, 2004).

9. Shane Leslie, review of *Ulysses*, *Quarterly Review* (October 1922), reprinted in Deming, *James Joyce: The Critical Heritage*, Vol. I, p.207; Mary Colum, 'The Confessions of James Joyce', *Freeman* (19 July 1922), reprinted in Deming, *James Joyce: The Critical Heritage*,

Vol.I, p.232; Random House publishers, 'How to Enjoy James Joyce's Great Novel *Ulysses*', *Saturday Review of Literature*, 10 February 1934, pp.474–5; Jeff Danziger, cartoon in *International Herald Tribune*, 24 July 1998, p.7; Dettmar, 'James Joyce and the Great Books', paragraph 4.

10. *Ulysses* divides into eighteen units, but the usual novelistic term 'chapters' has often seemed inadequate as a name for them. They are more discrete than typical chapters in novels – there is usually a gap of unaccounted-for time between the end of one and the start of the next, sometimes a few minutes and sometimes several hours, and each one can seem more like a self-contained unit than a section of an ongoing novel. Joyce used the terms 'adventure' and 'episode' rather than 'chapter' to describe these eighteen units, and 'episode' seems as good a term as any to use for them. For a sampling of Joyce's remarks, see his letters regarding the 'Circe' episode (LI, 141, 142, 146, 149, 150; LIII, 15, 19–20, 31). He used the Homeric names for the episodes in many letters and in the two schemas for *Ulysses* that he prepared in 1920 and 1921: the 1920 schema is reproduced in Richard Ellmann, *Ulysses on the Liffey* (New York: Oxford University Press, 1972), twelve unnumbered pages following p.187, and the 1921 schema in Gilbert, *James Joyce's 'Ulysses'*, p.30. Gilbert uses the names throughout his book-length study of *Ulysses*, a practice that many subsequent critics have followed. There has been some dispute as to whether or not *Ulysses* is a novel. Joyce seems to have stopped using the term 'novel' for *Ulysses* as he worked on it; see A. Walton Litz's speculations about considering *Ulysses* as a novel in 'The Genre of *Ulysses*' (1974), reprinted in Mary T. Reynolds (ed.), *James Joyce: A Collection of Critical Essays* (Englewood Cliffs, NJ: Prentice Hall, 1993), pp.109–17, esp. p.111. Here I have defined 'novel' loosely as a full-length work of prose fiction and have used the term for *Ulysses*.

11. We don't know how this came about: maybe Joyce planned all along to include details about the characters' ancestors and backgrounds but to give them only near the end, or maybe he decided only as he was writing *Ulysses* to include them. Hans Walter Gabler makes this second claim and argues that, because most of the rest of the book had already been set up in type when Joyce decided to include the details, the only place that he – an obsessive reviser who added details to the text at every possible opportunity – could do so was in the last two episodes. Gabler, 'Afterword', in *Ulysses: A Critical and Synoptic Edition*, ed. Hans Walter Gabler with Wolfhard Steppe and Claus Melchior, 3 vols (New York: Garland, 1984), Vol.III, p.1891. See also Hugh Kenner, *Ulysses* (1980; rev. ed., Baltimore, MD: Johns Hopkins University Press, 1987), Ch. 8: 'The Aesthetic of Delay', esp. pp.79, 80–1.

12. Don Gifford with Robert J. Seidman, *'Ulysses' Annotated: Notes for James Joyce's 'Ulysses'* (Berkeley, CA: University of California Press, 1988), p.93. Shortly afterwards the narrator uses 'thing' again – 'The priest came down from the altar, holding the thing out from him' (U, 5.417–18) – this time echoing Bloom's ignorance of the word 'missal' (Gifford and Seidman, *'Ulysses' Annotated*, p.96).

13. In a clever analysis of Joyce's narrative technique, which sometimes goes so far as to

let the vocabulary of the character being described permeate the narration, Hugh Kenner terms it the 'Uncle Charles Principle', basing the name on the narrator's treatment of a minor character who appears near the beginning of Chapter 2 of *Portrait*. The term has become standard for Joyce's method. Kenner, *Joyce's Voices* (Berkeley, CA: University of California Press, 1978), Chapter 2: 'The Uncle Charles Principle', esp. pp.18, 21. For a judgement that Joyce's method is an artistic failure because it fails to offer sufficient guidance to the reader, see Wayne C. Booth, 'The Problem of Distance in *A Portrait of the Artist*', in *The Rhetoric of Fiction* (1961; 2nd edn, 1983), reprinted in James Joyce, *A Portrait of the Artist as a Young Man: Text, Criticism, and Notes*, ed. Chester G. Anderson (New York: Viking, 1968), pp.455–67, and Mark A. Wollaeger (ed.), *James Joyce's 'A Portrait of the Artist as a Young Man': A Casebook* (Oxford: Oxford University Press, 2003), pp.59–72.

14. David Sipress, cartoon in *The New Yorker*, 20 September 1999, p.129.
15. Joyce quoted in Budgen, *James Joyce and the Making of 'Ulysses'*, p.291.
16. Joyce quoted in ibid., p.15; Pound, 'Paris Letter', reprinted in *Pound/Joyce*, p.197; Gorman, *James Joyce*, p.45 [cited in *JJ*, 46]; Joyce quoted in Budgen, *James Joyce and the Making of 'Ulysses'*, p.15.
17. Arnold Goldman, *The Joyce Paradox: Form and Freedom in His Fiction* (London: Routledge and Kegan Paul, 1966).
18. Budgen, *James Joyce and the Making of 'Ulysses'*, pp.52, 107.
19. Gifford and Seidman, *'Ulysses' Annotated*, p.33.
20. Gilbert, *James Joyce's 'Ulysses'*, p.30.
21. David Hayman, *'Ulysses': The Mechanics of Meaning* (Madison, WI: University of Wisconsin Press, 1982 [1970]), esp. pp.93–5.
22. Arnold Bennett, 'James Joyce's *Ulysses*', *Outlook* (29 April 1922), reprinted in Deming, *James Joyce: The Critical Heritage*, Vol.I, p.220.
23. Gilbert, *James Joyce's 'Ulysses'*, p.30.
24. Michael Groden, *'Ulysses' in Progress* (Princeton, NJ: Princeton University Press, 1977), *passim* and p.60.
25. Budgen, *James Joyce and the Making of 'Ulysses'*, p.264.
26. Gifford and Seidman, *'Ulysses' Annotated*, p.98.
27. Ewa Ziarek discusses the complex issues of fidelity and memory in 'The Female Body: Technology and Memory in "Penelope"', in *Molly Blooms: A Polylogue on 'Penelope' and Cultural Studies*, ed. Richard Pearce (Madison, WI: University of Wisconsin Press, 1994), pp.264–84.
28. Terry Eagleton, *Literary Theory: An Introduction*, 2nd edn (Minneapolis, MN: University of Minnesota Press, 1996), p.71.
29. Richard Ellmann, 'Preface' to *Ulysses: The Gabler Edition*, ed. Hans Walter Gabler with Wolfhard Steppe and Claus Melchior (New York: Vintage, 1986, 1993), p.ix.
30. A recent discussion of Bloom's Jewishness is in Cormac Ó Gráda, 'Lost in Little Jerusalem: Leopold Bloom and Irish Jewry', *Journal of Modern Literature*, 27, 4 (Summer 2004), pp.17–26. In *The Years of Bloom: James Joyce in Trieste, 1904–1920* (Dublin: Lilliput

Press; Madison, WI: University of Wisconsin Press, 2000), John McCourt documents how Joyce constructed Leopold Bloom by superimposing aspects of various Jewish men he knew in Trieste on to an Irish character.

31. For example, Kimberly J. Devlin and Marilyn Reizbaum (eds), *'Ulysses': En-Gendered Perspectives* (Columbia, SC: University of South Carolina Press, 1999); Christine Froula, *Modernism's Body: Sex, Culture, and Joyce* (New York: Columbia University Press, 1996); Suzette A. Henke, *James Joyce and the Politics of Desire* (London and New York: Routledge, 1990); Bonnie Kime Scott, *Joyce and Feminism* (Bloomington, IN: Indiana University Press, 1984) and *James Joyce* (Brighton: Harvester Press, 1987).

32. For example, Derek Attridge and Marjorie Howes (eds), *Semicolonial Joyce* (Cambridge: Cambridge University Press, 2000); Vincent J. Cheng, *Joyce, Race, and Empire* (Cambridge: Cambridge University Press, 1995); Enda Duffy, *The Subaltern 'Ulysses'* (Minneapolis, MN: University of Minnesota Press, 1994); Andrew Gibson, *Joyce's Revenge: History, Politics, and Aesthetics in 'Ulysses'* (Oxford: Oxford University Press, 2002); Michael Groden, 'Joyce at Work on "Cyclops": Toward a Biography of *Ulysses*', *James Joyce Quarterly 44, 2 (Winter 2007)*, pp.217–45; Declan Kiberd, *Inventing Ireland* (London: Jonathan Cape, 1995; Cambridge, MA: Harvard University Press, 1996); Dominic Manganiello, *Joyce's Politics* (London and Boston, MA: Routledge and Kegan Paul, 1980); Emer Nolan, *James Joyce and Nationalism* (London and New York: Routledge, 1995); Willard Potts, *Joyce and the Two Irelands* (Austin, TX: University of Texas Press, 2000).

33. For example, Cheryl Herr, *Joyce's Anatomy of Culture* (Urbana, IL: University of Illinois Press, 1986); R.B. Kershner (ed.), *Joyce and Popular Culture* (Gainesville, FL: University Press of Florida, 1996) and 'Cultural Studies of James Joyce', special issue of *European Joyce Studies*, 15 (2003); Garry Leonard, *Advertising and Commodity Culture in Joyce* (Gainesville, FL: University Press of Florida, 1998); Garry Leonard and Jennifer Wicke (eds), 'Joyce and Advertising', special issue of *James Joyce Quarterly*, 30, 4/31,1 (Summer/Fall 1993); Thomas Richards, *The Commodity Culture of Victorian England* (Stanford, CA: Stanford University Press, 1990), Chapter 5, 'Those Lovely Seaside Girls'.

34 See, for example, Michael Groden, *'Ulysses' in Progress*; 'Genetic Joyce: Textual Studies and the Reader', in Jean-Michel Rabaté (ed.), *Palgrave Advances in James Joyce Studies* (London: Palgrave Macmillan, 2004), pp.227–50 and 'Before and After: The Manuscripts in Textual and Genetic Criticism of *Ulysses*', in Michael Patrick Gillespie and A. Nicholas Fargnoli (eds), *'Ulysses' in Critical Perspective* (Gainesville, FL: University Press of Florida, 2006), pp.152–70.

35. See Groden, 'Joyce at Work on "Cyclops": Toward a Biography of *Ulysses*' and *'Ulysses' in Progress*, pp.169–70; Vanderham, *James Joyce and Censorship*; David Weir, 'What Did He Know, and When Did He Know It: The *Little Review*, Joyce, and *Ulysses*', *James Joyce Quarterly*, 37 (2000), pp.389–412, esp. p.405. Regarding *Ulysses* and copyright, see Paul K. Saint-Amour, *The Copywrights: Intellectual Property and the Literary Imagination* (Ithaca, NY: Cornell University Press, 2003), Chapter 5, 'James Joyce, Copywright: Modernist Literary Property Metadiscourse'; Robert Spoo, 'Copyright Protectionism

and Its Discontents: The Case of James Joyce's *Ulysses* in America', *Yale Law Journal*, 108, 3 (December 1998), pp.633–67, 'Copyright and the Ends of Ownership: The Case for a Public-Domain *Ulysses* in America', *Joyce Studies Annual*, 10 (1999), pp.5–62, 'Injuries, Remedies, Moral Rights, and the Public Domain', *James Joyce Quarterly*, 37 (2000), pp.333–51, and *Three Myths for Aging Copyrights: 'Tithonus', 'Dorian Gray', 'Ulysses'* (Dublin: National Library of Ireland, 2004); and 'James Joyce: Copyright, Fair Use, and Permissions: Frequently Asked Questions', written by Paul K. Saint-Amour, Michael Groden, Carol Shloss and Robert Spoo for the International James Joyce Foundation's Special Panel on Intellectual Property, *James Joyce Quarterly*, 44 (2007), pp.753–84.

36. Budgen, *James Joyce and the Making of 'Ulysses'*, p.69.

37. The marker was put up when Dublin celebrated the centenary of Joyce's birth in 1982. A plaque presumably would have gone up instead where the Blooms lived at 7 Eccles Street, but that building had already been demolished. The existing marker fulfils a prophecy in one of Bloom's fantasy/hallucinations in 'Circe', in which he becomes a city alderman and the late Lord Mayor of Dublin decrees 'That the house in which he was born be ornamented with a commemorative tablet' (15.1384–5).

CHAPTER SEVEN

Finnegans Wake:
Some Assembly Required

TIM CONLEY

His producers are they not his consumers? (FW, 497.1–2)

His friends assembled at the wake ... (song lyric, 'Finnegan's Wake')

While *Ulysses* was hailed as a great (if controversial) work in its day, *Finnegans Wake* was generally received with uncertainty, stupefaction and irritation, even by many who had supported the previous book most vigorously. Among the disenchanted were Ezra Pound, H.G. Wells, Rebecca West, Wyndham Lewis and, most vexing for Joyce, his brother, Stanislaus, and his patron, Harriet Shaw Weaver.[1] Within a year of the publication of *Ulysses*, T.S. Eliot pronounced the novel a work 'from which none of us can escape';[2] yet *Finnegans Wake* seems to escape us still, eluding even rudimentary classification. Some call it a novel, some call it poetry, though Joyce himself usually referred to it non-committally as a 'book', and sometimes more tellingly as a 'monster'.[3] Like *Ulysses*, the *Wake* appeared in serialized segments (under the extremely apt title 'Work in Progress') for years before the completed book itself appeared. However, the arrival of the first edition in 1939 was altogether eclipsed by the threat of fascism and the outbreak of war. An affronted Joyce intimated to Beckett that the war could be avoided by reading his new book.[4]

Joyce's seemingly flippant remarks are often worthy of a serious double-take. Consider, as a brief example, his given reason for seeing Homer's Ulysses as a greater hero than Christ, who, Joyce said, 'never lived with a woman'.[5] On the face of it, this seems like nothing more than a cheap sexist wisecrack – and yet it can also be interpreted (if we are willing to look beyond the sexism, though not necessarily condone or even forget it) as an altogether feminist criticism of the construction and connotations of heroism and masculinity. Ulysses is better-rounded, even more egalitarian than Christ, who generally seemed to prefer the company of men. This example is especially worth bearing in mind because it reflects the very method of Finnegans Wake, wherein any pronouncement – even a single word – can be seen to express two entirely antithetical meanings simultaneously. When we talk about what something in the Wake 'means', we are invariably confronted with the co-existence of a contrary meaning.

If, in seriously considering Joyce's claim about avoiding war by reading the Wake, we set aside the fact of Joyce's disproportionate self-importance, we are left to ponder how a book could possibly prevent a war. Such a book would certainly have to possess some fantastic qualities. Even a combination of immense popularity and international circulation with a capacity for diverting a great many serious-minded people (even those not usually drawn to books) would not be enough: after all, neither The Da Vinci Code nor the latest Harry Potter volume halted the invasion of Iraq. No, a book that would stop a world war would have to be not only far more popular and infinitely more absorbing than these examples, but effectively transformative and uniting. It would have to be for the world and about the world and even, I think, by the world.

Here the three criteria Wallace Stevens offers as 'Notes Toward a Supreme Fiction' are usefully precise: it must be abstract; it must change; it must give pleasure. Stevens's poem, which appeared just a few years after Finnegans Wake, significantly ends with a conception of conscious being as 'a war between the mind / And sky, between thought and day and night'. This is 'a war that never ends' and yet 'your war ends':[6] our individual lives and thoughts are discontinuous sub-routines within a larger, ever-running programme. Stevens's 'war' is an existence, whereas the war raging while he writes the poem is just an occurrence. The Wake affirms: 'the world, mind, is, was and will be writing its own runes for ever' (19.35–6). Added to Stevens's criteria is an outrageous fourth: it must be endless. Writing and the efforts at expression are unending because they are manifestations of the ceaseless tension and slippage between the imagined and the real. Joyce posits a 'world mind' capable of sustaining total contradictions and containing multitudes of meaning. This is a sleeping mind and *Finnegans Wake* can be read as a dream, its disorienting language a dream-language. The unconscious is a 'hothel' or 'boardelhouse' (586.18; 186.31; a blend of 'hotel' or 'boarding house' with 'brothel' or 'bordello') with both history (the things we have done) and desire (the things we wish we had done and would yet like to do) as restless tenants and regular customers. Insofar as it can be said to be a story about anything – and it is, as I'll explain, a story about anything and nothing, too, but also not a story at all – *Finnegans Wake* is a never-ending story about such a hotel. At least, according to some people.

This poor sort of description likely seems frustratingly nebulous or evasive to readers who like, and perhaps even depend upon, identifiable and distinct settings and characters, well-delineated plots, with a beginning, middle and end, and, of course, a recognizable language for its expression. *Finnegans Wake* has none of these, or if it does, they have – as Joyce's father said upon seeing Constantin Brancusi's highly abstract portrait of the artist – changed a great deal. The book begins and ends, if those verbs may be used, in mid-sentence, so the end of its reading is 'neverreached' (523.14). It has 'characters' in the sense that, as Jed Rasula has observed, there is, besides the 'psychological and calligraphic' definitions of the term, 'a corresponding parallelism of "letter" as both epistolary and alphabetical':[7] the typographical forms that signify morphemes and phonemes as well as entire words and phrases are themselves the *Wake*'s heroes. These 'characters', however, have no fixed addresses and their locations in space and time lack immoveable deictic markers. When did or will they do this or that? 'They always did: ask the ages. What bird has done yesterday man may do next year, be it fly, be it moult, be it hatch, be it agreement in the nest' (112.9–11). Narrative's constituent variables stay variable or, more precisely, are treated as variations on a theme.

Complicating things further, the *Wake*'s polyvocality is as near to omnivocality as makes no difference. In *Ulysses* a distinctive narrative framework is used for each chapter – a scheme whose constancy affords readers some comfort. Once it is understood or even just faintly supposed, for example, that the stylistic eccentricities or aberrations found in a given chapter are peculiar to it, the reader may assume that he or she need not worry that a given perspective and technique will radically change until the next chapter begins. The reader's situation turns out to be stickier than that, of course (Joyce nearly always seems to sabotage his own structures). For instance, in the 'Nausicaa' episode the reader first encounters a parody of the kind of prose one finds in adolescent romances, but the perspective does in fact shift suddenly (to that of a spent Bloom) and questions linger about who devises the initial parody (is the purple prose Joyce's rendering of Gerty's purple thoughts, or is Bloom projecting a fantasy narrative on to his fantasy image?). Yet these incongruities and displacements pale in comparison to the *Wake*, where a phenomenal 'Everybody' ('one sum and the same person' [FW, 606.28]) is speaking and the tone and manner of narration can change from paragraph to paragraph, if not sentence to sentence. Now we hear a droning, patronizing, professorial voice, and then a gossipy, superstitious, proverb-mangling one; here a soapbox oration, there a whispered rosary.

In her book, *The Decentered Universe* of Finnegans Wake, Margot Norris writes: 'The singularity of individual experience – its uniqueness – is undermined by the replication of events and the instability of characters. The causal relationship of events in novelistic narration is replaced in *Finnegans Wake* by contiguous associations on the order of psychoanalytic free associations.'[8] Joyce may have been deeply ambivalent about the clinical practice of psychoanalysis ('I can psoakoonaloose myself any time I want' [FW, 522.34–5]), but he was never uninterested in the evolving discourse itself. The *Wake* is sometimes shocking, flush as it is with incest, adultery, kidnapping, rape, patricide, voyeurism and urolagnia. In fact, sexual, murderous and scatological innuendoes enjoy a polymorphous perversity Freud could only dream about. (Yet despite the sheer density of naughty stuff in its pages, *Finnegans Wake* never attracted the censors' breathy attentions the way *Ulysses* did. Maybe they were unsure, when they peeked into it, that what they thought they saw and heard there really was there.) The *Wake* treats readers as its dreamers, thereby allowing itself to disown and even fling back any recriminations at patently dirty-minded interpreters: 'a baser meaning has been read into these characters the literal sense of which decency can safely scarcely hint' (FW, 33.14–15).

Because the *Wake* attempts to emulate a collective unconscious, so its 'ideal reader' is necessarily a collective capable of dreaming its dream. Such a collective ought not to be imagined as a chorus, singing a single note in unison – quite the contrary. Responses to the *Wake* are discordant and sometimes cacophonous. Psychoanalysis has neither exclusive nor totally conclusive claims on dreams. All comers are welcome in Joyce's strange hotel (the word comes from 'medieval Latin *hospitāle* "place where guests are received"'[9]), and every literary approach and theory will, like a visitor to any other hotel, feel at home yet ill at ease, too.

Finnegans Wake spawns prevarications, qualifications, tautologies, paronomasia and digressions[10] in those who attempt to discuss it (and this essay will prove no exception). Sam Slote contends that 'the only possible statement of definitude is that the *Wake* is "destined to be odd's without ends" (FW, 455.17–18): an odd iteration iterated oddly and perpetuated perpetually'.[11] I here propose to add two 'loose carollaries' (294.6) to this 'statement of definitude'. First, insofar as the *Wake* is an *omnium gatherum* of disparate and unusual odds and ends, it represents a mass of building materials for readers, with which they are encouraged to construct provisional meanings. Second, because these materials are so disparate and unusual, this process of building necessitates cooperation between individual readers with individual skills, experiences, and perceptions. The single word that encompasses both of these linked suggestions is assembly, a theme explored in the following pages. Assembly is required for *Finnegans Wake* – the text is inert only 'till summone be the massproduct of teamwork' (546.15) – and for the larger-seeming purpose of ending war.

SOMETHING OUT OF NOTHING

(How to Make and Appreciate a Sandwich)
Samuel Beckett's much-quoted phrase from his contribution to *Our Exagmination* – '[Joyce's] writing is not about something; it is *that something itself*'[12] – is, on the one hand, probably the most compact and valuable

critical insight a student of Finnegans Wake may take to heart, and, on the other, a disarmingly unhelpful and vague assertion (one of Beckett's 'handful of abstractions').[13] The Wake's absolute resistance to paraphrase, its demand that readers immerse themselves in the language of the text without a workable glossary or singular, stable point of reference, suggests the culmination of one of modernist literature's boldest ambitions: the transcendence of mediation. Indeed, it could be argued that the recognition of the Wake as experience itself rather than representation of experience trumps mimesis and at least equals in audacity Marcel Duchamp's suave desecrations of aesthetic doxa.

Yet what is the 'something' to which Beckett refers? We may reasonably state that a given experience is not representative of something else, be it another experience or an abstraction, but in so doing we have not identified the experience. For example, a good sandwich need not be 'about' something, in that it need not be interpreted as a sign of a just and loving God, say, for the sandwich to be appreciated, even critically. The sandwich is the meal as assemblage, a compounding and layering of assorted foodstuffs, and the Wake is a similar construction of slices of words, sounds and symbols. Beckett suggests the following etymological ingredients:

Lex	=	Crop of acorns.
Ilex	=	Tree that produces acorns.
Legere	=	To gather.
Aquilex	=	He that gathers the waters.
Lex	=	Gathering together of peoples, public assembly.
Lex	=	Law.
Legere	=	To gather together letters into a word, to read.[14]

Margot Norris has pointed out that Heidegger highlights the false conception of logos as the origin of speech; the word connotes, rather, reading: 'to put one thing with another, to bring together, in short to gather'.[15] It is also worth recalling, in this context, how Rudolf Carnap evaluated Heidegger's Being and Time. Averse to those philosophies which he saw as linguistic abuses, Carnap expressed dissatisfaction with the notion of 'nothingness' (Nichts, Nichtheit and so on) and reduced Heidegger's thought to a faulty syllogism like this one: a sandwich is better than nothing; nothing is better than God; therefore, a sandwich is better than God. This intriguing sleight-of-hand with idioms, balancing the concrete against the abstract and the literal against the figurative or metaphorical, bears comparison with any number of the *Wake*'s most discombobulating formulations. Moreover this faux logical wordplay is worth bearing in mind should we wish to consider whether, given the undeniable incoherence found in its pages and its routine use of negations and contradictions, *Finnegans Wake* might be said to be made up of 'nothing' rather than 'something'. Heidegger suggests that the concept of 'nothing' is the very root of our anxiety about being in the world:

> Everyday discourse tends towards concerning itself with the ready-to-hand and talking about it. That in the face of which anxiety is anxious is nothing ready-to-hand within-the-world. But this 'nothing ready-to-hand', which only our everyday circumspective discourse understands, is not totally nothing. The 'nothing' of readiness-to-hand is grounded in the most primordial 'something' – in the world.[16]

Finnegans Wake would likely be a terror for Carnap: a nothing sandwich! Joyce's book is 'Putting Allspace in a Notshall' (455.29), gluttonously packing within the contained space of a book as much meaning as possible and in the process squeezing out all of the definition. Words like 'muffinstuffinaches' (225.11) and 'pourquose' (18.31) and 'isocelating' (165.13) and 'hopsadrowsy' (597.23) will seem both familiar and strange, 'like' this or that other 'real' word (i.e., one with a definition, one that means 'something') but not the same and, it would seem, signifying 'nothing'.[17]

In his aphorism, Beckett neglects to say what he means by 'something', which might seem like answering the question 'How is your sandwich?' with instructions on how the sandwich is made, rather than simply stating how the sandwich tastes; but such an answer can be interpreted as a purposeful conflation of *being* and *doing*. (When I ask my friend, 'How are you?' he understands that I am not asking what quality of person he is but 'How are you *doing*?') The sandwich is as good as its production and its enjoyment: the experience of the sandwich is a process. Beckett does say, at the very beginning of his essay, that 'the contemplation of a carefully folded ham-sandwich' is 'soothing'.[18] Eating the sandwich is only one way of experiencing a sandwich: in fact, it might be called a rather predictable and even lazy way of experiencing it. And just as there are different tastes, there are different approaches to eating. Rebecca West, who accused Joyce of being 'entirely without taste',[19] is rebuked by Beckett for her own bad table manners: 'she might very well wear her bib at all her intellectual banquets'.[20] The metaphors here are not simply gustatory but focused on how one *prepares* to dine. West wears a bib, expecting to be served and fed. Yet the fullest pleasures of a sandwich comprise the very act of its assembly, and perhaps a moment of admiration for the constructed item before eagerly gripping it in one's hands and disassembling it (even deconstructing it).

Finnegans Wake is a picnic of 'sangwidges' (142.1), a smorgasbord laid out for 'gormandising and gourmeteering' (407.1–2) readers. Certainly there is plenty of ingestion in the book. Just as Leopold Bloom is introduced by the recitation of his dietary preferences in Ulysses (he 'ate with relish the inner organs of beasts and fowls' [U, 65]), long lists of favoured food and drink signal this or that emergent personality in the Wake, and distinctions in preferences are distinctions between these 'characters'. Thin Shem's 'lowness creeped out first via foodstuffs' (FW, 170.25) and his wining and dining habits mark him as an uneven combination of fussy and cheap: 'he would sooner muddle through the hash of lentils in Europe than meddle with Irrland's split pea' (171.5–6) but is willing to imbibe 'some sort of rhubarbarous maundarin yellagreen funkleblue windigut diodying applejack squeezed from sour grapefruice' (171.16–18). Bulky Shaun, by contrast, likes expensive items in immense quantity, but is also given to some ceremonial fasting: 'meals of spadefuls of mounded food, in anticipation of the faste of tablenapkins, constituting his threepartite pranzipal meal plus a collation' (405.30–2). The old saw 'you are what you eat' approaches literal truth when the embattled brothers are called Burrus and Caseous (161.12; butter and cheese, as well as the Roman traitors Brutus and Cassius, who are themselves a kind of snack for the devil in Dante's Inferno). Consumption and production are, like these 'contrairy' (620.12) brothers, the 'sehm asnuh' (620.16; a wonderful anagram suggesting 'same anew' or 'same as new') twins in *Finnegans Wake*. These processes (for character in the *Wake* is transformation and work is ever in progress) resemble, dissemble and reassemble one another, in very much the same way that writing and reading, writers and readers do.

A MULTIPLICITY OF PERSONALITIES INFLICTED ON THE DOCUMENT

(How Not to Write a Book by Yourself)
In a key moment in *Heart of Darkness*, Marlow hesitates in narrating his Congo adventure to say: 'We live, as we dream — alone'.[21] There are two different meanings a reader may take from this haunting phrase of Conrad's, and they are at least antithetical to each other if not altogether mutually exclusive. The first offers horror: consciousness is the curse of solitude and individuality is absolute. Marlow falters in telling his tale because 'it is impossible to convey the life-sensation of any given epoch of one's existence — that which makes its truth, its meaning'.[22] One's feelings and experiences are exclusive to oneself and are thus incommunicable. A second interpretation, however, emerges from the recognition of a paradox signalled by Marlow's use of the pronoun 'we'. This common paradox appears in both the anxious lover's question, 'when can we be alone together?' and the customary translation of the Irish nationalist shibboleth *sinn féin*, 'ourselves alone' (variations of which are plentiful in the *Wake*). That is, although my own subjectivity encloses me tightly, I am not at all alone in this condition, since absolutely everyone else is likewise stuck in themselves. What's more, I can communicate this fact to others, as even Conrad does to his readers. If his listeners aboard the yawl do not pay the closest attention to his yarn, nor does Marlow seem to realize that he is not just literally but on this metaphysical point precisely in the same boat as they are. *Finnegans Wake* reminds us that we are all lost together, 'in the same boat of yourselves' (FW, 370.17).

Received wisdom about modernism, which takes its cue from the first of these interpretations, emphasizes tropes of alienation and isolation, embodied by the disaffected, exiled author. This interpretation does carry considerable weight — one need only think of how lonely Stephen Dedalus lurks about wishing he were the Count of Monte

Cristo, in much the same way that Little Chandler in 'A Little Cloud' longs to be recognized for his distinguished and especially Celtic melancholy – but its girth does get in the way of other ways of thinking about writers such as Kafka, Woolf, Stein, Proust and Joyce. Indeed, as I will discuss below, this conception of authorship and the experience of modernism imposes upon the reader, who may well feel compelled to assume a similar posture and suppose that the best way to read *Ulysses* is alone, preferably in a tower if one is available.[23]

In his autobiography, Eugene Jolas recalls Joyce denying that he alone was the author of *Finnegans Wake*:

> [Joyce] seemed to be constantly on the look-out, listening rather than talking. 'Really, it is not I who am writing this crazy book', he said in a whimsical way. 'It is you and you and that girl over there and that man in the corner.' One day I found him in a Zurich tea-shop laughing quietly to himself. 'Have you won the *gros lot*?' I asked. He explained that he had asked the waitress for a glass of lemon squash. The somewhat obtuse Swiss girl looked puzzled. Then she had an inspiration: 'Oh, you mean Lebensquatsch?' she stammered. (Her German neologism might be translated as 'life's piffle'.)[24]

Sure enough, the waitress's lovely invention appears in the *Wake*: 'I'll go for that small polly if you'll suck to your lebbensquatsch' (270.left 1). It is worth noting that the judgement of 'obtuse' is Jolas's and not necessarily Joyce's. What the *Wake* reports of the word-thieving habits of Shem the Penman is true of Joyce himself: 'All the time he kept on treasuring with condign satisfaction each and every crumb of trektalk, covetous of his neighbour's word' (172.29–30); 'Who can say how many pseudostylic shamiana, how few or how many of the venerated public impostures, how very many piously forged palimpsests slipped in the first place by this morbid process from his pelagiarist pen?' (181.36–182.3).

I have elsewhere proposed an understanding of the *plural* authorship of *Finnegans Wake*, in distinction from both the conception of the solitary modernist genius-creator and Roland Barthes' formulation of the 'dead' author.[25] In my view, both of these latter notions of authorship unduly circumscribe acts of interpretation by ignoring the material history of textual production and posing the problem of authorship specifically and exclusively in metaphysical and even theological terms. Without restating the whole of that argument here, let me illustrate the kind of understanding of authorship that the *Wake* itself – so flush as it is with questions about who is doing the writing – endorses with an analogy.

Probably the most famous scene in the Marx Brothers' film *A Night at the Opera* (1934) is that of the overcrowded steamship cabin. One after another functionary squeezes into the tiny cabin with the brothers: tray-bearing stewards, the engineer, the engineer's assistant, another passenger looking for her lost aunt, and so on. Finally, when the eminently scandalizable Margaret Dumont comes to call on Groucho, the critical mass is achieved and everyone tumbles out into the hall with a great crash. There are many good jokes bandied about before this climax, perhaps the best of which is Groucho's reply to a woman asking if he wants a manicure: 'no, come on in'. The marvellously absurd gratuitousness of this gesture encapsulates how we might best conceive of Joyce's authorship of the *Wake*.[26] Just as all textual sources were welcome, so too were others invited to contribute – the more, the merrier. 'Work in Progress' was practically an industrial production (an assembly line, though not a straight one) involving amanuenses, typists, patrons, translators, critics, journal editors and of course printers, all of whose reactions to the ongoing work were themselves integrated into it. It has recently been discovered that even Joyce's wife, Nora – long thought to be more or less entirely removed from the making of her husband's books – was among the earliest takers of dictation for the nascent *Wake*, a book she championed after his death as more important than *Ulysses*.

Danis Rose writes that Joyce 'wrote the book piece by piece as he went along; there was no original all-embracing ground-plan'.[27] Indeed, Joyce had expressed concern that he had perhaps 'oversystematized *Ulysses*',[28] and the composition of *Finnegans Wake* can be seen as, if not an abandonment of systems, a sounding of disharmony between and among conflicting systems. An 'original' pun is further obscured and occasionally even buried under another layer of puns as one draft overwrites another. The conceit of drunken speech neither trumps nor disallows that of infantile babble in attempts to explain or understand the slurred and garbled language; Vico's *ricorso* is of no greater or lesser structural or conceptual significance than the stations of the cross or the rise and fall of Parnell. No single context for any word of the *Wake* can be divorced from, or privileged over, any other: 'Every talk has his stay ... and all-a-dreams perhapsing under lucksloop at last are through. Why? It is a sot of a swigswag, systomy dystomy, which everabody you ever know anywhere at all doze' (FW, 597.19–22). Sam Slote finds a '*desistance* of constitution' in the *Wake*;[29] I would say, rather, a desistance of exclusion. All authors are welcome to lay claims to the *Wake*.

In 'The Author as Producer', Walter Benjamin envisions a kind of writing continually and expressly aware of the circumstances of literary and cultural production:

> What matters ... is the exemplary character of production, which is able, first, to induce other producers to produce, and, second, to put an improved apparatus at their disposal. And this apparatus is better, the more consumers it is able to turn into producers – that is, readers or spectators into collaborators.[30]

Benjamin's essay, prepared as an address to the Institute for the Study of Fascism, was written in 1934, the same year that *A Night at the Opera* hit the screens and when Joyce was at work on the 'Nightletter' chapter of *Finnegans Wake* (II.2). There we find children producing marginal notes – titles, tunes, doodles, mnemonics, questions, jokes and innuendoes– apparently within the pages of a school textbook (itself covering a melange of subjects, from geography to grammar), perhaps writing or annotating a letter. These responses and correspondences make the chapter a virtual palimpsest, the most overt example of a general principle of composition in the *Wake*. One good letter deserves another: 'please too write, won't you' (458.18–19). The proliferating responses and meanings to the text are 'returnally reprodictive of themselves' (298.17–18).

CONSUMPTION AS PRODUCTION

(*How to Build a Leaning Tower*)
However learned and hardy, the individual reader faces considerable

disadvantages when tackling the *Wake* alone and unassisted. Such an ambitious reader needs to be, for one, an awesome polyglot, familiar with (for example) Norwegian, Albanian, French, Persian, Magyar, Latin, Russian, Welsh, Finnish and of course Irish, along with many other languages. Besides extensive reading in several centuries of the literatures and philosophies of Europe and an encyclopaedic awareness of Irish history, geography and culture, this inexhaustible super-reader probably ought to have excellent knowledge of the world's rivers and religions, nursery rhymes, the Napoleonic wars, architecture, early radio, Egyptian funeral rituals, flower names and meanings, Euclidean geometry, the Russian revolution, opera and folk songs, astronomy, the occult, heraldry and entomology – for starters, at any rate. Moreover, if one heeds the recommendations of the many published and usually well-meaning guidebooks and introductions to the *Wake*, there are entire libraries of texts (should one call them 'pretexts'?) to be studied forwards and backwards before one even attempts reading the *Wake* itself: Freud, Vico, Yeats, Ibsen, Blake, Ellmann's biography, all of Joyce's other published and unpublished writings, and the list continues. The *Wake* jokes that what it needs is 'an ideal reader suffering from an ideal insomnia' (FW, 120.13–14) and, most cheekily, further recommends that such a reader have 'patience' (108.8). These are, of course, impossible demands – as impracticable and as conceited as the expectation that a world war should cease for the sake of reading a book. Yet, if we allow that this 'ideal reader' with these varied abilities and qualifications could be a population rather than an individual, the often-emphasized difficulties (and even infeasibility) of reading the *Wake* fade in direct relation to how broadly we define this pluralized readership. Inclusivity and diversity will yield a wider array of knowledge and insight and thus make for richer reading.

The idea of reading as a solitary activity, dependent on the attentiveness and imagination of the individual reader, prompted Marshall McLuhan to outline the differences between print and other media, including radio, film and television. The so-called 'hot' media of books and newspapers have different effects on their consumers than the 'cool' electronic mass media, effects which in McLuhan's view were not merely cultural but psychological and even physiological.[31] Textual people tend towards schizophrenia (the result of entertaining multiple voices and perspectives within one mind), while oral/aural societies are tribal.[32] *Finnegans Wake* particularly excited McLuhan – his habit of quoting from it grew with and in each book he wrote – because it stands as a direct challenge to these differences. The *Wake* mimics the mass media (radio broadcasts, quiz shows, telephone calls, vaudeville acts, classified ads in newspapers) and demands to be both seen and heard.[33] A good example of this conflation of media can be found in III.3, where an exchange of dialogue suggests an auction ('Sold! I am sold!' [500.21]), a stage play ('Act drop ... Curtain up' [501.07]), a radio transmission ('Tune in and pick up the forain counties' [500.35–6]), and a telephone conversation ('Hellohello! ... Am I thru' Iss? Miss? True?' [501.04]). *Finnegans Wake* is an 'allnights newseryreel' (489.35) and 'radiooscillating epiepistle' (108.24) at the same time that it is a book. It is a broadcast to the world, made in a distorted jumble of the world's languages, crying out: 'Calling all downs. Calling all downs to dayne. Array! Surrection!' (593.02). The lack of apostrophe in Joyce's title marks it as an imperative, that we are the Finnegans being called to the wake (or to awake, even to resurrect, ourselves). *Wake* readers form a remarkable, paradoxical-seeming hybrid: a tribe of individuated listeners.

Where Benjamin argues that writers should, in their work, comprehend the production of that writing, *Finnegans Wake* compels readers to see reading as production, and investigate the phenomena of 'making sense' of language and text. Whereas *A Portrait of the Artist as a Young Man* arguably ends with the suggestion of its own conception – Stephen Dedalus is off to write the book that has just ended[34] – the *Wake* truly does represent a chronicle of its own production, including references to its own publication history and mixed reception. It anticipates the troubles it will cause readers, and puts them in the material terms of book production: 'you need hardly spell me how every word will be bound over to carry three score and ten toptypsical readings throughout the book of Doublends Jined' (FW, 20.13–16). Besides placidly giving their lives to studying the book (the biblical allowance of 'threescore years and ten' appears in Psalm 90, which concludes with emphasis on 'the work of our hands'), readers are invited to weigh and compare the efforts behind writing and reading it.

The first part of this task can mean immersion in the details of Joyce's life, any number of which have their reflections in the *Wake* (for example, the schizophrenic daughter motif stems from Lucia Joyce's own psychological condition), or having a 'genetic' awareness of the manuscript's evolution. In Joyce's notebooks, for example, we can sift through myriad bits and scraps of data that he saw fit to record (like 'Lebensquatsch'): these are the flotsam and jetsam Joyce would use to 'plotsome to getsome' (*FW*, 312.18). Happily, their recent publication means more access to these treasures and throwaways for more people, and thus guarantees a greater assembly in both senses of the word.[35]

The second part is harder to generalize because it is still taking shape: readers' production of the *Wake* is ongoing. Different readers have different objectives and objections. Some read for plot (really, some do!), some look for allegory, some readers go in for the sounds and laughs. Consider, for example, the following passage from I.5, the 'mamafesta' chapter:

> one who deeper thinks will always bear in the baccbuccus of his mind that this downright there you are and there it is is only all in his eye. Why?
>
> Because, Soferim Bebel, if it goes to that, (and dormerwindow gossip will cry it from the housetops no surelier than the writing on the wall will hue it to the mod of men that mote in the main street) every person, place and thing in the chaosmos of Alle anyway connected with the gobblydumped turkery was moving and changing every part of the time: the travelling inkhorn (possibly pot), the hare and turtle pen and paper, the continually more and less intermisunderstanding minds of the anticollaborators, the as time went on as it will variously inflected, differently pronounced, otherwise spelled, changeably meaning vocable scriptsigns. (118.15–28)

Interpretations of passages like this one are rather like the Tower of Babel, to which it refers: they are built by many working in cooperation, and they grow from the ground up. A reader with Hebrew (or, as poor substitute, a copy of McHugh's alternately useful and frustrating

Annotations[36]) will translate *soferim* as 'writers'. Another reader might remark on how visual metaphors in words and expressions such as 'all in his eye' (suggestive of 'all in my eye', foolishness), 'hue' (colour), 'mote' (in one's eye) are contrasted with aural ones: 'inflected' and 'pronounced' and 'vocable'. Inspired, a third reader may remember having somewhere heard the phrase 'the eyes are the windows to the soul' and ask whether it has some relevance to 'dormerwindow', to which another reader could respond with notice that the French verb *dormir*, 'to sleep' lies within that compound word. The reader who ventures this passage aloud – always an excellent idea with the *Wake* – may be unsure about how to pronounce, say, 'baccbuccus' or 'chaosmos'. Sooner or later (and most probably recurrently), these readers come to realize that the passage itself represents their own efforts at making sense of the text: aware that 'downright' explication is impossible, they have become 'anticollaborators', building 'upwrong' (if you will) a tower of unstable meaning and moving parts.

The text makes us aware (at times uncomfortably aware) of our own agendas and their limitations. Certainty stays at a minimum and every new reading experience with the *Wake* seems to change the rules of the interpretive game, however slightly. In contemplating this accumulative sort of exegesis, wherein awareness of the materiality of words and print can achieve a manic quality (the tower can go higher and higher), Walter Benjamin, the metaphysician of the literal, is again worth consulting. Susan Buck-Morss outlines the careful distinctions between allegorical readings and Kabbalist ones, as they came to be understood by Benjamin:

> The whole thrust of humanity's moral obligation is a cognitive one, that is, to overcome ignorance of God by interpreting nature in terms of the divine sparks within it. The broken unity of both nature and language dictates the specifics of the interpretive method. Kabbalist exegesis is antisystemic. Each interpretive fragment has, monadologically, its own center; the macrocosm is read with the microcosm.[37]

I have claimed that the narrative elements of *Finnegans Wake* are best understood as variations on a theme, and the book's composition a revolt against systems. Accordingly, reading the *Wake* is a performance based upon variation and – the comparison to jazz becomes apparent – improvisation, which is also, like Kabbalist exegesis, 'antisystemic'. Jazz's tonal conversation and the intellectual exchange of ideas and translations, however passionate and argumentative or diffuse and digressive they may become, inevitably produce continuous music and meaning: 'As you sing it it's a study' (*FW*, 489.33).

SEWING A DREAM TOGETHER

(How to Stop Warring and Love the 'Wake')
In the traditional folk song 'Finnegan's Wake', the eponymous hero is mistaken for dead after drunkenly falling from a ladder. He is rolled up in a sheet and laid out for a wake, which gathering quickly becomes drunken and boisterous. When at last the revellers spill whiskey (from the Irish *uisce beatha*, literally 'water of life') on Finnegan, he awakes amazed: '*Thanam o'n dhoul*, do ye think I'm dead?' Joyce's obsession with the re-emergence of the dead extends from the uncertainties about Father Flynn (dead at the opening of 'The Sisters' but at the story's end 'wide-awake and laughing-like to himself' [*D*, 10]) and the unexpected spectre of Michael Furey in 'The Dead' to Bloom's wandering thoughts about gramophone recordings of voices of the deceased and novel ways to avoid premature burial in 'Hades'. In the *Wake*, Joyce repeatedly revisits and rewrites this song of farcical resurrection to examine from every possible angle its absurdity and wonder. As our everyman hero lies 'bursted to the wurld at large, on the table round' (*FW*, 498.24), he is 'circumassembled by his daughters in the foregiftness of his sons' (498.27–8) until at last he is 'healed cure and embalsemate, pending a rouseruction of his bogey' (498.36–499.1). Death and rebirth are simultaneous here; destruction and construction occur together. The betrayed and crucified Christ is reconfigured and revived by those apostles who write their remembrances; those faithful who kill the false Buddha (because any Buddha one meets on the road to enlightenment must be false) bring themselves nearer a newly conceived Buddha; keepers of a vigil ensure that death has occurred and the spirit is renewed by their prayers.

The *Wake*'s theme of resurrection ('rouseruction' blends the lyrics 'a row and a ruction soon began' with hints of 'Rosicrucian' mysticism) is indistinguishable from those of revolution, destruction and reconstruction. Another guise of the fallen Finnegan is Humpty Dumpty, an egg whose sundering begins the universe (as a Hindu creation myth has it). It is interesting that only adults – never children – find it strange or ridiculous that all the king's horses would be assisting in the re-assembly. This is because children know what headstrong adults can easily forget: in a desperate situation, you need all the help you can find.

The tag-line of the redemption-fantasy film *Field of Dreams* (1989) –'if you build it, they will come'– contains a causal (if/then) logic that *Finnegans Wake* eschews. We come together to build the meanings of the *Wake*, but which follows or results from the other remains an open question.[38] This is, indeed, the problem for all conceptions of Utopia, including those of a world without war: is societal transformation brought about by changes within its individuals, or vice versa? Giambattista Vico, who mapped out a cyclical history that is shared by all, commended students of his *New Science* 'to live a decent and just humanity in the world of nations'.[39] That 'decent and just humanity', to which *Finnegans Wake* addresses itself, requires assembly.

Will reading the *Wake* prevent a war, as Joyce suggested? Waging war is considerably more desperate than the task of reading *Finnegans Wake* – a fatuous statement but a truth worth remembering and repeating, for both of these wholly different, otherwise uncomparable nightmares are, each in their own ways, so overwhelming as to make those in their thrall lose perspective and even hope. Of these nightmares, though, as Conrad's Marlow would attest, it is something to have a Joyce.

NOTES

1. All are absorbed into the *Wake*. For example, Lewis's criticism of the 'mind of James Joyce' in *Time and Western Man* and his unexpected attack on 'Work in Progress' gave fuel to the theme of space–time connections – W. Lewis, *Time and Western Man*, ed. P. Edwards (Santa Rosa, CA: Black Sparrow Press, 1993), pp.73–110. Lewis and Stanislaus Joyce are two of the many sources for Shaun, the fraternal foil for Shem, while Weaver is more obliquely winked at as 'the fiery goodmother Miss Fortune' (*FW*, 149.22–3).
2. T.S. Eliot, 'Ulysses, Order, and Myth', in *Selected Prose of T. S. Eliot*, ed. Frank Kermode (London: Faber and Faber, 1975), p.175.

3. R. Ellmann, *James Joyce, New and Revised Edition* (New York: Oxford University Press, 1982).

4. Ibid., p.728.

5. F. Budgen, *James Joyce and the Making of 'Ulysses'* (Harmondsworth: Oxford University Press, 1972), p.191.

6. W. Stevens, 'Notes Toward a Supreme Fiction', in *The Palm at the End of the Mind: Selected Poems and a Play*, ed. Holly Stevens (New York: Vintage, 1972), p.233.

7. J. Rasula, 'Finnegans Wake and the Character of the Letter', *James Joyce Quarterly*, 34, 4 (1997), p.523.

8. M. Norris, *The Decentered Universe of 'Finnegans Wake': A Structuralist Analysis* (Baltimore, MD: Johns Hopkins University Press, 1976), p.11.

9. J. Ayto, *Dictionary of Word Origins* (New York: Arcade, 1990), p.287.

10. Also, as you will have noticed, compulsive list-making. The *Wake* thrives on lists, very much in the way the narratively outsized chapters of *Ulysses* (particularly 'Cyclops' and 'Ithaca') do, and a significant, sympathetic portion of *Wake* scholarship is given to indexing and collating.

11. S. Slote, 'Nulled Nought: The Desistance of Ulyssean Narrative in Finnegans Wake', in *James Joyce Quarterly*, 34, 4 (1997), p.538.

12. S. Beckett, 'Dante... Bruno. Vico.. Joyce', in *James Joyce/'Finnegans Wake': A Symposium. Our Exagmination Round His Factification for Incamination of Work in Progress* (London: Faber and Faber, 1972), p.14.

13. Ibid., p.3.

14. Ibid., p.11. J. Bishop, *Joyce's Book of the Dark, 'Finnegans Wake'* (Madison, WI: University of Wisconsin Press, 1987), pp.200–1, provides an even more expansive 'etymological chart' for the root *leg-, including such varied and lovely words as legibility, horologe, logarithm, lesson, sacrilege, legacy, allegation and elegance.

15. Norris, *The Decentered Universe of 'Finnegans Wake'*, p.69.

16. M. Heidegger, *Being and Time*, trans. John Macquarrie and Edward Robinson (Oxford: Blackwell, 2001), p.232. The question of whether *Finnegans Wake* can be said to constitute, express, or even approximate 'everyday discourse' gives one great pause. The instinctive answer is probably no, and the reasons given could include the complexities or the uniqueness of the text; or perhaps the conceptual-thematic understanding (most ably outlined by Bishop) of the book as 'everynight life' (*FW*, 17.33), the antithesis to quotidian consciousness. Yet the cockeyed translations, the spoonerisms and malapropisms, the stuttered and lisped half-utterances are reminiscent of language as it really is experienced on a daily basis – imperfectly articulated and transmitted ('bi tso fb rok engl a ssan dspl ina' [124.7–8]) and just as imperfectly received and understood.

17. For further discussion of 'nothing' and negation, see the essays of Jean-Michel Rabaté, Fritz Senn and Dirk Van Hulle in C. Jaurretche (ed.), *Beckett, Joyce and the Art of the Negative* (Amesterdam: Rodopi, 2005). For considerations of *Finnegans Wake* as 'nonsense', see Brett Bourbon's 'The "'Twitterlitter"' of Nonsense: *Askesis at Finnegans*

Wake', *James Joyce Quarterly*, 39, 2 (2002), pp.217–32 and my '"Oh me none onsens!":
Finnegans Wake and the Negation of Meaning', *James Joyce Quarterly*, 39, 2 (2002),
pp.233–49.

18. Beckett, 'Dante... Bruno. Vico.. Joyce', p.3.

19. Quoted in W.C. Williams, 'A Point for American Criticism', in *Our Exagmination Round
His Factification for Incamination of Work in Progress*, p.173.

20. Beckett, 'Dante... Bruno. Vico.. Joyce', p.13.

21. J. Conrad, *Heart of Darkness* (Harmondsworth: Penguin, 2000), p.50.

22. Ibid.

23. It is this altogether romantic notion of authorship that smiles on the attribution of
these last words: 'is there one who understands me?' (*FW*, 627.15). Regardless of
whether Joyce actually melodramatically quoted the *Wake* on his deathbed, the
answer is no – no *one* does, but many together might.

24. E. Jolas, *Man from Babel*, ed. Andreas Kramer and Rainer Rumold (New Haven, CT: Yale
University Press, 1998), p.166.

25. See T. Conley, *Joyces Mistakes: Problems of Intention, Irony, and Interpretation* (Toronto:
University of Toronto Press, 2003), pp.40–58.

26. The joke makes one naturally think of Samuel Beckett's account of his taking
dictation from Joyce one day when a knock came at the door. When Joyce said,
'Come in', Beckett transcribed the instruction, and afterwards, when he read it back,
'Joyce thought for a moment, then said, '"Let it stand"' – Ellmann, *James Joyce, New and
Revised Edition*, p.649.

27. D. Rose, *The Textual Diaries of James Joyce* (Dublin: Lilliput Press, 1995), p.x.

28. Ellmann, *James Joyce, New and Revised Edition*, p.702.

29. Slote, 'Nulled Nought', p.536.

30. W. Benjamin, 'The Author as Producer', trans. Edmund Jephcott, in Michael W.
Jennings, Howard Eiland and Gary Smith (eds), *Selected Writings, Volume 2: 1927–1934*
(Cambridge, MA: Harvard University Press, 1999), p.777. Benjamin offers Brecht's
epic theatre as an example of the kind of materially self-aware art he is seeking, but
he might have looked into 'Work in Progress'. Indeed, a comparison could be made
between Brecht's project and Joyce's. Brecht's governing principle, that the 'spectator
must prove that he is not enslaved to the actor, as much as the actor must not be
incarcerated by the spectator', runs a parallel course to Joyce's erasure of the
demarcations between writer and reader – N. Bracker, 'The Signifier as Siren – Kafka,
Brecht, Joyce and the Seduction of the Text', *Intertexts*, 4, 2 (2000), p.187.

31. M. McLuhan, *The Gutenberg Galaxy: The Making of Typographic Man* (Toronto: Signet, 1962),
pp.34–48.

32. This last insight is obvious to anyone who, having gone without watching television
for a season or more, meets with friends who have had no such deprivation and
who thus collectively share a common language (even the intonations are agreed
upon) that seems entirely foreign to their disconnected friend.

33. For more on this subject, see D.F. Theall, *James Joyce's Techno-Poetics* (Toronto: University

of Toronto Press, 2007), and J.A. Connor, 'Radio Free Joyce: *Wake* Language and the Experience of Radio', in *Sound States: Innovative Poetics and Acoustical Technologies*, ed. Adaliade Morris (Chapel Hill, NC: University of North Carolina Press, 1997), pp.17–31.

34. 'Arguably' because the unpublished and adrift Stephen of *Ulysses* suggests otherwise.

35. V. Deane, D. Ferrer and Geert Lernout (eds), *James Joyce: 'Finnegans Wake' Notebooks at Buffalo* (Amsterdam: Brepols, 2001–).

36. R. McHugh, *Annotations to 'Finnegans Wake'*, 3rd edn (Baltimore, MD: Johns Hopkins University Press, 2006).

37. S. Buck-Morss, *The Dialectics of Seeing: Walter Benjamin and the Arcades Project* (Cambridge, MA: MIT Press, 1989), p.236.

38. Fritz Senn once remarked to me that Joyceans are generally lonely people. He did not say that reading Joyce together makes us (or simply might make us) less lonely, but I feel less lonely for knowing that I'm not alone.

39. G. Vico, *The New Science*, 3rd edn, trans. Thomas Goddard Bergin and Max Harold Frisch (Ithaca, NY: Cornell University Press, 1984), p.428.

CHAPTER EIGHT

Joyce in Theory/Theory in Joyce

CHRISTINE VAN BOHEEMEN-SAAF

I t all began at a symposium hosted by the Johns Hopkins Humanities
Center in October 1966, the aim of which was to explore the impact
of contemporary 'structuralist' thought on critical methods in the
humanities. Among the participants were the French psychoanalyst
Jacques Lacan who presented the paper, 'Of Structure as an Inmixing of
an Otherness Prerequisite to Any Subject Whatever', and the French
philosopher Jacques Derrida, whose 'Structure, Sign, and Play in the
Discourse of the Human Science' changed the nature of the conference
itself.[1] These two French thinkers heralded the transition from a 'structuralist' to a 'post-structuralist' perspective which relinquishes the concept of a privileged origin, a fixed boundary and even linear temporality.
They are important to us, because each was profoundly involved with
Joyce's *Finnegans Wake*. Although they became famous for their dispute
about the nature of the 'letter' in Poe's 'The Purloined Letter', this discussion might just as well have revolved around the nature of the 'letter' of
Finnegans Wake.[2] Each wrote important essays on Joyce, whose text offered
them a concrete example on which to found their respective theories.
Post-structuralist theory expanded the body of topics and texts which
might be taken into consideration when doing literary work; and with
this relinquishing of the aesthetic came a mode of inquiry that brings the
traditional mimetic, formalist or expressive understandings of the literary
text into crisis. It no longer holds the view that the literary work is a
reflection (more or less perfect) of an objective and stable real world which
it captures as in a mirror. Its effect on the profession was so profound that
a closer look at the relationship between Joyce and theory is warranted.

Even before the advent of theory, the works of Joyce had been a 'happy huntingground' for structuralism and reception-aesthetics, new approaches to the literary text which predominated in the 1960s and 1970s. Wolfgang Iser, David Lodge, Franz Stanzel, as well as many others, used Joyces's narratives as a resource in their analysis of the reader's response (Iser) or the nature of modern narrative (Lodge, Stanzel). Indeed, Joyce's experimental textuality made him an almost inescapable test case, not only in anglophone writing, but also on the Continent. Although it has often been observed that Joyce, who was a master in marketing his own work, very carefully planned its own reception, even he could not have foreseen that his rich and sometimes wilful violations of the conventions of realist writing would provide generations of cultural critics, each in a new and different manner, with the material to argue new approaches, to adstruct their views, and to gradually explore the very grounds of literary representation as well as of human identity itself. Wolfgang Iser, for example, found Joyce significant because his work afforded a demonstration that it is what is not included in the narrative – the absences or emptinesses – which allow the reader to imaginatively project herself into the text.[3] Precisely because Joyce's works were so useful to the professors, his status grew so that the label 'Joyce' steadily gained currency. Joyce's name, next to that of Proust, proliferates in commentary and theoretical reflection of all descriptions, from Lukács and Adorno to Fredric Jameson, from Carl Gustav Jung to Julia Kristeva, from Umberto Eco to Gilles Deleuze. Especially since the late 1960s, reference to Joyce seemed inescapable, as if the use of the name of Joyce had become a warrant of seriousness, or avant-garde distinction. It should be noted, however, that 'Joyce' was used for widely divergent views on human subjectivity, on representation, and many other topics. As we shall see, Derrida, Lacan and Lyotard turned to Joyce for very different purposes. Perhaps the Joycean text, which is characteristically ambiguous and ambivalent, proved so useful as a resource owing to its very undecidability.

JOYCE AND PARIS

When Joyce moved to Paris in 1920, prodded by Ezra Pound, the great moderator of the Modernist movement, the city – where he would stay

for twenty years – was the crossroads of the creative avant-garde. After the
Paris publication of *Ulysses* by Shakespeare & Co. in 1922, his reputation
was assured, and Joyce himself did not hesitate to compare himself to
Picasso.[4] Passages from 'Work in Progress' were published in *transition*,
founded in 1917 by Eugene Jolas, which also featured Picasso, Man Ray,
Braque, Gide, Rilke and Tristan Tzara.[5] Jolas begins his essay 'The
Revolution of Language and James Joyce' with the words:

> The Real metaphysical problem today is the word. The epoch when
> the writer photographed the life about him with the mechanics of
> words redolent of the daguerreotype, is happily drawing to its close.
> The new artist of the word has recognized the autonomy of language
> and, aware of the twentieth century current towards universality,
> attempts to hammer out a verbal vision that destroys time and space.[6]

Because Joyce was seen to be part of the great drive 'to make it new'
which produced such experimental movements as Cubism, Dadaism
and Surrealism, his name was an international label of innovation, long
before it became the name of the great twentieth-century Irish writer.
The link between theory and Joyce, in fact, goes back to the 1930s and
Joyce's stay in Paris, where his name lingered on in French intellectual
circles after the Second World War. It is said that Lacan (who was deeply
interested in Symbolism) heard a reading of Joyce's work in translation,
and had met Joyce himself in Adrienne Monnier's bookshop between
1917 and 1921. To him, and his contemporaries, *Finnegans Wake* was the
equivalent in literature of Picasso's painterly experiments with representation. When Hélène Cixous met Jacques Derrida in Paris in 1962, their
topic of conversation was James Joyce, the subject of her dissertation. In
1963 she was introduced to Lacan, who was then looking for someone
to help him cope with Joyce's works. From the first, then, Joyce's
modernity was linked to an undecidable realm where creation can
scarcely be distinguished from destruction, where form and formless-
ness are well-nigh inseparable, where the nature of the word (literature,
writing, the letter) is centrally at issue. Richard Ellmann began his biography with the famous words: 'We are still learning to be James Joyce's
contemporaries, to understand our interpreter.'[7] We might see the rise and
development of theory as the *effect* of the Joycean text on the humanities.

Our understanding of literature (and of philosophy and psychoanalysis) has changed as we have grown attuned to Joyce's pedagogy in *Finnegans Wake*. The critical debate around Joyce itself partakes of the textual action of Joyce's œuvre, and is not static.

FROM THE NEW CRITICISM TO STRUCTURALISM

The earliest criticism of Joyce (1907–41), as collected in Deming's two volumes in the Critical Heritage Series, mainly consisted of appreciation and attempts to elucidate the texts, at a time when literary criticism had not yet become the prerogative of the universities.[8] As the New Criticism became the dominant mode of address in the American universities and Leavisite approaches flourished in Great Britain, Joyce was not central to their projects. His narratives were too unwieldy to serve as illustrations of the intricacy of artistic form. Leavis excluded Joyce from his Great Tradition, finding the writing style pernicious and inorganic. Although the New Criticism appears to have contributed to the linguistic turn ('nothing but the text'), in classroom practice literary criticism remained a humanist pursuit, based on a mimetic understanding of the text and the notion of authorial consciousness (the implied author) as origin. The summary of current approaches to *Ulysses*, which S.L. Goldberg offered in *The Classical Temper* of 1969, suggests that what most baffled the New Critics was the absence of the familiar feature of authorial presence on which to base their interpretation. The responses range from the view of *Ulysses* as 'a naturalistic Irish comedy, the apotheosis of the bar-room joke'; the exemplification of 'indifference to all moral values ... by its implicit nihilism'; the expression of a 'mystical, esoteric or metaphysical belief'; the 'pessimistic rejection of modern life'; to the 'optimistic acceptance of life as it is'.[9] Each view, including that of Goldberg himself, approaches Joyce's work from the assumption that, however imperfectly, it mirrors an objective world. New Critical and Leavisite readings understood narrative fiction as a mirroring re-presentation of an outside, anterior and foundational world and tended to evaluate it aesthetically, in terms of its accuracy and moral perspective.

Although there were critics like Hugh Kenner whose *Dublin's Joyce* (1955) listens to the discursive nature of Joyce's language, the first major scholarly approach to Joyce's work, which was neither philological nor stylistic but structuralist, was not published until 1974. Margot Norris's *The Decentered Universe of 'Finnegans Wake': A Structuralist Analysis* locates Joyce in relation to the linguistic turn.[10] She studies the text through Claude Lévi-Strauss's structural model of myth, Freud's psychoanalysis, René Girard's notion of mimetic envy, and points to repetitive aspects of narrative form, informative themes, deconstructive technique, etc. in a radically non-mimetic reading of the work. Although Norris used the term 'structuralist' in her subtitle, her anti-essentialist, non-linear approach unweaves even Lévi-Strauss's concept of structure and veers toward Derrida and Lacan. In the mid-1970s the current distinction between 'structuralism' and 'post-structuralism' had not yet arisen. It is not surprising that Norris's innovation of Joyce studies should have been inspired by *Finnegans Wake*, a text which, as Tim Conley notes earlier in this collection, challenges any mimetic understanding.

Meanwhile, narratology, the structuralist theory of narrative, had encountered the limits of its theoretical presuppositions in confrontation with Joyce's *Ulysses*. Originally formulated in France by Gerard Genette, and popularized internationally by Seymour Chatman, narratology starts from the assumption that a narrative text is to be analyzed through different layers and categories, each of which are clearly distinguishable. When *Ulysses* was scrutinized through the lens of Genette's theory, however, it proved impossible to point to a distinct or unifying consciousness to which the narrative might be attributed. In 1978, Kenner had spoken of 'Joyce's Voices', pointing out that Joyce bends the third-person discourse of the narrator to accommodate the mind, education or personality of the person who is the object of description. In Joyce studies, his term, 'the Uncle Charles principle', came to replace the linguistic denomination of 'free-indirect speech'. Kenner noted the perspectival abyss which Joyce's strategy of disappearing behind his handiwork sets up; but his concluding chapter, 'Beyond Objectivity', could not resolve the phenomenon, nor did he draw the conclusion that Joyce specializes in undecidability. Instead, Kenner fell back on the mythic notion of an 'eternal Ausonian Muse' to make sense of Joyce.[11] Thus Kenner, who saw the problem, remained locked in a humanist model. The struggle to locate a unified agency to which the phenomena of the text might be attributed continued to occupy American critics like David Hayman (who coined the term 'the arranger' to replace 'narrator') and John P. Riquelme. In France, meanwhile, Roland Barthes, in an analysis of Balzac's novella *Sarrasine* had concluded that it is 'language which speaks, not the author'.[12] The author, the text and the readers alike are made up of the totality of quotations available in a culture which is without beginning or end. Celebrating 'the death of the author', Barthes freed the reader from the constraints of origin, identity, mimesis, and initiated a whole new manner of reading which generated its own terminology. Instead of the 'work' of literature, we speak of 'textuality', on the assumption that the work of literature is constructed from language which has no motivated connection to the world. This view of the rhetoricity of language leads to the notion that all texts derive from the archive of earlier texts. The 'origin' of the text is thus its intertextuality, and not the genius of the writer.

THE ADVENT OF THEORY

The first sustained reading of *Ulysses* in the new mode was Colin MacCabe's 1978 *James Joyce and the Revolution of the Word*. In this work, then a controversial Cambridge dissertation, MacCabe draws on a whole range of theorists, including Derrida and Lacan, to argue that traditional criticism of Joyce ('banal liberal humanism') preserves Joyce unread.[13] It is only when a representational theory of language is relinquished that various new positions from which meaning becomes possible open themselves up. As his title indicates, MacCabe's ultimate claim is the political nature and effect of Joyce's texts. They are revolutionary because, as he claims, they investigate the breaches and disruptions in traditional discourse, opening up an area of desire and perversion. In a series of readings of separate chapters of *Ulysses*, the reader is introduced to the new theoretical ideas. The exposition is clearly intended to convert the novice to theory, but its drawback is that MacCabe fails to discriminate between philosophical (Derrida), psychoanalytic (Lacan) and political (Althusser, Mao Tse-tung) influences, so that the effect is sometimes confusing.

Crucial to MacCabe's approach is the thesis that there is no metalanguage. An interpretation or a reading of a text is not the application of theory to literature. The relationship between reader and text, theory and literature is transferential. The theory is read by the literary text as much as vice versa. In their 'Introduction' to *Post-Structuralist Joyce: Essays from the French* (1984), Derek Attridge and Daniel Ferrer also insist on this point:

> It is impossible to exert any mastery over [Joyce's text], its shifts are such that you can never pin it down in any definitive place – it always turns up again, laughing, behind your back. In fact, the aim is not to produce a *reading* of this intractable text, to make it more familiar and exorcise its strangeness, but on the contrary to confront its unreadability.[14]

Post-Structuralist Joyce, which includes essays by Cixous and Derrida, is generally seen as the central document in the history of 'Joyce and Theory', although it opted to exclude Lacan on the grounds of difficulty. The collection of essays offers a number of different models for approaching Joyce without claiming to be definitive. As the 'Introduction' suggests, the idea is 'to look at the mechanisms of [Joyce's] infinite productivity; not to explore the psychological depths of the author or characters, but to record the perpetual flight of the Subject and its ultimate disappearance'.[15]

Post-Structuralist Joyce was published in the same year that Jacques Derrida and Julia Kristeva were invited to speak at the International James Joyce Symposium in Frankfurt am Main. The decades after the mid-1980s witnessed the flowering of theory in Joyce studies, before political and other constraints would enforce what we now call the 'ethical turn'. In order to trace the differences within theory, and to explain the backlash of the 1990s, I will focus on the addresses given at Joyce Symposia by Lacan (1975), Derrida (1984) and Lyotard (1988).

LACAN ON JOYCE

On 16 June 1975 members of the International James Joyce Foundation had gathered in the grand amphitheatre of the Sorbonne University for the opening of the fifth symposium by the famous French psychoanalyst, Jacques Lacan. He began with the excuse of not being in true form. This address, entitled 'Joyce le Symptôme', dismayed many in attendance, because the speaker seemed to be addressing his own followers over the heads of the Joycean audience. Full of Joycean wordplay, Lacan's speech relied on previous knowledge of his ideas, and concluded with the announcement that his seminar of the coming year would be devoted to Joyce. Although seemingly incomprehensible, patient scholarship over the years has revealed the significance of Lacan's perspective(s) on Joyce.

Lacan's text addresses the issue of communication through Roman Jakobson, but not without a touch of Heidegger. His first claim is that in speaking of Joyce the Symptom, he is giving Joyce his proper name 'in the dimension of naming'.[16] The name signifies the opening up of the space which makes it possible to name things with words. The name is also the link which ties the individual to culture and language. The peculiarity of Joyce, for Lacan, is that, through writing, Joyce succeeded in making his own name immortal while this very writing also displays the symptomaticity of his insertion in language. This view of Joyce, based on *A Portrait of the Artist* and *Finnegans Wake*, allowed Lacan, throughout his career, to evolve a theory about the topology of subjectivity which would keep changing over the decades. In 1975, highlighting the playfulness of the *Wake*, Lacan noticed that the work lacks meaning and is unreadable in a conventional sense, but radiates with the sheer ecstatic enjoyment (*jouissance*) of its writer. The text of *Finnegans Wake* is also not analyzable in a psychoanalytic sense, nor do we read it because it captures our unconscious. Lacan does not even find Joyce sympathetic; he is fascinated by Joyce's peculiar practice of writing which shatters and litters the letter while conveying *jouissance*. Lacan's central example is, '*Who ails tongue coddeau, aspace of dumbillsilly*' (FW, 15.18) which should be articulated as French: '*Où es ton cadeau, espèce d'imbécile*' ['where is your present, you idiot'].[17] When we get the point, we laugh. Unheard of (and unheard) here, Lacan points out, is the fact that the translinguistic homophony rests upon writing conforming to English spelling. The letter is not language itself, and someone who uses the letter in this manner interrogates the grounds of our relationship to language.

Lacan had invoked Joyce and the littering of the letter already in his 1956 Seminar on Poe's 'The Purloined Letter', to indicate that a letter is a sign, both message and material object. Here Lacan returns to this issue. The central question is: Why did Joyce publish *Finnegans Wake?* Why did he send the letter which has no message? The fact of publication is crucial to Lacan's epithet 'the symptom', because in publishing his work-in-progress, making it public, Joyce triggered the effect of the symptom, its essence and its abstraction. The only thing which attaches us to *Finnegans Wake* is its ecstatic joy – not meaning, not content, not even unconscious sympathy or identification. The *Wake* is a 'funferal' without link to conventional communication (FW, 120.10). If language speaks us, if the unconscious is structured like a language, and if writing can make the name, Joyce's strategy of writing in the *Wake* is the sheer manifestation of that fact. It is this feat of the absolute detachment of writing from meaning-making which made Joyce important to Lacan as a symptomatic exemplification of how subjectivity relates to language.

Whereas Lacan emphasizes that Joyce's style allows the filtering into written communication of the ecstatic joy (*jouissance*) which he relates to an absolute reality outside our being in language, in the concluding paragraphs of the piece he also points towards a new reading of Joyce which he would develop over the coming years, and which would make him revise his spelling of 'symptôme' as 'sinthome'. The example of Joyce offers, in fact, a revision of the very topology of human subjectivity. Lacan had used the three orders of the Imaginary, the Symbolic and the Real to demonstrate how the individual subject links to culture. He now adds a fourth order, the 'Sinthome', which is inspired by Joyce's peculiar relationship to the Imaginary and to writing. Writing *was* Joyce's ego, Lacan claims in his Seminar. The 'Sinthome' then is the peculiar way in which Joyce knots together the Imaginary, the Symbolic and the Real in order to keep afloat as a writing human being. If a 'symptom' relates to the subject as the effect of an unusual inscription in culture, the 'Sinthome' reverses that relationship; it is the signifying formation which lends the subject its ontological consistency. The term 'Sinthome' plays on 'symptom' but also on 'saint homme' [holy man].

Lacan's views on Joyce have gained currency in cultural studies owing to Slavoj Žižek's application of them, as in *Enjoy Your Symptom! Jacques Lacan in Hollywood and Out.* Thanks to the explanatory work of a number of critics, most notably Jean-Michel Rabaté, the significance of Lacan's work for Joyce is now unquestionable.[18] Instead of an oddity,

Finnegans Wake is now a document in the history of modern subjectivity. The importance of the name, the use of the three (later four) orders, and especially the issues of gender to which Lacan's work gives rise have made themselves widely felt in Joyce criticism. Even our reading of a realist text like *Dubliners* has deepened. We now read the stories not only as portraits of Dublin types, but also as explorations of the nature of human consciousness itself.[19] The increasing experimentalism in *Ulysses* is no longer perceived as the author's wilful teasing of the reader, but as the natural process of his development in the direction of the exile from meaning-making. Thus theory opened up new perspectives on Joyce's text which have added to its cultural value. We are far removed from the concern with Homeric parallels, the father–son theme, the unreliability of the narrator, the number of lovers of Molly Bloom, which preoccupied the 1960s.

DERRIDA ON JOYCE

The story of Derrida's involvement with Joyce is more widely known than that of Lacan, though it, too, is the history of a relationship which frames a whole career. Unlike Lacan, who used Joyce as grist for his mill but seems not to have been personally engaged with Joyce's fiction, Derrida testifies to direct influence and he never changed his mind on Joyce. From his first comments in the 'Introduction' to Husserl's *The Origin of Geometry* where he introduces Joyce as an instance of writing which differs from Husserl's conception, Derrida kept mentioning Joyce. In a footnote to 'Plato's Pharmacy', for example, he points out that his piece is nothing but a footnote to *Finnegans Wake*. Derrida even imitated aspects of Joyce's textual experimentation, as in *Glas*, or the Babelization of the postal system in *The Post Card*. In his 1984 Frankfurt address, Derrida chose, unexpectedly, to present a reading of *Ulysses* rather than *Finnegans Wake*. 'Ulysses Gramophone: *Hear say yes in Joyce*' is a sustained meditation on a number of themes: the postal system, the way of our being-there as a being at the telephone where the doubleness of the act of communication is already inscribed in the voice, the untranslatability of the pun in the French expression L'oui-dire/L'ouï-dire ('hear say yes') which bears on the tension between the heard and the read, and the notion of 'competence' as a Joyce scholar. Derrida wound back and forth between these themes and quotations from *Ulysses* to demonstrate the internal reduplication implicit in the 'yes' which 'must reiterate itself, must archive its voice in order to give itself once again to be heard.'[20]

One of Derrida's points is that '[t]he desire for memory and the mourning implicit in the word *yes* set in motion an anamnesic machine'.[21] Joyce's texts are an archive of previous texts, functioning as a storehouse of Western culture. It is as if Joyce deliberately pre-empted all attempts at imitation by making his text so all-inclusive that everything is already contained in it, including even our interpretations of *Ulysses*. 'Yes, everything has already happened to us with *Ulysses* and has been signed in advance by Joyce.'[22] Again and again, throughout his career, Derrida confessed his dismay at confronting such a forbidding precursor who exhausted all possibilities of invention, and is forever reducing him to being in his debt. On the other hand, Joyce made evident what has always already been implicit in our human link to our cultural tradition:

> Now with the event signed by Joyce a *double* bind has become at least explicit (for we have been caught in it since Babel and Homer and everything else that follows): on the one hand, we must write, we must sing, we must bring about new events with untranslatable marks – and this is the frantic call, the distress of a signature that is asking for a *yes* from the Other, the pleading injunction of a counter-signature; but on the other hand, the odd novelty of every other *yes*, of every other signature, finds itself already phono-programmed in the Joycean corpus.[23]

After Joyce, there is no originality. The special feature of Joyce's *Ulysses* is its postal and programophonic technologies, which are intended to keep generations of university professors at work; and Joyce was uniquely astute in preprogramming the afterlife of his own work and name. Derrida is admittedly writing in the wake of Joyce, and he finds 'Joyce's ghost always coming on board', even in the final years of his life/career.[24] The essay included in *Post-Structuralist Joyce* focuses particularly on the ambivalence with which Derrida thinks of Joyce as an *event* of writing which is of 'such plot and scope that henceforth you have only one way out: *being in memory of him*'.[25]

Derrida's significance for Joyce studies was likened by Bernard Benstock to 'the storming of the Bastille'.[26] That claim was overstated. In the American academy, Derrida's post-structuralism was quickly naturalized as a practice of textual analysis which bore the name 'deconstruction'. A deconstructive reading of a text painstakingly analyzes the use of binary oppositions in the service of argumentation, and points out the contradictory nature of the act of privileging one over the other. Derrida's work on Joyce, however, is *not deconstructive*. Instead, it shows that the Joycean text is itself a deconstructive, disseminating machine – a machine which teaches one to read with much greater attention to the implications of strategies of textuality. The perception that everything in Joyce is surrounded by invisible quotation marks gained currency; and critics began to study the function of blanks or the effects of undecidability, without irritable reaching after fact. Thus Joyce scholarship grew attuned to the notion that Joyce's text is already read and decoded, and that it reads the reader.

THE ETHICAL TURN

What unites Lacan and Derrida in their view of Joyce is the focus on the reader and on the *effect* of the text. The difference between them is that they hold different notions of the materiality of the letter and the nature of its effect. Each views the community of Joycean experts with bemused envy. The heritage of theory, then, is a view of Joyce as a textual machine which forces the reader to (re-)produce it and to generate more and more commentary, in the awareness that the text is also a web in which one will be trapped, because it precludes any possibility of certainty. Indeed – and this is among the objections raised against French theory – it appears to turn literary criticism into a playful and value-free activity which may be intellectually stimulating and deeply sophisticated, but which also fails to relate to the very pressing social and political concerns of our world. Is theory not an élitist and ultimately trivial pursuit? The fact is that from the very first, a number of Joyce scholars tried to preserve the political and ethical relevance of the text in the face of the difficulties thrown up by theory. As we noted, MacCabe's aim had been to unleash Joyce's revolutionary potential; Patrick McGee's *Paperspace: Style as*

Ideology in Joyce's 'Ulysses' (1988) managed to explore the socio-ideological significance of Joyce's styles from a post-structuralist perspective; and my own 'Joyce, Derrida, and the Discourse of "the Other"', delivered after Derrida's reading at the Frankfurt conference, pointed to the deconstructive effect of gender in both Joyce and Derrida.[27]

The years 1987–88 also witnessed two notorious debates. In France, the relation of Heidegger's work to his Nazi connections raised wide concern. In the United States, the discovery of Paul De Man's youthful publications in a pro-Nazi Belgian newspaper shocked the academy. Although it is sometimes argued that these two events enforced the recognition of the ethical limitations of theory, the truth is that from within post-structuralist philosophy there had been a movement to 'establish an ethics compatible with postmodern philosophy's suspicion about positive or universal claims from the standards of reason, nature, and law'.[28] Derrida's first two essays on Lévinas are an instance, but the most obvious example is Lyotard's *The Differend* (1983), which preceded the backlash.

This notion of the *differend* articulates a discursive deadlock found in situations of hegemonic domination: 'In the differend, something "asks" to be put into phrases and suffers from the wrong of not being able to be put into phrases right away.' Discourse may be haunted by another, unspoken and unspeakable voice which remains silent. 'What is at stake in literature, in a philosophy, in a politics perhaps, is to bear witness to differends by finding idioms for them.'[29] Lyotard had casually mentioned Joyce in contrast to Proust as the modernist writer who represented the unrepresentable in fiction, but his real contribution to Joyce studies is 'Going Back to the Return', delivered at the 1988 Joyce Symposium in Venice. In contrast to Derrida (who is silent on the subject) and Lacan (who appears to have avoided it deliberately), Lyotard points to the problem of sexual difference as the central question posed by Joyce's text. The unspeakable situation of the differend surfaces in *Ulysses* as the fact of sexual difference. 'If there is so much sex in *Ulysses*, it is not because Joyce is unduly obsessed by it … It is there because the text of the Homeric homecoming, even if it returns via the Biblical exodus, cannot avoid coming up against that difference, that most ancient, internal obstacle which hinders the return, prevents it and ceaselessly returns to it.'[30] Although he is pointing to a moment of unde-cidability in Joyce's text, Lyotard is not doing theory; he is practising philosophy. The *aporia* around which Joyce's text revolves, according to Lyotard, is not the mere (and politically meaningless) effect of language or textuality, but a point at which language and consciousness touch upon justice.

The work of Lyotard seems to have been much less influential in Joyce studies than that of Derrida and Lacan, but it is there, in Joseph Valente's *James Joyce and the Problem of Justice: Negotiating Sexual and Colonial Difference*, for instance. Although James McMichael only refers to Lyotard in a number of footnotes, it is obvious that *Ulysses and Justice* was inspired by the opening which Lyotard provided. Similarly influenced by Lyotard, and explicitly engaged with the ethical responsibility of wit-nessing oppression, is my *Joyce: Derrida, Lacan and the Trauma of History* which reads the absence of the Irish mother tongue as the traumatic differend which generated Joyce's writerly experiments. Most explicit in taking an ethical turn was, perhaps, Patrick McGee. Although influenced by Derrida, and not Lyotard, *Telling the Other: The Question of Value in Modern and Postcolonial Writing* challenges the conventional separation of the aesthetic from the ethical, and shows how literature, in its resistance to the fram-ing effect of an institution, can open up a space of otherness which breaks through our fixed social and professional identities.[31]

AFTER THEORY

Since the 1980s Joyce criticism has moved in a number of very different directions. Most radical, perhaps, is the change in the work of the French editor of *Post-Structuralist Joyce*. Daniel Ferrer now professes the genetic study of literary texts which scrutinizes the process of composi-tion by means of drafts and other textual documents. Safely concrete and seemingly value-free, genetic criticism is incontrovertibly scholarly, and seemingly far removed from the undecidabilities of theory. Nevertheless, it was theory which prepared its way by abolishing the hierarchy between the valorized aesthetic, authorized literary work, and its unauthorized pre-texts. Indeed, most of the current historicizing and contextualizing cultural studies approaches to Joyce owe a debt to theory. Its dismantling of aesthetic privilege revealed the discursive nature of the literary text, allowing its placement in the context of the large framework of cultural discourses – from advertising to fashion, from obstetrics to political theory. In a different manner, gender studies and queer studies have profited greatly from reading strategies derived from Derrida, while the attention to the relationship between body and language in recent Joyce scholarship would not have arisen without Lacan. One might, in fact, claim that the majority of critical approaches after the 1980s were made possible by the advent of theory. Thus the once undecidable relationship between Joyce and nationalism was opened up for discussion, owing to the influx of theoretical thought from post-colonial critics (such as Homi Bhabha, who was himself profoundly influenced by Derrida). Although theory, as theory, is no longer a controversial item, that is because it has transformed our habits of reading so completely as to have become almost imperceptible. Here and there one may hear a voice which calls for another turn, a turn to a renewed and less hegemonic concept of the category of the aesthetic.

NOTES

1. See R. Macksey and E. Donato (eds), *The Structuralist Controversy: The Languages of Criticism and the Sciences of Man* (Baltimore, MD: Johns Hopkins University Press, 1970).

2. For the rivalry around the *Wake* see C. van Boheemen-Saaf, 'Purloined Joyce', in *Re: Joyce: Text, Culture, Politics*, ed. John Brannigan, Geoff Ward and Julian Wolfreys (Houndsmills and London: Macmillan, 1998), pp.246–58. The discussion around Poe is summed up by Barbara Johnson, 'The Frame of Reference: Poe, Lacan, Derrida', in *The Purloined Poe*, ed. J. Muller and W.J. Richardson (Baltimore, MD: Johns Hopkins University Press, 1988), pp.213–51.

3. W. Iser, *The Act of Reading: A Theory of Aesthetic Response* (Baltimore, MD: Johns Hopkins University Press, 1978).

4. R. Ellmann, *James Joyce: New and Revised Edition* (New York: Oxford University Press, 1982), p.594.

5. See N. Fitch (ed.), *In Transition: A Paris Anthology* (New York and London: Anchor Books Doubleday, 1990).

6. In S. Beckett *et al.*, *James Joyce/'Finnegans Wake': A Symposium/Our Exagmination Round His Factification For Incamination Of Work In Progress* (1929; rpt. New York: New Directions, 1972), p.79.

7. Ellmann, *James Joyce*, p.3.

8. R.H. Deming (ed.), *James Joyce: The Critical Heritage*, 2 vols (London: Routledge and

Kegan Paul, 1970).

9. S.L. Goldberg, *The Classical Temper: A Study of James Joyce's 'Ulysses'* (London: Chatto and Windus, 1961), pp.20–1.

10. M. Norris, *The Decentered Universe of 'Finnegans Wake': A Structuralist Analysis* (Baltimore, MD: Johns Hopkins University Press, 1974). Note that R. Scholes had published an essay entitled: 'Ulysses: A Structuralist Perspective', in *Fifty Years: 'Ulysses'*, ed. T.F. Staley (Bloomington, IN: Indiana University Press, 1974), pp.161–72.

11. H. Kenner, *Joyce's Voices* (Berkeley, CA: University of California Press, 1978), p.99.

12. R. Barthes, 'The Death of the Author', trans. Stephen Heath, in *The Norton Anthology of Theory and Criticism*, ed. V.B. Leitch (New York and London: W.W. Norton and Co., 2001), pp.1466–70, p.1467.

13. C. MacCabe, *James Joyce and the Revolution of the Word* (London: Macmillan, 1978), p.3. The year 1978/79 also saw a special number of the *James Joyce Quarterly*, entitled 'Structuralist/Reader Response Issue', which fails to address the implications of French thought.

14. D. Attridge and D. Ferrer (eds), *Post-Structuralist Joyce: Essays from the French* (Cambridge: Cambridge University Press, 1984), p.10.

15. Ibid.

16. The title of the address was 'Joyce le Symptôme', and the text is included in the 2005 edition of Lacan's seminar of 1975/76. Jacques Lacan, *Le Séminaire, livre XXIII: Le sinthome*, ed. Jacques-Alain Miller (Paris: Du Seuil, 2005), pp.161–9, p.162.

17. Ibid., p.166.

18. J. Rabaté, *Jacques Lacan: Psychoanalysis and the Subject of Literature* (Houndsmills and New York: Palgrave, 2001).

19. G.M. Leonard, *Reading 'Dubliners' Again: A Lacanian Perspective* (New York: Syracuse University Press, 1993).

20. J. Derrida, 'Ulysses Gramophone: Hear say yes in Joyce', in *James Joyce: The Augmented Ninth*, ed. B. Benstock (New York: Syracuse University Press, 1988), pp.27–77, p.44.

21. Ibid., p.44.

22. Ibid., p.48.

23. Ibid., p.49.

24. The quotation is from 'Two Words for Joyce', in Attridge and Ferrer (eds), *Post-Structuralist Joyce*, pp.145–58, p.149. See J. Derrida, 'La veilleuse ('… au livre de lui-même')', in J. Trilling, *James Joyce ou l'écriture matricide* (Belfort: Éd. Circé, 2001), pp.7–32.

25. Derrida, 'Two Words for Joyce', p.147. The most sustained exploration of the Derrida–Joyce relationship is A. Roughley, *Reading Derrida, Reading Joyce* (Gainesville, FL: University of Florida Press, 1999).

26. B. Benstock, Introduction to *The Augmented Ninth*, p.5.

27. P. McGee, *Paperspace: Style as Ideology in Joyce's 'Ulysses'* (Lincoln, NE: University of Nebraska Press, 1988); C. van Boheemen, 'Joyce, Derrida, and the Discourse of "the Other"', in Bernard Benstock (ed.), *The Augmented Ninth*, pp.88–103.

28. B.R. Voloshin, 'The Ethical Turn in French Postmodern Philosophy', *Pacific Coast*

Philology, 33, 1 (1998), pp.69–86, p.69.

29. J. Lyotard, *The Differend: Phrases in Dispute*, trans. G. van den Abbeele (Minneapolis, MN: University of Minnesota Press, 1988), p.13.

30. J. Lyotard, 'Going Back to the Return', in R.M. Bolletieri Bosinelli, Carla Marengo and Christine van Boheemen (eds), *The Languages of Joyce* (Philadelphia, PA and Amsterdam: John Benjamins, 1992), pp.193–211, p.209.

31. P. McGee, *Telling the Other: The Question of Value in Colonial and Postcolonial Writing* (Ithaca, NY: Cornell University Press, 1992).

CHAPTER NINE

Joyce's Bodies

KATHERINE MULLIN

Joyce's preoccupation with the body is notorious. *Ulysses'* fame stems almost as much from its reputation as a 'dirty book', banned for much of the twentieth century in many English-speaking countries, as for its prominence as a foundational text of experimental modernism. Its reputation for obscenity was established before its publication and even that fellow Modernist pioneer, Ezra Pound, quailed before his friend's explicitness. Attempting to steer the 'Calypso' episode of *Ulysses* through the *Little Review*, Pound pleaded with Joyce to tone down the closing passage describing Leopold Bloom's morning visit to the outside privy. Advising Joyce to 'Leave the stool to Geo. Robey. He has been doing down where the asparagus grows for some time', Pound tried to caution him over what was proper to literary art, and what was beyond the pale.[1] George Robey was an English music hall comedian, known for his innuendo-laden skits on bodily functions, and to Pound, Joyce was in danger of tainting his writing with similar vulgarity. Yet, for Joyce, the representation of all aspects of the body, in all its 'lowness', was integral to his creative project. In depicting Bloom 'at stool' (U, 4.465), Joyce self-consciously pushed at the boundaries of what could be shown in literary fiction by recording what would inevitably be labelled 'obscene'. The word 'obscene', as Joyce well understood, derived from the Latin '*ob scena*' or off-stage. By flaunting the obscene, he declares his intention that, for him, no subject must necessarily remain behind the curtain. For Pound, this insistence on describing the body's most taboo functions threatened to compromise artistic credibility, yet Joyce himself considered his unflinching inclusion of those details most writers chose to omit a vital marker of his broader aesthetic ambitions. Many readers of Ulysses feel that they know Leopold Bloom more fully than any other character in fiction, and the novel's somatic explicitness plays a crucial part in forming that pungent sense of intimacy. This chapter is, however, concerned with more than simply demonstrating that Joyce's interest in the body is central to his modernist experimentation with the form of the traditional realist novel. It will explore how, throughout his career, Joyce posited a complex and modulating relationship between bodies and texts. After all, the bodily moment which so unsettled Pound is, tellingly, also a literary moment. 'He liked to read at stool' (4.465), the narrator tells us, and the 'old number of Tit-Bits' (4.467) Bloom selects has a double use: 'He tore away half the prize story sharply and wiped himself with it' (4.537). This kind of frisson between the body and the text is, indeed, one of Joyce's most sustained concerns, as, from Dubliners to Finnegans Wake, bodily explicitness is increasingly mapped on to radical fictional innovation.

Joyce's troubling interest in the body and its dark places may have disconcerted Pound, but it was heralded as early as 1906, when the struggling young author, unknown and adrift in Trieste, fulminated against a climate of prudishness dominating his home-town. The immediate cause of his wrath was an article in the Irish nationalist journal Sinn Féin deploring the 'venereal excess' of those British soldiers barracked in Dublin who spent their evenings in the city's red light district.[2] Joyce was particularly incensed to learn that the journalist was the poet and critic Oliver St John Gogarty, his former companion in his own brothel adventures, later fictionalized as Buck Mulligan in Ulysses. Writing to his brother Stanislaus, Joyce castigated Gogarty's 'lying drivel about pure men and pure women and spiritual love and love for ever' as 'blatant lying in the face of truth' (LII, 192). In retaliation, he promised to 'put down a bucket in my own soul's well, sexual department' and 'in my novel [inter alia] … plank the bucket down' before his appalled literary associates back in Dublin. What interests me here is not so much Joyce's declaration of intent to write his sexual autobiography in Stephen Hero, later revised into A Portrait of the Artist as a Young Man, as the way in which the body and its unpalatable preoccupations are presented as the proof, even the guarantor, of a new literary authenticity. On the threshold of his career, Joyce flaunts his writing as a form of bracing, liberating indecent exposure. The body, even its 'sexual department', is to be hauled up and displayed as an antidote to the prudish disingenuousness of his contemporaries. Through representing the body and its concerns openly and without obfuscation, Joyce vows that his writing will transcend and rebuke the intellectual and aesthetic dishonesty of his literary rivals.

In 1906, Joyce was sporadically at work on *Stephen Hero*, but he was also revising and completing many of the *Dubliners* short stories, composed between 1904 and 1907 but only published, after many travails with timid publishers, in 1914.[3] The publishers' recalcitrance was in the main due to Joyce's unblushing concern with the body, since the collection places it at the heart of its exploration of a national malaise. *Dubliners* famously diagnoses the city of Joyce's birth as 'the centre of paralysis' (*LII*, 134), and the extent to which that paralysis extends to the bodies of its characters is one of its sustained themes, introduced and reprised in the three stories of childhood which begin the collection.[4] The first of these, 'The Sisters', presents paralysis as both a literal and a metaphoric affliction as the young narrator ambiguously mourns the passing of his friend and sometime tutor, Father Flynn, who has died after a long and mysterious illness resulting in a 'third stroke' (D, 7). 'The heavy grey face of the paralytic' (9) haunts the youth as he remembers the old man's physical frailties: 'his stupefied doze' (10), 'his large trembling hand' (10), 'his big discoloured teeth' (12), and the tongue which lolls 'upon his lower lip' (12) when he smiled. The spectre of Father Flynn's paralytic, hideous yet nonetheless compelling body dominates the story, and inspires a kind of sympathetic response in the boy-narrator. Recalling the old man's palsied trembling and final inertia, the boy repeatedly attempts to discipline his movements and gestures: 'I crammed my mouth with stirabout for fear I might give utterance to my anger' (9); 'I went in on tiptoe' (13); 'She pressed me to take some cream crackers also but I declined because I thought I would make too much noise eating them' (13). Paralysis in this story seems almost contagious, and it accordingly bleeds into the next, also concerning a young boy's troubling encounter with a disconcerting old man.

Bodily freedom is ostensibly the aim of the young narrator in 'An Encounter', as he and two school-friends plan 'a day's miching' (D, 20), prompted by 'a spirit of unruliness' distilled from 'the literature of the

Wild West' (18). This quest for 'wild sensations, for the escape which those chronicles of disorder alone seemed to offer me' (19) is, however, soon curtailed, firstly by their exhaustion, and secondly by the two boys' chance meeting with a character only named as a 'queer old josser' (26). The man appears when both boys are 'too tired' to do more than rest in a field and indulge in 'jaded thoughts' (24, 25), and, like Father Flynn, his physical mannerisms are suggestive of paralysis. He walks towards them, away from them, and then back again 'with one hand upon his hip' and 'very slowly ... so slowly that I thought he was looking for something in the grass' (25). His curious gait is shadowed in the hypnotic circularity of his obsessive monologue on the whipping of boys: 'His mind, as if magnetised again by his own speech, seemed to circle slowly round and round its new centre' (27). This physical and mental paralysis recalls Father Flynn; the queer old josser's fantasy of administering 'a nice warm whipping' (27) to young boys also looks back to the former story's interest in how the young narrator attempts to discipline and control his own wayward body. These themes are confirmed in 'Araby', Dubliners' third and final 'story of childhood', which also creates a counterpoint between youth and age, discipline and desire. The story's protagonist is poised on the cusp between the carefree days of childhood, where 'we played till our bodies glowed' (29), and a stifling adolescence overwhelmed by a futile erotic obsession with a girl named only as 'Mangan's sister' (30). As he watches his beloved covertly from an upper window, he glimpses only fragments of her body – 'the soft rope of her hair' (30), 'the white curve of her neck' (32), the silver bracelet which she turns 'round and round her wrist' (32) – and his attempts to court her by bringing her a gift from the Araby charity bazaar are initially frustrated by his ineffectual aunt and drunken uncle, then later by his late arrival and the stifling atmosphere of the bazaar itself. Although the narrator feels that 'my body was like a harp and her words and gestures were like fingers running upon the wires' (31), like the boy-narrators of 'The Sisters' and 'An Encounter', he comes to learn that his body must be cramped and thwarted, since to hope for fulfilment is to find oneself 'driven and derided by vanity' (36).

The body under constraint is thus a sustained theme of all three of Joyce's stories of childhood. The 'nice warm whipping' which so excites the queer old josser is the most blatant instance of all the stories' depiction of the inhibition of young bodies which might otherwise long to glow in vigorous play, or ramble across Dublin on a truant expedition, or even eat cream crackers with abandon. The narrator's fear that the strange old man might 'seize me by the ankles' (28) as he gets up to leave only emphasizes the way in which all three boy-protagonists find their bodily impulses repeatedly thwarted by their elders in Joyce's 'centre of paralysis'. The three stories are, however, not simply concerned to delineate Dublin as a place of inevitable corporeal restraint; they are also insistent in mapping that restraint on to the reading imagination. For physical repression is repeatedly accompanied by complementary attempts, frequently by those same disciplining elders, to regulate or prescribe their access to stories. In 'The Sisters' the boy hears 'stories about the catacombs and about Napoleon Bonaparte' (11) and certain mysteries of Catholic doctrine from Father Flynn, yet another elderly man, Old Cotter, is quick to damn such knowledge as 'bad for children … because their minds are so impressionable' (9). Similarly, in 'An Encounter' the boy finds his access to fiction is contested by two men. Firstly, Father Butler dismisses his pupils' penny-dreadful story papers as 'wretched stuff' (19) and threatens Leo Dillon with the cane for reading them; later the queer old josser attempts to establish his authority by recommending Scott, Moore and Lytton before asserting that 'there were some of Lord Lytton's works which boys couldn't read' (23). In 'Araby' the protagonist's dead-end romantic fantasies are filtered through a variety of texts belonging to an older generation: the dead priest's bequeathed copies of 'The Abbot by Walter Scott, The Devout Communicant and The Memoirs of Vidocq' (29), his uncle's favourite poem 'The Arab's Farewell to his Steed' (34), and even the nineteenth-century Irish poet James Clarence Mangan, who hovers behind the shadowy figure of 'Mangan's sister'. In all three stories the boys' access to novels, poetry, magazines and other stories are circum-scribed through the mediation of older authority figures. Reading is persistently associated with regulation – either through censorship or prescription – and those inhabiting inhibited, whipped or frustrated bodies inevitably find their access to literature similarly controlled or withheld.

If, in the collection's first three stories, Joyce meticulously relates bodily to textual paralysis, then that imbrication of body with narrative continues throughout *Dubliners'* later tales of adolescence, maturity and public life. Eveline Hill's physical catatonia at the North Wall quayside, where 'passive, like a helpless animal' (43) she refuses to board the emigration ship which might carry her to a new life in Buenos Ayres with her lover Frank, has much to do with the myriad of competing fictions which haunt this seemingly slight story. Within the text, Eveline is half-fascinated, half-bewildered by Frank's 'tales of the terrible Patagonians', or song 'about the lass that loves a sailor', uncertain whether to believe him or her father, who dourly counters with 'I know these sailor chaps' (40). On the silent margins of the story, as I have argued elsewhere, hover other cautionary tales of duped and destitute Irish emigrants to South America, or of 'white slaves' dumped in the brothels of Argentina, which a woman of Eveline's age and time could scarcely have ignored.[5] These narratives, all jostling with one another to inform Eveline's great decision, induce an unmistakeably somatic response: 'Her distress awoke a nausea in her body'; 'Her hands clutched the iron in frenzy' (42). Her response is not merely paralysis, but an aphasic blankness as she gives Frank 'no sign of love or farewell or recognition' (43). A similar moment of paralysed estrangement occurs in 'A Painful Case', when Mr Duffy's reading suddenly puts him off his dinner: 'One evening as he was about to put a morsel of corned beef and cabbage into his mouth his hand stopped. His eyes fixed themselves on a paragraph in the evening paper' (125). Here, even more explicitly that in 'Eveline', a narrative evokes a response viscerally located in the body, emphasized by the close focus upon hands and eyes. The story, indeed, prepares for this connection between body and text through the advertisement for Bile Beans Mr Duffy has, 'in an ironical moment' (119), pasted to the cover of his private journal. Bile Beans were a popular 'tonic laxative', and Mr Duffy's attempt at writing is an appropriately sluggish, constipated process: 'In these sheets a sentence was inscribed from time to time' (119). No wonder, then, that the story of Mrs Sinico's fate affects his digestive processes: 'The whole narrative of her death revolted him' (128). Both 'Eveline' and 'A Painful Case', in very different ways, depict characters whose bodies articulate the traumatic and paralysing effects of the texts they consume.

Elsewhere in *Dubliners*, bodies and texts repeatedly blur into one another. Literary success and sexual desire are conflated in 'A Little

Cloud', where Little Chandler's envy of his successful friend Ignatius Gallagher, now 'a brilliant figure on the London Press' (76), is partly bound up with his thwarted ambitions to delight London reviewers with his poetry 'of the Celtic school' (80), and partly animated by Gallagher's boasts about 'the vices of many capitals' (85). Little Chandler would doubtless relish the literary career of Gabriel Conroy in 'The Dead', who reviews books for the London *Daily Express*, but for Conroy this success is also entwined with sexual humiliation. The flirtatious Irish Nationalist Molly Ivors first chides him as a 'West Briton' (216) while they dance, and later, his wife Gretta inadvertently underlines this rebuke by deflating his advances through her grief over her West of Ireland lover, Michael Furey. Sexual disappointment is bound to a different kind of narrative in 'Clay', in which Maria's 'mistake' in performing an abbreviated version of the song 'I Dreamt that I Dwelt in Marble Halls' embarrassingly draws her listeners' attention to her pitiable spinsterhood. Indeed, Maria's inadvertent compression alludes to her own corporeal insignificance: her 'diminutive body' (113) is mirrored in her diminutive version of her song. Maria's 'tiny quavering voice' (118) contrasts sharply with the virtuoso performance of another inappropriate song by an elderly spinster: Julia Morkan's rendition of 'Arrayed for the Bridal' in 'The Dead'. In Julia's case, however, the very beauty of her voice supplies an ironic tension foregrounding the singer's terminal exhaustion: 'To follow the voice, without looking at the singer's face, was to feel and share the excitement of swift and secure flight' (220), the narrator tells us, and Gabriel later recalls 'that haggard look' (254) presaging her death. This moment, the collection's sole exhilarating instance of artistic transcendence of that torpor which otherwise bounds the world of *Dubliners*, is compromised by the failing body which inexorably tethers the artist to earth. The collection thereby ends as it began, with death. Father Flynn's counterpart is not only the body of Michael Furey, lying buried beneath the 'crooked crosses and headstones' (256) of Galway's lonely churchyard, but, less obviously, the doomed Julia Morkan. Both stories parallel the death of the body with the termination of narrative. In 'The Sisters', Father Flynn loses those powers of story-telling which have so enthralled the young narrator: his sister Eliza reports him 'talking to no one and wandering about by himself' or 'sitting up by himself in the dark in his confession-box, wide awake and laughing-like softly to him-self' (17). Julia Morkan's death is also marked by a silencing. A gifted coloratura soprano, her career is cut short through Pope Pius X's 1903 decree excluding women from church choirs. Together, the stories underline the collection's sustained and intricately nuanced meditation upon the symbiotic relationship between the regulation of the body and the stifling of the text.

Amid *Dubliners'* gallery of bullied children, thwarted celibates and unhappy spouses, Julia Morkan is arguably the collection's sole artist. Others – Little Chandler, Maria, Mr Duffy, Kathleen Kearney, Gabriel Conroy – might aspire to their moment of creativity through after-dinner speeches, private writings or performances of songs, but only Julia achieves it. Her sorry fate, anticipated in 'The Dead' but confirmed in *Ulysses* by both Bloom and Stephen Dedalus, underlines how the somatic constriction Joyce so relentlessly describes as peculiar to Dublin is potentially fatal to the artist. That problem forms one of the chief themes of *A Portrait of the Artist as a Young Man*, the book eventually issuing from Joyce's 1906 threat to flaunt his 'sexual department' before a prudish Dublin literati. Whereas *Dubliners* delineates the stifling symbiosis between the body and all kinds of narratives – from old men's stories through newspaper reports to popular songs – *A Portrait* is ostensibly concerned not so much with the processes of narrative consumption as with the alchemy of artistic production. Yet, as in *Dubliners*, Joyce begins by showing how a child is taught to associate the inhibition of the body with the regulation of the text. Indeed, the first page of the novel associates Stephen Dedalus's first lesson in bodily restraint with the bowdlerization of a song he has learnt to call his own. 'O, the wild rose blossoms / On the little green place' (P, 7) is a sanitized version of the popular ballad 'Lilly Dale' (1852), in which the word 'place' has been substituted for 'grave' in order to transform a song about desire, loss and death into a palatable nursery rhyme. Stephen himself, however, has modified the song further, lisping 'O, the green wothe botheth' (7), inviting much speculation about what a 'green rose' might signify. Is the flower appro-priately Irish, as might befit this first act of creation? Might it, more darkly, hint at the green carnation worn by Oscar Wilde, an Irish artist whose martyrdom for his sexual transgressions animated one of Joyce's

Triestine essays (CW, 201–5)? These questions hang in the air as the coloured narrative moves on to 'When you wet the bed first it is warm then it gets cold' (P, 7). Stephen's first attempt to find his own voice is thus repeatedly entwined with his attempt to regulate his wayward body. As in Dubliners, the opening episode of A Portrait immediately problematizes the relationship between body and text.

This early intimation that Stephen's artistic progress will be closely bound up with his body is sustained throughout the novel. At Clongowes School still more compelling somatic secrets interrupt his attempts to comprehend the mysteries of language. When two lines from the Litany of the Blessed Virgin Mary, 'Tower of Ivory. House of Gold', baffle Stephen, he interprets the words through his friend Eileen's 'long thin cool white hands' and her 'fair hair' which 'streamed out behind her like gold in the sun' (48). Accessing language by mapping it on to the body comes naturally to Stephen, but the strategy fails him when he is called upon to decipher the still more mysterious word 'smugging'. Learning that some of his school-fellows are to be flogged for this obscurely named crime, Stephen muses, 'What did that mean about the smugging in the square' (47), wondering if the transgression has something to do with the graffiti of the walls of the 'square', or school latrines: 'Perhaps that's why they were there because it was a place where some fellows wrote things for cod?' (48). What 'smugging' actually means is still a subject of some dispute, and I have argued elsewhere that it most plausibly signifies some form of collective masturbation, the focus of an abiding anxiety throughout boys' public schools in Britain and Ireland at the time.[6] Crucially, however, the word's suggestive indeterminacy invites a telling frisson between bodily and textual transgression. A forbidden text, for Stephen here as much as for the boy in 'An Encounter', is loosely associated with corporal punishment, and, at some dimly understood level, with sexual desire.

These associations between writing and the abject sexual body are inevitably sharpened in adolescence. In the second chapter Stephen travels with his father to Cork and visits the university where the older man once studied. There, father and son tour the anatomy theatre, where Mr Dedalus seeks out the initials he once carved on a desk. Anatomy and inscription are, however, bound together in a second sense when

Stephen finds another carving which devastatingly speaks to his own sexual anxieties: 'On the desk he read the word *Foetus* cut several times into the dark stained wood' (101). This 'sudden legend', suggestive of an abortive or sterile sexuality, seems to publish his own 'mad and filthy orgies' (103) to the world, and his mortification increases as he reads into '[t]he letters cut in the stained wood of the desk' the stigmata of his own 'bodily weakness and futile enthusiasms' (103). Stephen's tendency to map the body on to writing, already established at Clongowes, here takes on the weight of epiphany as the connection between word and body becomes intensely personal. What is at stake here is not simply adolescent sexual panic, but Stephen's half-grasped understanding of the inextricable relationship between his physical and his creative life. Indeed, the word 'Foetus' itself takes on a quasi-corporeal form in this episode, as it 'capered before his eyes as he walked back across the quadrangle' (102). It follows, therefore, that Stephen should choose to spend some of the money gained from his schoolboy literary successes, 'the moneys of his exhibition and essay prize' (109), on losing his virginity with one of Dublin's many prostitutes. The second chapter closes with his dramatic turn from finding solace in literature, particularly 'the soft speeches of Claude Melnotte' (112), to seek out 'sin with another of his kind' (113). As '[t]he verses passed from his lips', displaced by 'the inarticulate cries and the unspoken brutal words' (113) of desire, Stephen is nonetheless unable to leave behind the world of language as he compares his 'cry for an iniquitous abandonment' to 'the echo of an obscene scrawl which he had read on the oozing walls of a urinal' (114). This is the third of the novel's pointed conflations of sexuality with graffiti, recalling both Stephen's childhood misunderstanding that 'smugging' is forbidden writing on the lavatory walls, and his encounter with the word 'Foetus' in the Cork lecture theatre.

As the third chapter of the novel unfolds, Stephen's future as an artist is shown to be dependent upon his ability to resist and, ultimately, reject cultural incitement to regulate his body's wayward appetites. Father Arnall's infamous hell-fire sermon ironizes the Christian doctrine of the Word made flesh through its relish for the physical. His command of the language of bodily disgust inspires a somatic response in Stephen, who leaves the sermon beset by 'Bodily unrest and chill and weariness'

JAMES JOYCE

(155), and subsequently disciplines himself into a regime of strict denial. This system of physical constraint, however, connects to a familiar form of narrative circularity. Like the old man in 'An Encounter', Stephen too slips into a pattern of monologic repetition as his life 'circled about its own centre of spiritual energy' (168). His religious practices – most notably reciting the rosary or attending confession – ensnare Stephen in a stifling cycle of 'confess and repent and be absolved, confess and repent again and be absolved again, fruitlessly' (174) as he repeats the same words time and again. This sense that the body's suppression crushes and stifles creativity – and is thereby fatal to the development of the artist – is underlined at the close of the fourth chapter when Stephen, having rejected a religious life, perceives his alternative vocation embodied in the form of the bird-girl. The bathing young woman is both artist's muse and erotic spectacle, and Stephen's response to her hovers ambiguously between aesthetic reverence and ardent desire: 'His cheeks were aflame; his body was aglow; his limbs were trembling' (172). This epiphany, closing the fourth chapter and apparently betokening Stephen's future artistic destiny, points the way to the reconciliation of body and text in the young artist's future career. Yet, as the fifth and final chapter reveals, Stephen cannot so easily put aside a mistrust of the body that compromises his aesthetic ambitions.

Stephen's predisposition to view the body and art as irreconcilable is evident in his 'applied Aquinas' (238) theory of aesthetics. During his ambulatory lecture to Lynch, he insists that the 'kinetic' arts are 'pornographical or didactic' in exciting 'desire or loathing', and are therefore 'improper arts' (233). To illustrate his thesis, Stephen invokes a sequence of examples which repeatedly exclude the body from his own personal theory of art. He begins by casting out the 'pierced heart' (233) of the girl fatally wounded in the hansom cab from his definition of the tragic. Next, he refutes Lynch's suggestion that his desire for the Venus of Praxiteles is a bona fide artistic response, dismissing his reaction as 'simply a reflex action of the nerves' (234). With 'Let us take woman' (237), Stephen moves on to a convoluted attempt to divorce sexual attraction from artistic appreciation in an effort to articulate a clear distinction between 'eugenics' and 'esthetic' (237). The final flourish of Stephen's tendency to isolate art from the body is evident in the example he chooses to explain the three aesthetic elements of *integritas, consonantia* and *claritas*:

> Stephen pointed to a basket which a butcher's boy had slung over
> his head.
> - Look at that basket, he said.
> - I see it, said Lynch.
> - In order to see that basket, said Stephen, your mind first of all
> separates the basket from the rest of the visible universe which is
> not the basket. The first phase of apprehension is a bounding line
> drawn about the object to be apprehended. (241)

Stephen's theory of art here accomplishes the decapitation of the butcher's
boy: his explication depends upon the erasure of the boy's unruly body
from the picture. In this erasure, I would suggest, is rooted much of the
narrative's notorious ironic distance from its protagonist. The much-
debated artistic merits of his villanelle depend in part upon the tension
between Stephen's aesthetic theories and the blatantly erotic processes of
its composition. 'O! In the virgin womb of the imagination the word
was made flesh', thinks Stephen, but 'the temptress of his villanelle',
awakening from her 'odorous sleep' with a 'look of languor' (254),
states the radical extent of the narrative's interrogation of this biblical
trope. This moment of creation is suggestive not so much of divine inspi-
ration as of autoerotic fantasy, and even the form of the villanelle, through
its layers of rhythmic repetitions, implies masturbation. The villanelle
episode thus refutes Stephen's own aesthetic theorizing by locating the
body at the heart of artistic practice. The theme is further elaborated in
Ulysses, where Joyce's ironic meditation upon 'the word made flesh' is
confirmed and deepened within both the form and the content of the
novel.

I began by noting how the fourth episode of *Ulysses*, in which readers
first meet Leopold Bloom, invokes a controversial frisson between the
body and the text. The moment when Bloom wipes his backside with
Philip Beaufoy's prize-winning *Tit-Bits* story summarizes the novel's
sustained challenge to the anti-somatic aesthetic theory that Stephen
outlines in the final chapter of *A Portrait of the Artist as a Young Man*. At one
point during Stephen's disquisition, Lynch asks him, 'Are you laughing
in your sleeve?' (P, 209), and it might seem that even if Stephen himself is sincere,

then his creator is far from it. For *Ulysses* persistently associates literature with the body and its functions, in moments too numerous to list here in full detail. The 'Telemachus' episode, for instance, begins the novel with Buck Mulligan, Haines and Stephen vigorously attending to the needs of their bodies – breakfasting, contemplating a dip in the Forty Foot bathing pool – while reciting poetry, blasphemously quoting scripture, debating the Irish Literary Revival and discussing *Hamlet*. Bodies and texts are similarly entangled for Molly Bloom, who starts her day in 'Calypso' with breakfast in bed, a letter from her lover Blazes Boylan, and a discussion of her recent reading. Oblivious to Stephen's condemnation of the 'kinetic' arts which excite desire, Molly's tastes tend towards the 'pornographical' as she dismisses *Ruby: Pride of the Ring* for having 'nothing smutty in it' (U, 4.355) and requests 'another of Paul de Kock's. Nice name he has' (4.357). Molly's literary preferences are but one example of *Ulysses'* fascination with how reading might become embedded within the body, a point elaborated later in 'Wandering Rocks' when Bloom is browsing a bookstall for a suitable gift for his wife. He is drawn to *Aristotle's Masterpiece*, an eighteenth-century illustrated work of anatomical instruction and sexual folklore, then to James Lovebirch's flagellant novel *Fair Tyrants*, before finally choosing a book offering a more palatable vision of the sexual body. *Sweets of Sin* which, with its flagrant erotics of 'queenly shoulders and heaving embonpoint', is 'More in her line' (10.606); but all of the 'smutty' books Bloom fingers incite a physical response.

For Bloom, not only reading, but writing also is closely mapped on to the physical, as his clandestine erotic correspondence with Martha Clifford demonstrates. Martha has answered an advertisement Bloom placed in the *Irish Times* for a 'smart lady typist to aid gentleman in literary work' (8.326–7), and in 'Lotus Eaters' Bloom collects her letter from the Westmoreland Row Post Office. The correspondence is secret and anonymous – Bloom has concealed his name and address, and Martha may have concealed hers – but their lack of physical contact only emphasizes the extent to which sexuality is displaced on to the letters which pass between them. No wonder, then, that Bloom contemplates using Martha's letter as a masturbatory stimulus when he lies in his bath.[7] This frisson between writing and the body applies not only to Martha's letter, but also to the prose style of *Ulysses*, increasingly so towards the closing third of the novel. Joyce's mounting interest in the body and its taboos can be read alongside the contested process of *Ulysses*' serial publication. Episodes of the novel were published serially in the New York magazine *The Little Review* and, predictably, the journal was beset by censors. In January 1919 the New York Society for the Suppression of Vice confiscated the 'Lestrygonians' number of the magazine; the 'Scylla and Charybdis' episode was their target in May that year, followed by the suppression of the thirteenth 'Nausicaa' episode in August, an event precipitating the legal trial in February 1921 which would in effect ban *Ulysses* from the English-speaking world. Meanwhile, Joyce was composing the latter third of the book, from 'Nausicaa' onwards, during months when he was keenly attentive to news of his novel's legal skirmishes in New York. In this context, the novel's escalating tendency towards somatic explicitness might look like provocation. In particular, episodes fourteen, fifteen and eighteen entangle bodies and texts together both in their content and, most interestingly, in their form.

'Oxen of the Sun', the fourteenth episode, presents blatant correspondences between its subject matter and style. As Bloom, seeking news of Mina Purefoy's labour, joins Stephen Dedalus, Buck Mulligan and their medical student friends in the ante-room of the Rotunda maternity hospital, the narrative maps the modulating language of the episode on to the woman's labouring body. The chapter moves through evolving styles of English literary prose, tracing its chronological development from Anglo-Saxon to the present day. Loosely arranged in nine sections corresponding to the nine months of pregnancy, the word is once again made flesh. 'Oxen of the Sun' prepares us for a variation on this mapping of the body on to the text in the fifteenth episode, 'Circe'. Arguably the most difficult and sexually disturbing chapter, 'Circe' is frequently read as an exploration of dreams, hallucinations and fantasies, as 'Nighttown' stages Bloom's and Stephen's subconscious thoughts and fears. Yet the revelation of the dark places of the mind is accompanied by the exposure of the dark places of the body. Acts which are kept off-stage elsewhere in the novel – notably Boylan's afternoon in bed with Molly – are paraded in 'Circe', where readers are invited to join Bloom and 'apply your eye to the keyhole and play with yourself while I just go through her a few times' (15.3788–9). This flirtation with pornography reaches its peak in the notorious sequence where Bloom is transformed into a woman and gynaecologically displayed before eager bidders by Bello Cohen: '(*he bares his arm and plunges it elbowdeep into Bloom's vulva*) There's fine depth for you! What, boys? That give you a hardon? (*he shoves his arm into a bidder's face*)' (15.3088–91). This, often startling, preoccupation with flaunting the body is, however, paralleled through the chapter's form as the narrative unexpectedly changes genres from fiction to drama. Austin Briggs and others argue that 'Circe' is best understood as a film script, since many of its incidents – such as Virag unscrewing his head and placing it under his arm, or a singing soap flying through the sky – might most plausibly be enacted through camera trick or animation.[8] The very impossibility of staging 'Circe' draws attention to how drama relies upon transforming actors' bodies into spectacle. The episode's obscene content thus reflects its form, testing the limits of what the body can plausibly represent.

The final 'Penelope' episode, however, most flamboyantly asserts the novel's subtension of body and text. Molly Bloom's monologue is notoriously preoccupied with her own physicality, as she ponders food, drink, clothes, her waning beauty, her sexual past and future, childbirth, breastfeeding and death. It is, equally notoriously, written in a form which seems to filter the text through her voluptuous body. During her monologue, Molly discovers she is menstruating: 'have we too much blood up in us or what O patience above its pouring out of me like the sea anyhow he didn't make me pregnant as big as he is I don't want to ruin the clean sheets I just put on' (18.1122–5). The tide of liquid from her body has been repeatedly indexed to the seamless outpouring of her words, her eight long, unpunctuated sentences labelled a 'flow' by almost all critics, who frequently 'resort to metaphors of rivers, streams and liquids' in defining the episode's style.[9] This sense in which Molly's body seems to merge with her text in the closing pages of *Ulysses* offers an appropriate conclusion to a novel which has, from its beginning, been concerned to destabilize any perceived division between the somatic and the aesthetic. While Stephen Dedalus, in the fifth chapter of *A Portrait*, seeks to isolate art from the body in his lecture on aesthetics, *Ulysses*, like *Dubliners* and *A Portrait*, asserts the centrality of the body to its literary experiment. Whereas in *Dubliners* and, to a degree, in *A Portrait*, acts of reading and acts of writing are persistently associated with corporal restraint and inhibition, *Ulysses* offers an alternative, more optimistic vision of the word made flesh. Through ending the novel with Molly's flow, *Ulysses* celebrates the imbrication of the body with the text, placing bodily matters resoundingly at the heart of its literary experiment.

Joyce's final novel, *Finnegans Wake* (1939) might, at a first glance from a puzzled reader, appear to continue Molly's monologue through its opening lines: 'riverrun, past Eve and Adam's, from swerve of shore to bend of bay, brings us by a commodious vicus of recirculation back to Howth Castle and Environs' (*FW*, 1.1–3). Here too, the language of 'flow' evokes bodily fluids, while the idea of 'recirculation' suggests not only a river, but also blood circulating through the body. Bodies, and their fluids, are indeed somewhere at the heart of *Finnegans Wake* and its obscure, convoluted 'plot', if plot we can call it. The challenge of making sense of Joyce's compendious and confounding novel is ever so slightly lessened if one understands the basic family story buried somewhere within the novel's midden-heap of language. *Finnegans Wake* concerns a family: a father, Humphrey Chimpden Earwicker or HCE, his wife, Anna Livia Plurabelle or ALP, their two warring twin sons, Shem the Penman and Shaun the Postman, and their desirable daughter, Issy. These five characters have multiple identities and permutations, allowing a claustrophobic, incestuous and intensely somatic pattern of allegiances and conflicts to build up between them. HCE desires his daughter, and, at some point (the novel insinuates though never confirms) has engaged in an act of sexual voyeurism with her, which may, or may not, involve covertly watching as she urinates. The precise nature of this crime has been witnessed by a third party, and is detailed in a lost letter, maybe written by Shem and transmitted by Shaun. Whether this letter will ever come to light is the closest the novel gets to a whodunit. Thus, although we might be at sea in *Finnegans Wake*, we are also, in a sense, in familiar territory. Joyce's final novel, like his previous three fictions, is absorbed by the questions arising from transgressive bodies and their relationships to unstable texts.

This chapter is not the place to venture too far into the vast landscape of *Finnegans Wake* and will instead confine itself to the seventh chapter of the first book, which is devoted to Shem the Penman, a character Joyce blatantly introduces as his own alter-ego: 'Shem is as short for Shemus as Jem is joky for Jacob' (169.1). That Shem is, in a sense, 'Jem' or 'James', is made clear when we learn more of his previous literary career: he is responsible for 'his usylessly unreadable Blue Book of Eccles' (179.26–7) (the first edition of *Ulysses* had a bright blue cover; 7, Eccles Street is Bloom's home address), and pages 186 to 187 contain puns on the names of all the *Dubliners* short stories. The chapter demands to be read as Joyce's own playful meditation upon his literary career and its reception, and it focuses upon the author's bodily abjection. Written from the perspective of a hostile critic, the narrative illustrates 'the noxious pervert's perfect lowness' (174.35–6) as manifested through both his body and his writing. The chapter provides an encyclopaedic account of Shem's physical shortcomings. '[H]is lowness creeped out first via foodstuffs' (170.25–6), since, like the typist in T.S. Eliot's *The Waste Land*, he prefers to eat from tins. A coward, he 'disliked anything anyway approaching a plain straightforward standup or knockdown row' (174.5–6), and his personal hygiene leaves much to be desired: the narrative details 'the foxtrotting fleas, the lieabed lice, the scum on his tongue, the drop in his eye, the lump in his throat' (180.18–20) and notes that few 'dared whiff the polecat at close range' (181.23–4). Shem's 'lowness', however, is simultaneously articulated through his writings, about which the polemical narrator is still more vitriolic. Shem's work is fake, fraudulent and plagiarized: 'Who can say how many pseudostylic shamania, how few or how many of the most venerated public inpostures, how very many piously forged palimpsests slipped in the first place by this morbid process from his pelagiarist pen?' (181.36–182.3). Yet what is at stake here is the very 'morbid process' by which Shem writes, a process which collides the 'lowness' of his body with the 'lowness' of his work. Denied 'romeruled stationery' (185.5) by his publishers 'Robber and Mumsell, the pulpic dictators' (185.1–2) and 'Father Flammeus Falconer' (185.4) – Joyce's references are to the renegade publisher of *Dubliners*, George Roberts at Maunsel & Co. and his printer, John Falconer – Shem is cast upon his own resources, making 'synthetic ink and sensitive paper for his own end out of his wit's waste' (185.7–8). The intricacies of this manufacture are coyly couched in cod-

Latin, 'cloaked up in the language of the blush-fed' (185.9–10) to evade the censors, but reveal that the 'indelible ink' (185.26) is made from a mixture of his faeces and urine, and then used to write upon 'every square inch of the only foolscap available, his own body' (185.35–6). This, then, is *Finnegans Wake*'s primal scene of writing, where the body and the text merge into one, indivisible and indistinguishable from one another.

The moment returns us to Ezra Pound's advice to Joyce that he 'leave the stool to Geo. Robey' and turn away from the abject body towards subject matter more fit for high art. Pound was not alone in his unease over Joyce's somatic preoccupations. Virginia Woolf also dismissed *Ulysses* in a 1922 diary entry as the work of 'a queasy undergraduate scratching his pimples', damning it as 'an illiterate, underbred book, the book of a self-taught working man, and we all know how distressing they are, how egotistic, insistent, raw, striking and ultimately nauseating'.[10] Woolf's recourse to tropes of acne and nausea to describe the pungency of Joyce's writing could easily belong in the seventh chapter of *Finnegans Wake*. There Joyce gleefully pastiches reactions like Woolf's and Pound's, insisting instead on the centrality of the body, in all its unpalatable vulgarity, to his art. It is a position sustained, in multiple ways, throughout Joyce's literary career, from *Dubliners* and *A Portrait of the Artist as a Young Man*, where the suppression of the physical is repeatedly linked to the stifling of the creative imagination, through to *Ulysses* and *Finnegans Wake*, where bodies and texts become increasingly enmeshed. For Pound, for Woolf and for the appalled narrator of the 'Shem the Penman' episode of *Finnegans Wake*, Joyce's fascination with the body and its 'nameless shamelessness' (182.14) placed him beyond the pale of high modernism, exposing him as 'in his bardic memory low' (172.28). Yet those bodily preoccupations today place Joyce at the heart of what has recently been named 'low modernism', where he continues to unsettle, to surprise and even to shock.[11]

NOTES

1. Letter dated 29 March 1918 in F. Read (ed.), *The Letters of Ezra Pound to James Joyce, with Pound's Essays on Joyce* (New York: New Directions, 1965), p.131. For a full account of Pound's attempts at editorial interventions in *Ulysses*, see P. Vanderham, *James Joyce and Censorship: The Trials of 'Ulysses'* (Basingstoke: Macmillan, 1998), pp.18–28.

2. O. Gogarty, 'Ugly England', Sinn Féin, 15 September 1906, p.3. Gogarty was contributing to a sustained campaign in nationalist circles to highlight the supposedly lower standard of sexual morality in Britain than in Ireland. I have discussed Joyce's interest in this debate at length elsewhere in K. Mullin, 'English Vice and Irish Vigilance: The Nationality of Obscenity in Ulysses', in Joyce, Ireland, Britain, ed. A. Gibson and L. Platt (Gainesville, FL: University of Florida Press, 2006), pp.68–84.

3. 'The Sisters', 'A Painful Case', 'Two Gallants' and 'A Little Cloud' were all in the process of composition or revision during 1906.

4. Joyce divided Dubliners into four discrete sections: 'childhood, adolescence, maturity and public life. The stories are arranged in this order' (LII, 134).

5. See K. Mullin, 'Don't Cry for Me, Argentina: "Eveline" and the Seductions of Emigration Propaganda', in Semicolonial Joyce, ed. D. Attridge and M. Howes (Cambridge: Cambridge University Press, 2000), pp.172–200.

6. See K. Mullin, James Joyce, Sexuality and Social Purity (Cambridge: Cambridge University Press, 2003), pp.83–115.

7. In the 'Nausicaa' episode later in the novel, Bloom recovers from his masturbatory encounter with Gerty MacDowell with the remark, 'Damned glad I didn't do it in the bath this morning over her silly I will punish you letter' (13.785–6).

8. A. Briggs, 'Roll Away the Reel World, the Reel World: Circe and Cinema', in Coping With Joyce: Essays from the Copenhagen Symposium, ed. M. Beja and S. Benstock (Columbus, OH: Ohio State University Press, 1989), pp.149–56. For the role of animation in 'Circe', see K. Williams, 'Ulysses in Toontown: Vision Animated to Bursting Point in Joyce's "Circe"', in Literature and Visual Technologies, ed. J. Murphet and L. Rainford (Basingstoke: Palgrave, 2003), pp.96–112.

9. For an account of the critical reception of the chapter, and a fascinating problematization of the centrality of the 'flow' metaphor in readings of 'Penelope', see D. Attridge, 'Molly's Flow: the Writing of "Penelope" and the Question of Women's Language', Joyce Effects: On Language, Theory and History (Cambridge: Cambridge University Press, 2000), pp.91–116.

10. V. Woolf, entry for 16 August 1922, in A. Bell and A. McNeillie (eds), The Diary of Virginia Woolf, Volume 2: 1920–1924 (London: Hogarth Press, 1978), pp.188–9.

11. C. MacCabe's introduction to the recent 'Low Modernism' issue of Critical Quarterly, 46, 4 (2004), p.ii, edited by Rachel Potter and David Trotter, notes how Joyce is 'the most constant point of reference' in the essays which follow.

CHAPTER TEN

Joyce's Afterlives: Why Didn't He Win the Nobel Prize?

AARON JAFFE

Let's begin with the short answer: James Joyce didn't win the Nobel prize, because he was dead when it was most likely to be awarded to him. He was never formally proposed for the prize[1] and it was not until the mid-1940s that the Academy felt disposed enough to innovators of transatlantic modernism to arrive at an interpretation of Nobel's legacy favourable to the post-Joycean age: beginning in 1946 with Hesse, then Gide, then Eliot, then Faulkner, and ending with Beckett in 1969, the latest of late modernists (the period of laureates which Kjell Espmark designates as the dawn of 'new competence for the difficult mission'[2]). Had Joyce survived his perforated ulcer and the war, he would have surely made the trip to Stockholm once in those twenty-three years.[3] As it is, the oversights include the likes of Zola, Ibsen, Twain, Tolstoy, James, Hardy, Conrad, Proust, Fitzgerald, Woolf, Stein, Dreiser, Cather, Brecht, Auden, Bowen, Nabokov, Borges, Calvino and other writers of the Nobel era who had obtained some degree of cosmopolitan exposure and prestige before their deaths. Joyce may be this category's most glaring omission. One reason to assert this is the frequency with which Joyce's name and its all-too-remarked-upon omission punctuates Nobel ceremonies, beginning with Sinclair Lewis in 1930 and climaxing with Eliot in 1948. The name of Joyce endures, hanging uncannily above an empty stage in 1969, with Beckett hiding from the 'catastrophe' in Africa.[4] It greets Soyinka importunely, arriving as the first African laureate in 1986 to be told his work traces a 'great European' tradition instantiated by James Joyce.[5] Over and again, Joyce's afterlife is his good name serving the present as a durable literary standard, a touchstone for probing the preciousness and confirming the value of the coin of the realm of world literature.

What would the Nobel medallion have done for Joyce? A question like this leads to the tantalizing, if wholly fantastic, enterprise of alternate history. Imagine Nobel-augmented fame and fortune (40,000 in non-inflation adjusted dollars in 1923) helping Joyce bypass the lunacies of patronage and coterie culture, or, more equivocally perhaps, mutating his 'industrial evolution', in Fritz Senn's phrase, under the more permissive watch of his initial literary executors.[6] The hypothetical literary output of a later, last Joycean phase may be anyone's guess, but one item in this expanded Joycean universe seems certain: a speech on that cosmopolitan platform in Stockholm. What would have been said? Consider a flamboyant refusal, an inspired *non serviam* born of new taste for apricot cocktails and postwar discussions in Café Les Deux Maggots.

Maybe it is best, after all, to leave it at just that the missing Nobel represents a principle of *more Joyce*. Of all the constraints implied by Nobel's will – a death drive, to be sure – it's this single cardinal principle, transformed by years of practice and precedent into the solid institutional bedrock, that remains at once the most obvious and most arbitrary rule of the game: the Nobel follows a principle of life. The prize is at all costs to be awarded in the presence of the living author's body (if need be, with Harold Pinter, by video hook-up) not the posthumous corpus.[7] Yet paradoxically, because the prize deigns to honour the entire body of work – as if it were complete, as if the contribution had been registered in full – there remains to these ceremonies a distinct echo of the genres of obituary and last rites.

Also afoot is something we could call the sportscaster effect: the award-givers, we have been assured, are apprized of all world-class contests, the import of all feats and records for the 'history books', and so on. The illusion of absolute spectator competence is essential to the spectacle. As James English points out in his superb study of the contemporary phenomenon of cultural prizes, the practice of awarding prizes in literature in the arts is twinned with the rise of competitive sports culture as a global vernacular.[8] Fittingly, the Olympic movement begins in 1896, the same year as Nobel's bequest (and incidentally four years before the initial running of Gordon Bennett Cup, the sporting event which comes to Ireland in 1903 and which gives Joyce his subject matter in his story 'After the Race'). One thinks of the now ubiquitous *Ulysses* marathon readings on Bloomsday.[9] Prize winning – and competition more generally – provides a simplified accounting ledger for locally recorded value elements (winners and losers, merits and demerits, credits anddebits) to go global.

How and why did the name of Joyce, the great Nobel omission, come to serve as a leading synecdoche for the kind of world-class literary value as enshrined *par excellence* in the Nobel mission? Some answers can be found sifting the Joycean biographical and bibliographical record for leads about how Joyce felt about literary prizes and their role in presenting the names of author-genius as rightful claimant to cosmopolitan, trans-local value. Here, *Stephen Hero* is an invaluable resource, because it contains the organizing matrix of the Joycean *career*. Other answers require a broader consideration of the form, function and ideological substrate of the Nobel prize. This chapter will examine both fields, reading early scenes of Joyce's prize consciousness side-by-side with a survey of presentations, addresses and other materials from the Nobel archive.

In so many words, English's point is that prizes help to consolidate and to expand the cultural authority of the administrative subject (my phrase, not English's) in the twentieth century: mobilizing 'the whole middle-zone of cultural space, a space crowded not just with artists and consumers but bureaucrats, functionaries, patrons, and administrators of culture, vigorously producing and deploying such instruments as the best-of list, the film festival, the artists' convention, the book club, the piano competition'.[10] This zone, he observes, is a critical site of 'capital intraconversion', 'negotiating transactions between cultural and economic, cultural and social, or cultural and political capital'.[11] To examine the middle ground of a cultural condition occupied by the functionaries, luminaries, brokers, journalists and business operatives of culture, English steps back from literary authors and texts. Instead, he proposes a procedure of mid-range critical practices which effectively makes literary artefacts indistinguishable from their producers. This indistinctness is itself symptomatic of authorial self-fashioning *in extremis* and the maturity of

the historical controversy about authorship made famous by post-structuralism – that is, the redefinition of authorship as a mode of public
celebrity and celerity, from which prize culture first emerges.[12] For this
reason, the international sport of prizewinning depends on the constitutively omitted proper name of authorship, a matter which English, for
all his emphasis on literary prize culture, does not consider.

Understanding the connections between prizewinning in Joyce's
work, the omission of Joyce's name, and its durable prestige and cosmopolitan value has much to do with the problem of achieving critical
distance in times when the question of the literary is receding into pos-
terity. The question itself, as Gregg Lambert puts it, 'privileges the incre-
mental movement of hands across the pages of a printed book':

> The slowness of the preferred medium (the book, the text, the
> long and plodding duration of reading and re-reading, the metic-
> ulously careful argument, the uncertainty of all conclusion, the
> anxious citation of references, etc.) also express the privilege of a
> type of publicity that must be distinct from the speed, brevity,
> imprecision, of public media, and newspapers in particular.[13]

What remains perplexing is the continuing meaning and power of the
literary proper name in times when it sounds most tendentious – like a
distant, half-forgotten incantation. One senses an untimely emergence as
Joyce's name becomes the ubiquitous synecdoche for 'the greatest literary
genius of the age', which Morton Levitt puts this way: 'at a time when
many teachers of English fear growing illiteracy among our students,
James Joyce has become a cult figure of sorts'.[14] If not illiteracy exactly,
then a palpable indifference to the literary resides in our mass-mediated
cultures, for which Joyce nevertheless has come to stand shoulder to
shoulder with Shakespeare as literary ultimate, ultimatum and non plus
ultra.

The career of Joycean value stretches from 'Day of the Rabblement'
to Finnegans Wake, from Dublin ambitions to Zurich moulderings, from
the Anna Livia Departure Lounge to his citation as trivia initiation rite in
Martin Scorsese's The Departed. It is, furthermore, marked by the same
epochal structure of feeling about the literary – the literary as a cosmopolitan name for transcending located forms of necessity – that also led

Nobel to endow the prize. This chapter traces this complex trajectory; it is less interested in the sense of Joyce as an aggrieved party before the world court of literature than it is in the way the category of the great omission haunts the framework of prizewinning, by tracing the drift of Joyce's name in a post-literary social system.

PHYSICISTS

At a recent family gathering, I mentioned the question to my uncle: why didn't Joyce win the Nobel Prize for Literature? My uncle happens to be a physicist and suggested a better question: why not for physics?

Joyce winning the Nobel Prize for Physics is less far-fetched than it sounds. Theoretical physicists are well aware of Joyce's decisive role in this second esoteric domain of twentieth-century intellectual endeavour since he is implicated in the coinage of the term quark. First hypothesized and named in the mid-1960s by Murray Gell-Mann, the 1969 Nobel-laureate in physics, the quark is an elementary, subatomic particle, smaller than an electron, discoverable only by atom smashing. There are supposedly six 'flavours' of them, each coming with idiosyncratic electric charges of $+2/3$ or $-1/3$, so, in a way, quarks come in thirds; the line in Finnegans Wake mentions 'three quarks for muster mark'. Gell-Mann confirmed his literary debt in a 1978 letter to the editors of the OED.[15] What makes this coinage apt is its impossible feat of erudition: a triumphal bit of intellectual showmanship to give a hand in naming what turns out to be the most elemental of things to the epitome of lexical plenitude, the prolix Penman.[16]

The Joyce allusion has not escaped the notice of the Royal Swedish Academy of Sciences, the body which awards the Physics prize. In 1990, when awarding the prize to Jerome I. Friedman, Henry W. Kendall and Richard E. Taylor for taking us 'to the land of deep inelastic scattering where the colourful quarks and gluon first revealed themselves', Swedish academician Cecilia Jarlskog could not fail to mention that the word quark is borrowed from Wake, 'for most of us an incomprehensible masterpiece by the great Irish novelist James Joyce'.[17] 'Incomprehensible masterpiece' is a telling phrase in this context. Whereas comprehension apparently has little to do with greatness in literature, in physics, the 'most important tasks of [which] is to provide us with a clearer picture of the world we live in', being comprehendible is apparently another story, even if it does not preclude the occasional poetic flourish or erudite allusion.

According to my uncle, there is little controversy in physics about prizes – not as much as in literature, at any rate – because in this domain, there is a sense that every great contribution would be discovered by someone else in a few years. For every innovation or discovery worthy of an award, the names of many people whose work was essential to the effort do not accrue celebrity status. 'In literature the situation seems different', he wrote me, 'if Joyce had never lived I doubt anyone would have generated a comparable work of art. So individual achievement seems more singular.'[18] Another way of saying this is that in literature, genius matters institutionally – it matters to the institution of literature, because, unlike the other Nobel domains, the sovereignty of the name constitutes the institution of literature as such.

Proposing Joyce for a Nobel in Physics sounds somewhat akin to the lore about Albert Einstein endorsing Freud for a Nobel, but only if it were in literature not experimental medicine. One gets the sense that pushing Freud to the literature committee amounts to a disciplinary league relegation rather than a testimonial that he may be moving the literary arts in an 'ideal' direction – using the keyword of Nobel's.[19] What's remarkable here is the suggestion that Einstein's grey matter is so computationally extraordinary, it is equipped to propose nominations in all the Nobel fields. Roland Barthes says this about Einstein's brain as a 'mythical object':

> A photograph of Einstein shows him lying down, his head bristling with electric wires: the waves of his brain are being recorded, while he is requested to 'think of relativity' ... What this is meant to convey is probably that the seismograms will be all the more violent since 'relativity' is an arduous subject ... The mythology of Einstein shows him as a genius so lacking in magic that one speaks of this thought as of a functional labour analogous to the mechanical making of sausages, the grinding of corn or the crushing of ore: he used to produce thought, continuously, as a mill makes flour, and death was above all, for him, the cessation of a localized function: 'the most powerful brain of all has stopped thinking'.[20]

The closest analogue modernism has to this, as I have argued else-where, is Monroe reading *Ulysses*.[21] Rather than photographs of Einstein thinking, standing at the blackboard covered with complex equations (or, in the cartoons, 'chalk still in hand ... having written on an empty blackboard, as if without preparation, the magic formula of the world'), we get photographs of Marilyn struggling to puzzle Joyce's imprimatur out of 'Penelope'. The mytheme signifies the struggle of celebrity to auger 'Joyce' from his words, celluloid playing in the house of leaves. Like Einstein's brain, it is not finally a sign of heroism as invention – to be begun, finished, imitated and followed – but a more schematic and opaque enigma to be squinted at, like Nietzsche's abyss. If you could figure out a node to which to apply the electroencephalograph, what you would be measuring would be that void, the omission, the after-image *par excellence* of élite authorial value in an age of celebrity.

IDEALISTS

In 'The Art of Fiction', Henry James notes that too many popular novels end in too few ways: the overly predicable 'distribution at the last of prizes, pensions, husbands, wives, babies, millions, appended para-graphs, and cheerful remarks'.[22] James expands this point with a telling culinary metaphor: '[t]he ending of a novel is, for many persons, like that of a good dinner, a course of dessert and ices, and the artist in fic-tion is regarded as a sort of meddlesome doctor who forbids agreeable aftertastes'.[23] For authors themselves, however, the serving of desserts often comes at the beginning of the meal not the end. For the would-be doctors of fiction, the prize does not serve as symbolic money, some kind of accounts paid for work rendered or commodities exchanged. Instead, it functions as a talismanic rare-bit that inaugurates the rarified literary life in the first place, the insertion of the author's name in, what English calls, 'the economy of prestige'.[24] The prize comes first, followed by whatever attentions to the imprimatur this event occasions.

Prizewinning on a more modest scale plays a decisive role in Joyce's beginnings. With its inventory of scholastic prizes won, early publica-tions scored and assorted wampum garnered from prominent names in the literary establishment (Russell, Yeats, Lady Gregory, Archer, Ibsen,

Symonds), the prime mover of this phase seems to be the trophy cabinet, as it enlarges before expanding publics: from Clongowes Wood and Belvedere to University College and the postgraduate Dublin scene. In interpretive terms, the period serves not as a time of prefatory Bildung for subsequent successes but rather enacts a rehearsal in microcosm of the entire scope of the world-system of his reputation. If, as Jonathan Goldman writes, it seems 'as if James Joyce has always been a celebrity author', it may have something to do with the genetic terms Joyce himself supplies for the making of one's name.[25] 'There was a special class for English composition', he writes in Stephen Hero, 'and it was in this class that Stephen first made his name' (SH, 30). In Our Friend James Joyce, for example, Padraic Colum notes, as if on cue, that when he first met Joyce in 1901 or early 1902, he was 'already something of a celebrity', having made a name for himself with pamphlets and publications around Dublin.[26]

Whatever might be said against Richard Ellmann's governing contention that interpreting Joyce is essentially an exercise in biographical decoding – that his family 'relations appear in his books under thin disguises' – prizewinning is not the counter-argument.[27] It supplies solid bridgework between the biographical and literary domains, ready-made for Joyceans of all stripes to cross and re-cross. And, bracketing the ideologies of genius and prestige as expressive causes, it makes sense to read this dynamic not as the imposition of an intrusive biography on the literary texts, but as a secondary creation of the author himself. In other words, it is authored by Joyce, who stakes so much on the terms of prizewinning and privation that structure Portrait and Stephen Hero.

Rather than the stuff of standard chronological narrative, this logic provides a simplified schematics, a calculus of merit and demerit, for adding or subtracting distinction to the authorial name: attendance, examination, encomium, and local celebrity, on the one hand, and absence, transgression, punishment and local notoriety, on the other. At root, the defining feature of these transactional elements rest in their predisposition to accounting in the durable archives of primary, secondary, tertiary educational institutions, the legendary 'permanent record', which serves biographers as a choice archival destination, once they have sifted the primary materials and interviewed the living informants. Not surprisingly, then, there is an undercurrent of double-entry booking-keeping in much of the early events in the Ellmann biography. This undercurrent extends to an actual ledger Ellmann adds to the mystical storehouse of Joycean schoolboy paraphernalia, to be paired, perhaps, with the great celestial cash register of *Portrait*: when 'he lent [prize] money generously and imprudently to brothers, sisters, and parents, he entered the sums carefully in an account book'.[28] The idea of Joyce's account book (and his 'meticulous', if sometimes preposterous efforts to balance it) provides a counterpoint to the red ink – bills, debts, mortgages, rents in arrears – that trails the name of his lay-about father, John Joyce. The father forswears honouring his debts to shopkeepers; the son pays out his IOUs in honourable mentions in his literary works, jiggering the accounts of the symbolic order in Dantescan fashion. The difference between father and son lies in the axiological register the son keeps, where merits and demerits are recorded and tallied.[29]

Against the factors which may subtract from his total reputation (the increasing impoverishment of Joyce's family and Ellmann's portrait of the artist as young freeloader), is a counter-current of prizewinning. Joyce in fact won multiple prizes in his school years, and because they were dispensed over multiple years, he drew prize-funds continuously.[30] In 1897 and 1898 he won the best composition for his grade in the whole of Ireland. Referring to the 1894 winnings, Ellmann writes:

> The money was paid by the government to John Joyce, who turned it over to his son to spend as he liked … James had no difficulty, even at the age of twelve, in falling in with his father's ideal of light-hearted improvidence … He took his father and mother to theaters and restaurants, sparing no expense. The family tasted again the luxuries it could no longer afford, and did so thereafter every year that James won an exhibition. He thereby attained a sense of his own generosity so pervasive that, when asked to contribute to the family's support a few years later, he replied self-righteously, 'I have done enough'.[31]

Behind this seemingly reckless spending is not so much profligate lassitude as an insistence that the prize belongs in the realm of the jubilee and, as such, remains outside the usual necessities of domestic economy. Joyce's response in Paris in 1903 to a rejection from George Russell speaks to this logic:

> So help me devil I will write only the things that approve them-
> selves to me and I will write only what I can. It is the same way
> with boots. O, I have reveled in ties, coats, boots, hats since I came
> here – all imaginary! So damn Russell, damn Yeats, damn
> Skeffington, damn Darlington, damn editors, damn freethinkers,
> damn vegetable verse and double damn vegetable philosophy.[32]

There is a bit of Huck Finn's 'All right, then, I'll go to hell' in this vow. More to the point, it echoes the audacious valediction at the end of *Portrait*, Stephen's determination 'to forge in the smithy of [his] soul the uncreated conscience of [his] race' (P, 276).

Yet, this rejection of the literary establishment is leveraged on a veritable cargo cult of things such as ties, coats, boots and hats. *Portrait's* pulp idealism remains – superhuman artistic consciousness overleaping the nets of language, nationality and religion in a single bound – but here the idealism is fully consonant with the workings of commodity fetishism. In effect, what is taking shape in imaginary form in the smithy of young Joyce's soul and circulating alongside the boots – evolving out of its leathery brain grotesque ideas, far more wonderful than shoe-making – is his own literary name. Proper literary names understood adjectivally – as imprimaturs, as authenticating, ontologizing restatements of an imagined synecdocal link between the formal work of the text and the mental state of the author – work a lot like Marx's commodities. The circulation of names as rarified, fungible elements in economies of pres-tige lets Joyce and other aspirants to modernist value, as I have argued elsewhere, plot 'a phantasmal escape through the imagined hazards of the literary present into transhistorical economies of valuation'.[33] Joyce's case also makes clear that this escape is not just a flight from the night-mares of history but also an exit from the accidents of the local – the uneven developments of a submodernity exemplified in the 'semi-colonial' (to use the current term of art in Joyce Studies) 'backwash', among 'the most belated race in Europe', as Joyce remarks in this period (CW, 70–1). The imprimatur is Joyce's ticket-of-leave to a modernity envisioned 'out in Europe' (SH, 36), the transnational cosmopolis, which, as Pascale Casanova has it, has as much to do with picking winners on the literary world stock-exchange as it does electing representatives to the world republic of letters.[34] Neither Eveline, nor Jimmy Doyle, nor James Duffy makes it out, because, in so many words, each loses this game.

Joyce's Parisian comment is decidedly archaic, with its apostrophe, its invocation of talismanic fancy goods made in the city, and its maledictions against existing literary names and cultural preoccupations. It reads, in sum, like a supernatural incantation, a seriocomic effort to conjure up authentic 'goods' from inauthentic 'bads'. And, for Joyce, the Irish literary marketplace is a marketplace of 'bads' that jeopardize his aspirations to play the cultural capital name game.[35] This is not understood in terms of the editors and agents, but ordinary readership and mass-audience structures. In 'The Day of the Rabblement', the pamphlet Joyce published in 1901 against philistinism and the Dublin literary establishment, he uses a cognate of fetish ('the contagion of its fetichism and deliberate self-deception') to the discredit of the audiences of the Irish Literary Theatre (CW, 71). Fetishism here means something like faddism. The troll-like rabblement is decidedly subhuman (or, maybe just pre-pubescent) in its herd-like conformity as well as its bestial affect: 'placid and intensely moral, [it] is enthroned in boxes and galleries amid a hum of approval − la bestia Trionfante − and those who think that Echegaray is "morbid", and titter coyly when Mélisande lets down her hair, are not sure but they are the trustees of every intellectual and poetic treasure' (CW, 70). Although Joyce's discontent was largely motivated by the gaudy artifice of the Celtic revival, significantly this is not mentioned anywhere in this particular essay. The real intellectual and poetic treasure, the proverbial pearls before the swine, come from future Nobel laureate dramatists from out in Europe, the Spaniard Echegaray (1904) and the Belgian Maeterlinck (1911), later joined, in the essay and in Nobel laurels alike, by the Norwegian Bjørnson (1903) the German Hauptmann (1912) and, of course, the Irishman Yeats (1923).

Bracketing the familiar élitism Joyce's essay exhibits, let's examine its stakes in what Joyce himself calls here and elsewhere 'artistic economy'. Curiously, he understands the national literary marketplace solely and perhaps definitively as a source of 'debased value': 'No man, said the

Nolan, can be a lover of the true or the good unless he abhors the multitude; and the artist, though he may employ the crowd, is very careful to isolate himself' (CW, 69). He calls this a 'radical principle of artistic economy', but it is strange economy indeed, since it seems to offer no quarter for exchange. Joyce's thinking is later developed, among other places, in Stephen's 'theories' of *Stephen Hero*, indexed to the *Rabblement* pamphlet by a shared thematic preoccupation with 'isolation [as] the first principle of artistic economy', a citation repeated in both texts:

> Stephen laid down his doctrine very positively and insisted on the importance of what he called the literary tradition. Words, he said, have a certain value in the literary tradition and a certain value in the marketplace – a debased value. Words are simply receptacles for human thought: in the literary tradition they receive more valuable thoughts than they receive in the marketplace. Father Butt listened to all this, rubbing his chalky hand often over his chin and nodding his head and said that Stephen evidently understood the importance of tradition. Stephen quoted a phrase from Newman to illustrate his theory.
>
> – In that sentence of Newman's, he said, the word is used according to the literary tradition: it has there its full value. In ordinary use, that is, in the market-place, it has a different value altogether, a debased value. 'I hope I'm not detaining you'.
>
> – Not at all, not at all!.
>
> – No, no …
>
> –Yes, yes, Mr Daedalus, I see … I quite see your point … detain … (SH, 30–1)

Here – in the encounter that later becomes the famous 'tundish' scene in *Portrait* – we are presented with two systems of value. The concern here is that Stephen gives words a particular cast as commodities and, what's more, figures them as names in a vocabulary of value. In the marketplace, words are not so much starved of value as they are debased by over-use, whereas in the literary tradition, they are aesthetically available, materials to be charged and recharged with jubilescent, surplus meaning.

By the time this exchange finds its way into *Portrait*, Joyce seems to have resolved some of the category confusion between semiotic and economic systems. Stephen's literary economic 'theories' are no longer being sounded but engaged in an 'esthetic discussion' (in fact, the word 'economy' is not mentioned once in the whole of Portrait). For comparison's sake, here is the scene from Portrait:

> One difficulty, said Stephen, in esthetic discussion is to know whether words are being used according to the literary tradition or according to the tradition of the marketplace. I remember a sentence of Newman's in which he says of the Blessed Virgin that she was detained in the full company of the saints. The use of the word in the marketplace is quite different. I hope I am not detaining you.
> – Not in the least, said the dean politely.
> – No, no, said Stephen, smiling, I mean …
> – Yes, yes; I see, said the dean quickly, I quite catch the point: detain. (P, 203)

In Portrait, the dean misses the point of a word and the word is named: detain (which incidentally means the dean is missing one of the principle innovations of Joyce's method, the turn to free, indirect discourse). In Stephen Hero, this missed point itself is missing; the word literary tradition charges with a surfeit of value – 'detain' – is never named. Indeed, in Stephen Hero, it seems more the case that the literary name itself – Newman – carries the weight of the point of Portrait about exemplary words. The proper name itself holds the literary tradition and demonstrates the pressing fact that Stephen's discussant – in this case, Father Butt – is oblivious to the point (as is the debased local, literary marketplace, the point of the Rabblement essay). That the actual reference from Newman – pace Stephen, the greatest writer of prose, or so he says in Portrait – is omitted demonstrates how the name falls on an undiscerning auditor, whose gesticulations ('rubbing his chalky hand often over his chin and nodding his head') can't help but recall the vacuous rabblement of the Irish Literary Theatre. Tundish isn't the word Stephen came to discuss ('[t]he question you asked me a moment ago seems to me more interesting'), and neither did he intend to discuss tradition per se but the differences in value between 'full' and 'ordinary' attention to names. Stephen's discourse in Stephen Hero adds this to more poignant presentation in Portrait: the point is not that names are like words but that *he treats ordinary words as if they were names*.

Newman is but one in a long line of 'hierarchs of initiation [who] cast their spells upon him', in the language of Joyce's original 'Portrait' essay.[36] From Bruno to Ibsen, these names fall on the ears of others in Joyce's writings like so many 'lump[s] of the ordinary' / 'lumps of earth' (P, 205). Again and again, his family, colleagues and, most importantly, his teachers and professors lose the game, by failing to the recognize the auratic names that fill out the lists of cosmopolitan literary tradition. The test is, perhaps, put unequivocally a few pages after the Newman encounter in *Stephen Hero*:

> Yes, yes, said Father Butt one day ... I quite see your point ... It would apply of course to the drama of Turgénieff?
>
> Stephen had read and admired certain translations of Turgénieff's novels and stories and he asked therefore with a genuine note in his voice:
>
> – Do you mean his novels?
>
> – Novels, yes, said Father Butt swiftly ... his novels, to be sure ... but of course they are dramas ... are they not, Mr Daedalus? (SH, 42–3)

This exchange shows Father Butt trying to bluff an understanding of the Russian master and exposing himself as unequal to Stephen. There are many such quiz-show moments scattered throughout Joyce's writing. 'The Day of the Rabblement', one of Joyce's earliest writings, begins with the riddle of 'the Nolan' (it's Bruno!) and ends with the three tantalizingly unnamed authors representing the triumvirate of the living literary tradition: (1.) the one dying in Christiana, that is, Ibsen; (2.) the author of *Michael Kramer*, Hauptmann; and (3.) the one whose 'hour may be standing by the door', who can be no one other than Joyce himself (CW, 72). The point of these schematic value structures is twofold: they foreground the incompetence of the local audience in contests of world literature, and they give the perquisite of the ultimate prize to Stephen/Joyce.

PACIFISTS

In a letter of 21 September 1920, in reference to the publication of *Ulysses*, Joyce facetiously proposes himself for a Nobel peace prize. Here is the translation of the letter originally written in Italian: 'a great movement is being prepared against the publication on behalf of puritans, English imperialists, Irish republicans and Catholics – what an alliance! Golly, I deserve the Nobel peace prize' (SL, 271). However tongue-in-cheek, Joyce does register the spirit of the award, the idea that it is given for work on a common cosmopolitan cause, 'the greatest benefit on mankind', even if the common cause is the suppression of Joyce's writings. A decisive factor in the dissemination of Joyce's name as transnational literary capital is the banning of his works in Anglophone nations: 'THE SCANDAL OF ULYSSES', as reported, for instance, interspersed with the racing results, by the *London Sporting Times*.[37] In effect, Joyce's name becomes international currency because it is contraband in so many national contexts while legal in places where English is not the primary tongue.

In terms of the Nobel prize, Sinclair Lewis, the first American laureate in 1930, serves as one of the earliest messengers of these controversies of omission. No mere banquet address, his Nobel lecture 'The American Fear of Literature', reports on the burden of reporting on the current state of American letters ('certain trends, certain dangers, and certain high and exciting promises in present-day American literature').[38] After a Menckenian excursus into various shades of the national boobocracy ('[d]uring the football season, a capable player ranks very nearly with our greatest and most admired heroes – even with Henry Ford, President Hoover, and Colonel Lindbergh'), and with an eye on the Nobel idealism clause (assurances that his 'most anarchistic assertion has been that America, with all her wealth and power, has not yet produced a civilization good enough to satisfy the deepest wants of human creatures'), he delivers a speech that measures his candidacy against his unsuccessful American competitors. Reviewing a roll-call of more thirty worthies from Wharton to Hemingway ('a bitter youth, educated by the most intense experience, disciplined by his own high standards, an authentic artist whose home is in the whole of life'), the pre-eminent oversight turns out to be Theodore Dreiser.[39] The imagined Nobel to Dreiser –

Lewis describes it as his 'fantasy' – ultimately amounts to a perverse wish to have a winner who would elicit more outrage than Lewis from the insular provinces of the American scene. Most telling for our purposes, however, is a strange, final incantation of the tantalizingly unnamed coming generation, the missing American expatriate modernists standing by the door, as it were, all organized by their fidelity to a certain Irishman: 'a dozen other young poets and fictioneers, most of them living now in Paris, most of them a little insane in the tradition of James Joyce, who, however insane they may be, have refused to be genteel and traditional and dull'.[40] Is Joyce's name wanting – has his hour not already come – if so much of Sinclair's script seems to be one Joyce approved in 1900?

When T.S. Eliot takes the stage in Stockholm in 1948, eighteen years after Lewis's Nobel – and only six years after Joyce's death – it is clear, however belatedly, that the hour of Joyce has finally arrived. In the presentation speech, Anders Österling cites Joyce for special commendation:

> [I]t may be recalled that ['The Waste Land'] appeared in the same year as another pioneer work, which had a still more sensational effect on modern literature, the much discussed Ulysses, from the hand of an Irishman, James Joyce. The parallel is by no means fortuitous, for these products of the nineteen-twenties are closely akin to one another, in both spirit and mode of composition.[41]

Österling's word 'pioneer' has been taken by Kjell Espmark from this speech as the headword for the entire period of Österling's leadership.[42] This comment is remarkable for its violation of the Nobel rule book. First, it claims to redress unheralded, but hardly unnoticed, work of the 1920s, somewhat undermining the legitimacy of the previous selections. Second, it cannot help suggesting Joyce's primacy of sorts over the purported winner: Joyce's work has 'a still more sensational effect on modern literature' than Eliot's. In this way, consonant with the modernist project more generally, the prize now enshrines a mode of distinction more like the one associated with the science prizes: innovation, discovery and improvement.

For his part, in accepting what he calls 'the highest international honour … bestowed upon a man of letters', Eliot does not mention Joyce. Instead, he provides an interesting 'interpretation of the significance' of the award:

> If this were simply the recognition of merit, or of the fact that an author's reputation has passed the boundaries of his own country and his own language, we could say that hardly any one of us at any time is, more than others, worthy of being so distinguished. But I find in the Nobel Award something more and something different from such recognition. It seems to me more the election of an individual, chosen from time to time from one nation or another, and selected by something like an act of grace, to fill a peculiar role and to become a peculiar symbol. A ceremony takes place, by which a man is suddenly endowed with some function which he did not fill before. So the question is not whether he was worthy to be so singled out, but whether he can perform the function which you have assigned to him: the function of serving as a representative, so far as any man can be, of something of far greater importance than the value of what he himself has written.[43]

It would be fruitful to compare Eliot's remarks from his Nobel address with the influential model of reputation he elsewhere delineates, from its echoes of 'Tradition in the Individual Talent' (1919) to the late iteration in 'Notes on the Definition of Culture' (1948) of the same moment as the address. Suffice it here to note the idealist causality by which reputations are not at all achieved through publicity, authorial agency, or even merit but idealist, quasi-religious sanctification. The prizewinner becomes representative of exemplary representativeness across, in the words of Eliot's late summa, 'the frontiers of culture [which] are not, and should not be closed'.[44] Despite the changes in the selection ideologies of the Swedish Academy so well charted in Espmark's book, it is almost inevitable that by its sheer historical weight the prize takes on, for Eliot, the character of 'existing monuments form[ing] an ideal order among themselves'.[45]

There has been much written about the infelicity of Nobel's specific charge to the Swedish Academy. Espmark writes, for instance, that '[t]he history of the literature prize is in some ways a series of attempts to interpret an imprecisely worded will'. The offending words are 'the most outstanding work in an ideal direction'.[46] More specifically, there are two words at issue, idealist and idealistic. Espmark and others have suggested that the latter sense of humane optimism defined the first three decades of the Literature prizes, and was, in fact, very much what the former Nobel had in mind: 'When [Nobel] spoke ... of an "idealistic tendency" he undoubtedly gave more scope to rebellious and independent dispositions than his interpreters understood'.[47] Whether or not Nobel sought to enshrine 'a polemical or critical attitude to Religion, Royalty, Marriage, [and] Social Order generally', as one of his confidants maintained, his wording became a mandate for assessing nominations based on a perceived eligibility for the spiritual elector of the lettered world.[48]

Recent appearances of Joyce's name at Nobel ceremonies have assumed a geopolitical cast that is less austere, more down-and-dirty, yet equally 'ideal' in the Kantian sense. Beginning with Nadine Gordimer (1991) and, even more poignantly, with Gao Xingjian (2000), 'Joyce' appears to shore up the idea of the winner as an exile from the nation-state. In a related vein, Joyce's name has been used to signify a locally situated cosmopolitanism, transcending national frontiers. Derek Walcott (1992), for example, invokes 'Joyce' to describe his native Port of Spain as 'a city ideal in its commercial and human proportions, where a citizen is a walker and not a pedestrian': 'Its docks, not obscured by smoke or deafened by too much machinery, and above all, it would be so racially various that the cultures of the world – the Asiatic, the Mediterranean, the European, the African – would be represented in it, its humane variety more exciting than Joyce's Dublin'.[49] A similar point is made in the most recent presentation speech to Orhan Pamuk regarding Istanbul (2006): 'You have made your native city an indispensable literary territory, equal to Dostoyevsky's St Petersburg, Joyce's Dublin or Proust's Paris – a place where readers from all corners of the world can live another life, just as credible as their own, filled by an alien feeling that they immediately recognise as their own.'[50] Joyce's Dublin both precedes Walcott's Port of Spain as the ideal semi-colonial agora, locally situated and thus exemplary of human situatedness, and it promises, like Pamuk's Istanbul, an imaginative refuge for strangers in a city-state on the world literary atlas. In effect, 'Joyce' again becomes a name for value intra-conversion between various localized city spaces and an imaginary cosmopolitics.

That the Nobel has come to this desideratum – warding off nationalism from the literary – is far from self-evident. The Swedish Academy is, after all, an institution similar in providence to other national entities modelled on the Académie française. 'An independent cultural institution, founded in 1786 by King Gustav III in order to advance the Swedish language and Swedish literature', reads the institutional self-description.[51] Independent in this case means that the institution does not have a duty to serve a particular political constituency. Since the Academy's founding, its charge has been above all else linguistic corpus maintenance in all its forms – spelling reform, commissioning of dictionaries and reference works, and the awarding of prizes for Swedish letters – all of which are wrapped up in the ideological projects of the age of nation-states. Initially, presented with the mission conferred by Nobel's will, some members of the Academy resisted because they feared it would transform their institution into 'a cosmopolitan tribunal of literature'. And, indeed, it did.

In practice, for all Nobel's cosmopolitanism, a principle of national turn-taking prevails. Ironically, it is nationality, as opposed to shared language, that becomes a critical consideration for an award explicitly created to overcome national difference in literary achievement ('the most worthy shall receive the prize, whether he is Scandinavian or not'). Here a further tension emerges between the national-political and the national-linguistic dimensions of the prize. With the particularities of its political emergence – irredentist secession at the end of the First World War – Ireland presents a particularly pressing case for the Nobel cause; it represents one of the exceptions to hegemonic triumphalism of literary Great Powers. Casanova calls this the Irish paradigm:

> [t]he distinctive quality of the ... case resides in the fact that over a short period a literary space emerged and a literary heritage was created in an exemplary way. In a space of a few decades the Irish literary world traversed all the stages (and the states) of rupture with the literature of the center, providing a model of the aesthetic, formal, linguistic, and political possibilities contained in the outlying spaces.[52]

Figure 1. Irish Nobel prizewinners.

Ireland's status as simultaneously exceptional, peripheral and exemplary in Casanova's World Republic of Letters makes the absence of Joyce's name (and image) among the four Irish prize-winners – Yeats and Shaw, on one side, and Beckett and Heaney, on the other – all the more striking. He is missed, for instance, in a block of four commemorative stamps, issued jointly by the Swedish and Irish postal services in 2004, but not, I would suggest, forgotten.[53] Casanova figures Joyce to be the paragon of the Irish national emergence, expressing 'Irish literary autonomy', but this is the wrong formula, as Joyce is decidedly flying outside the national literary air space, as the treaties are codified. If Shaw is the great assimilationist of national-linguistics (and, Joyce, after all, congratulated him on his prize), and Yeats is the great public man of national-politics, Joyce, exiled from both national language and national politics, represents the great omission missing in the centre.

CHECKLISTS

The US newsweekly *Time*'s recent checklist of 'the All-Time 100 novels' provides a handy way to situate the no-place of 'James Joyce' within or behind or beyond or above the literary cosmopolis.[54] The checklist itself exists somewhere between young Joyce's imaginary ledger of the literary tradition and the bookie scorecard for the international literary spectator sport of the Cause Nobel. Following the precept of alphabetical levelling, the novels are not ranked, comprising a roster of all-stars rather than a hierarchy of greats. The alphabetical omission of *Ulysses* between *Under the Volcano* by Malcolm Lowry – a novel which is obviously weighed heavily upon by Joyce – and *The Watchmen*, the graphic novel by Alan Moore and Dave Gibbons, led one *Slate* reviewer to suggest that 'when they coined the term "graphic novel" nobody mentioned that the novel in question was *Ulysses*'.[55] Again, Joyce represents the great, glaring omission, the inter-zone of all anxieties of élite literary value. As with the Swedish Academy, the list compilers have some rules that belie the ideals of their enterprise. It is limited to only anglophone novels, written since 1922, and so the Joycean pay-dirt and modernism's *annum mirabilis* are excluded from the contest by a technicality. The official explanation for this constraint is limiting the field to those appearing since the newsweekly's inaugural issue, which hit the stands, dated 3 March 1923. The 'All-Time 100' are, in fact, an All-Time 100.

What's curious is the overdeterminacy of Joyce's name in a project that so explicitly tries to keep him out. Forget the ways that Joyce's influence haunts the novels selected; look at how much Joyce and *Ulysses* regulate the framing of the project:

> Welcome to the massive, anguished, exalted undertaking that is the ALL TIME 100 books list. The parameters: English language novels published anywhere in the world since 1923, the year that TIME Magazine began, which, before you ask, means that *Ulysses* (1922) doesn't make the cut ...
>
> Lists like this one have two purposes. One is to instruct. The other of course is to enrage. We're bracing ourselves for the e-mails that start out: 'You moron! You pathetic bourgeoise insect! How could you have left off ... (insert title here)'. We say *Mrs Dalloway*. You say *Mrs Bridge*. We say *Naked Lunch*. You say *Breakfast at Tiffany's*. Let's call the whole thing off? Just the opposite – bring it on. Sometimes judgment is best formed under fire. But please, no e-mails about *Ulysses*. Rules are rules.[56]

The managing editor also weighs in to justify this exclusion: 'we picked 1923 – when TIME began publishing – as our starting point. And we focused on books written in English. That's why there is no *Ulysses* (published in 1922).'[57] One gets the idea from all this that Joyce has nothing to do with Time, but this is far from true. The importance of Time to Joyce's career – he was on the cover twice – has already been profitably assessed by Maurizia Boscagli and Enda Duffy.[58] More to the point, Joyce makes an appearance in the very first issue of 3 March 1923:

> Last year there appeared a gigantic volume entitled Ulysses, by James Joyce. To the uninitiated it appeared that Mr Joyce had taken some half million assorted words – many such as are not ordinarily heard in reputable circles – shaken them up in a colossal hat, laid them end to end. To those in on the secret the result represented the greatest achievement of modern letters – a new idea in novels.[59]

Less than one hundred years later, Time could be said to have finally caught up – if Joyce weren't peremptorily disqualified. Then and now, Joyce, the exemplary case, doesn't make the cut, because he is that cut, which, in so many words, is a cut in time itself.

NOTES

1. See K. Espmark, The Nobel Prize in Literature: A Study of the Criteria Behind the Choices (Boston: G.K. Hall, 1991), p.152. Even though Joyce himself was aware of one effort to bring his name to the attention of the Swedish Academy, he reports to Stanislaus on 20 March 1922 of a resolution of the Irish Minister of Publicity, Desmond FitzGerald, 'to send [his] name to Stockholm as a candidate for the Nobel prize'. Joyce is not too keen on his chances, commenting that FitzGerald 'will probably lose his portfolio without obtaining the prize' (LIII, 61). For an interesting account of this episode, including a possible reference to 'No bells for Joyce' in Finnegans Wake, see J. FitzGerald, 'Grandad, Joyce and The Nobel Prize', in Carla de Petris (ed.), Names and Disguises: Joyce Studies in Italy 3 (Rome: Bulzoni, 1991), pp.77–84. Espmark's insider's history of the Nobel literary criteria notes explicitly that no formal proposal was ever made for Joyce.

2. K. Espmark, 'The Nobel Prize in Literature', 3 December 1999. <http://nobelprize. org/nobel_prizes/ literature/articles/espmark/index.html>.

3. When presenting the 2005 Prize in Medicine for the discovery of the pathogens behind peptic ulcer disease, the Nobel committee noted the disease's role in Joyce's mortality 'still disappointed at the poor reception of his latest novel Finnegans Wake' – S. Normark, 'Presentation Speech, Nobel Prize in Physiology or Medicine 2005', 10 December 2005. <nobelprize.org/nobel_prizes/medicine/laureates/2005/ presenta- tio-speech.html>.

4. J. Knowlson, Damned to Fame: A Life of Samuel Beckett (New York: Grove Press, 1996), pp.504–5.

5. L. Gyllensten, 'Presentation Speech, Nobel Prize in Literature 1986', 10 December 1986.

<http://nobelprize.org/nobel_prizes/literature/laureates/1986/presentation-speech.html>.

6. E. Hemingway, '"Nobelman" Yeats', in *Dateline: Toronto: The Complete 'Toronto Star' Dispatches, 1920–24* (24 November 1923), pp.384–6. F. Senn, 'The Joyce Industrial Evolution According to One European Amateur', in *Joyce and the Joyceans*, ed. M. Levitt (Syracuse, NY: Syracuse University Press, 2002). I am thinking here of the late deformities inflicted on the Joyce estate by Stephen Joyce. On the topic of the Joyce industry – and what could now, perhaps, be described as the 'Joyce industry' industry – see Levitt's book; Joseph Kelly, *Our Joyce: From Outcast to Icon* (Austin, TX: University of Texas Press, 1998); and Sean Latham (ed.), 'Post-Industrial Joyce', *James Joyce Quarterly*, 41, 1 (Fall 2003/Winter 2004).

7. Technically, the prize has been awarded posthumously only if the author dies during the award year.

8. J. English, *The Economy of Prestige: Prizes, Awards, and the Circulation of Value* (Cambridge, MA: Harvard University Press, 2005), see, in particular, pp.249–63.

9. Although it has the flavour of postmodern syncretism, I take this also to be the sense of Boston's James Joyce Ramble, 'not your average trot': 'Along the race path of this morning's 10 kilometer race beginning at 11 o'clock in Dedham Center, some 40 professional actors clad in period 19th Century costumes read from the works of the Irish bard. Accompanied by the riot of Celtic bag-pipes, the run has more the feel of a Mummers' parade than the Boston Marathon' – J. Budris, 'Runners Ramble on in Joyce's Honor', *Boston Globe*, 25 April 1999. <www.ramble.org/pressroom/coverage/index.cfm?ac=details&NewsID=94>.

10. English, *Economy of Prestige*, p.12.

11. Ibid., p.10.

12. In a related vein, Franco Moretti, also invested in synthesizing formalist and sociological procedures, has recently called for the invention of 'distant' reading, 'a specific form of knowledge', driven by 'fewer elements [of inquiry, but] a sharper sense of their overall interconnection' – F. Moretti, *Graphs, Maps, Trees: Abstract Models for a Literary History* (New York: Verso, 2005), p.1.

13. G. Lambert, *Report to the Academy* (Aurora, CO: Davies Group Publishers, 2001), p.52.

14. Levitt, 'Introduction', *Joyce and the Joyceans*, p.xi.

15. *American Heritage Dictionary of the English Language*, 4th edn (New York: Harper Collins, 2000), <www.bartleby.com/61/67/Q0016700.html>. See also H. Kendall, 'Deep Inelastic Scattering: Experiments on the Proton and the Observation of Scaling', Nobel Lecture, Nobel Prize in Physics 1990, 8 December 1990. <nobelprize.org/nobel_prizes/physics/laureates/1990/kendall-lecture.pdf#search='joyce'>.

16. 'Don't forget', my uncle cautioned me, when I pushed him on the point over e-mail, 'the quark in Scandinavia is something like dull cottage cheese'. Fresh, unripened cheese, this quark, as Joyce well knew, I'm certain, comes in more than six flavours.

17. C. Jarlskog, 'Presentation Speech, Nobel Prize in Physics 1990', 8 December 1990.

<nobelprize.org/ nobel_prizes/physics/laureates/1990/presentation-speech.html>.

18. Personal communication with Robert L. Jaffe.

19. When asked to second Freud's nomination, Einstein apparently refused. See C. Stolt, 'Why did Freud Never Receive the Nobel Prize', *International Forum of Psychoanalysis*, 10 (2001), pp.221–6.

20. R. Barthes, 'The Brain of Einstein', in *Mythologies* (New York: Hill and Wang, 1972), pp.68–70.

21. A. Jaffe, *Modernism and the Culture of Celebrity* (New York: Cambridge University Press, 2005), pp.1–3.

22. H. James, 'The Art of Fiction', in *The Art of Criticism, Henry James on the Theory and the Practice of Fiction*, ed. W. Veeder and S. Griffin (Chicago, IL: University of Chicago Press, 1986), p.168.

23. Ibid., p.169.

24. Indeed, in this sequence, we see the implications of Bourdieu's idea of an 'economic world reversed': in this cultural field, the flow of value from consumers to producers has been reversed quite literally, whereby, in effect, the whereabouts of the literary commodity itself becomes not so much an afterthought as so much fodder for game shows. The élite commodity itself trails as the last arriving message, providing a legend of economic sequence rather than a topography of high and low, a fable about the way modernist work offers itself as an exemplary, cosmopolitan replacement for the localized, biographical self. P. Bourdieu, *The Field of Cultural Production* (New York: Columbia University Press, 1993).

25. J. Goldman, 'Joyce, the Propheteer', *Novel: A Forum in Fiction*, 38, 1 (Spring 2004), pp.78–103 (p.84). Goldman's essay offers a definitive account of how *Ulysses* – particularly the 'Scylla and Charybdis' episode – engineers a matrix for a 'textually generated presence of the author beyond the narrative', p.88. See my own brief consideration of this matter focusing on the Stephen/Joyce games in *Portrait* in *Modernism and the Culture of Celebrity*, pp.33–9. Less certain of durability of Joyce's branding, Joseph Kelly's richly archival reputation and reception history is also relevant to this line of critique, even if its summary and prescriptivist motive to 'abandon ... the author who we, for so long believed wrote Joyce's books', seems out of sorts with its rigorously descriptivist methods. Kelly, *Our Joyce*, p.11.

26. P. Colum and M. Colum, *Our Friend James Joyce* (Garden City, NY: Doubleday, 1958), p.10.

27. R. Ellmann, *James Joyce* (New York: Oxford University Press, 1982), p.11.

28. Ibid., p.40.

29. On the significance of Joyce's attitudes about economics, debts and money, see M. Osteen, *The Economy of 'Ulysses': Making Both Ends Meet* (Syracuse, NY: Syracuse University Press, 1995).

30. Ellmann, *James Joyce*, pp.40, 47, 51.

31. Ibid., p.40.

32. Ibid., p.121.

33. Jaffe, *Modernism and the Culture of Celebrity*, p.57.

34. P. Casanova, *The World Republic of Letters* (Cambridge, MA: Harvard University Press, 2004).

35. I am thinking here of Ulrich Beck's work on second modernity. See U. Beck, *Risk Society: Towards a New Modernity* (London: Sage, 1992), and, more recently, *Cosmopolitan Vision* (London: Polity, 2006).

36. Joyce, 'A Portrait of the Artist', in *The Workshop of Daedalus: James Joyce and the Raw Materials for 'A Portrait of the Artist as Young Man'*, ed. R. Scholes and R. Kain (Evanston, IL: Northwestern University Press, 1965).

37. B. Arnold, *The Scandal of Ulysses: The Life and Afterlife of a Twentieth Century Masterpiece* (New York: St Martin's, 2004), pp.vi–vii. There are many chroniclers of the scandal-publicity model of Joyce's reputation from the memoirists and biographers to the journalists of the Joyce Wars. Although Arnold's is not a book with much scholarly apparatus, it does provide a great bio-bibliography. On this thesis, see also J. Brannon, *Who Reads 'Ulysses'?: The Common Reader and the Rhetoric of the Joyce Wars* (New York: Routledge, 2003).

38. S. Lewis, 'The American Fear of Literature', Nobel Lecture, Nobel Prize in Literature 1930, 12 December 1930. <nobelprize.org/nobel_prizes/literature/laureates/1930/lewis-lecture.html>.

39. Ibid.

40. Ibid.

41. A. Österling, Presentation Speech, Nobel Prize in Literature 1948, 10 December 1948. <nobelprize.org/nobel_prizes/literature/laureates/1948/press.html>.

42. Espmark, *Nobel Prize*, p.72.

43. T.S. Eliot, Banquet Speech, Nobel Prize in Literature 1948, 10 December 1948, in *Nobel Lectures: Literature*, ed. H. Frenz (New York: Elsevier, 1969), p.436.

44. T.S. Eliot, 'Notes on the Definition of Culture', in *Christianity and Culture* (New York: Harcourt, Brace, Jovanovich, 1988), p.191.

45. T.S. Eliot, 'Tradition and the Individual Talent', in *Selected Prose of T.S. Eliot* (New York: Harcourt, Brace, Jovanovich, 1975), p.38.

46. Espmark, *Nobel Prize*, p.3.

47. Ibid. p.5.

48. Ibid., pp.4, 9.

49. D. Walcott, 'The Antilles: Fragments of Epic Memory', Nobel Lecture, Nobel Prize in Literature 1992, 7 December 1992. <nobelprize.org/nobel_prizes/literature/laureates/1992/walcott-lecture.html>.

50. H. Engdahl, Presentation Speech, Nobel Prize in Literature 2006, 10 December 2006. <http://nobelprize.org/nobel_prizes/literature/laureates/2006/presentation-speech.html>.

51. Swedish Academy <www.svenskaakademien.se>.

52. Casanova, *World Republic of Letters*, p.304.

53. See figure. For further discussion of Irish authors and these stamps, see Stephen M. Watt, 'On Retrofitting: Samuel Beckett, Tourist Attraction', in Jonathan Goldman and

Aaron Jaffe (eds), *Modernist Star Maps: Modernity, Celebrity, Culture* (Ashgate Press, forthcoming 2010).

54. R. Lacayo, and L. Grossman, 'The All-Time 100 Novels', *Time*, 16 October 2005 <www.time.com/time/2005/100books/>.

55. T. Shone, 'Fighting Evil, Quoting Nietzsche: Did the Comic Book Really Need to Grow up?', *Slate*, 30 November 2005 <www.slate.com/id/2131269/?nav=ais>; R. Lacayo, 'How We Picked the List', *Time*, 16 October 2005 <www.time.com/time/2005/100books/0,24459,our_choices,00.html>.

56. Lacayo, 'How We Picked the List'.

57. J. Kelly, 'TIME's 100 Best Novels', *Time*, 16 October 2005 <www.time.com/time/magazine/article/0,9171,1118369,00.html>.

58. M. Boscagli and E. Duffy, 'Joyce's Face', in *Marketing Modernisms*, ed. K. Dettmar and S. Watt (Ann Arbor, MI: University of Michigan Press, 1996), pp.133–59.

59. 'Shantih, Shantih, Shantih: Has the Reader Any Rights Before the Bar of Literature', *Time*, 1 (3 March 1923), p.12.

Select Bibliography

Any abbreviation used in the text (as detailed in the List of Abbreviations) is noted here in brackets following the full reference.

WORKS BY JAMES JOYCE

The Critical Writings of James Joyce, ed. Ellsworth Mason and Richard Ellmann (New York: Viking, 1959). (*CW*)

Dubliners: Text, Criticism, and Notes, ed. Robert Scholes and A. Walton Litz (New York: Penguin, 1968 [1914]). (*D*)

Exiles, with Author's Own Notes and an Introduction by Padraic Colum (London: Jonathan Cape, 1972 [1918]). (*E*)

Finnegans Wake (New York: Viking, 1939). (*FW*)

Giacomo Joyce, ed. Richard Ellmann (New York: Viking, 1968). (*GJ*)

Letters of James Joyce, Vol. I, ed. Stuart Gilbert. (New York: Viking, 1957). (*LI*)

Letters of James Joyce, Vols.II and III, ed. Richard Ellmann (New York: Viking, 1966). (*LII* and *LIII*)

A Portrait of the Artist as a Young Man: Text, Criticism, and Notes, ed. Chester G. Anderson (New York: Viking, 1968 [1916]). (*P*)

Poems and Shorter Writings, including 'Epiphanies', 'Giacomo Joyce' and 'A Portrait of the Artist', ed. Richard Ellmann, A. Walton Litz and John Whittier-Ferguson (London: Faber and Faber, 1991). (*PSW*)

Stephen Hero, ed. Theodore Spencer, John J. Slocum and Herbert Cahoon (New York: New Directions, 1963). (*SH*)

Selected Letters of James Joyce, ed. Richard Ellmann (New York: Viking, 1975). (*SL*)

Ulysses, ed. Hans Walter Gabler with Wolfhard Steppe and Claus Melchior (New York: Garland, 1984 [1922]). (*U*)

SELECTED WORKS ON JAMES JOYCE

Arnold. B., *The Scandal of 'Ulysses': The Life and Afterlife of a Twentieth-Century Masterpiece* (Chester Spring, PA: DuFour Editions, 2005).

Attridge, D., *Joyce Effects: On Language, Theory, and History* (Cambridge: Cambridge University Press, 2000).

Attridge, D. and D. Ferrer (eds), *Post-Structuralist Joyce: Essays from the French* (Cambridge: Cambridge University Press, 1984).

Attridge, D. and M. Howes (eds), *Semicolonial Joyce* (Cambridge: Cambridge University Press, 2000).

Bannon, J., *Who Reads Ulysses? The Common Reader and the Rhetoric of the Joyce Wars* (New York: Routledge, 2003).

Beckett, S. *et al.*, *James Joyce/'Finnegans Wake': A Symposium. Our Exagmination Round His Factification For Incamination Of Work In Progress* (New York: New Directions Books, 1972 [1929]).

Benstock, S. and B. Benstock, *Who's He When He's at Home: A James Joyce Directory* (Urbana, IL: University of Illinois Press, 1980).

Bishop, J., *Joyce's Book of the Dark, 'Finnegans Wake'* (Madison, WI: University of Wisconsin Press, 1987).

Booth, W., 'The Problem of Distance in *A Portrait of the Artist*'. In *The Rhetoric of Fiction* (Chicago, IL: University of Chicago Press, 1961; 2nd edn, 1983). Reprinted in James Joyce, *A Portrait of the Artist as a Young Man: Text, Criticism, and Notes*, ed. Chester G. Anderson (New York: Viking, 1968), pp.455–67.

Bosinelli, R. and Harold F. Mosher Jr (eds), *ReJoycing: New Readings of 'Dubliners'* (Lexington, KY: University Press of Kentucky, 1998).

Brian, M., '"A Very Fine Piece of Writing": An Etymological, Dantean, and Gnostic Reading of Joyce's "Ivy Day in the Committee Room"'. In *ReJoycing: New Readings of 'Dubliners'*, ed. R. Bosinelli and Harold F. Mosher Jr (Lexington, KY: University Press of Kentucky, 1998), pp.206–27.

Brivic, S., *Joyce's Waking Women: An Introduction to 'Finnegans Wake'* (Madison, WI: University of Wisconsin Press, 1995).

Brown, R., *James Joyce and Sexuality* (Cambridge: Cambridge University Press, 1985).

Budgen, F., *James Joyce and the Making of 'Ulysses'* (London: Oxford University Press, 1972).

Campbell, J. and H.M. Robinson, *A Skeleton Key to 'Finnegans Wake'* (New York: Viking Press, 1961).

Cheng, V., *Joyce, Race, and Empire* (Cambridge: Cambridge University Press, 1995).

Curran, C.P., *James Joyce Remembered* (New York: Oxford University Press, 1968).

Derrida, J., 'Ulysses Gramophone: *Hear say yes in Joyce*'. In *James Joyce: The Augmented Ninth*, ed. B. Benstock (New York: Syracuse University Press, 1988), pp.27–77.

Dettmar, K., *The Illicit Joyce of Postmodernism: Reading Against the Grain* (Madison, WI: University of Wisconsin Press, 1996).

Devlin, K. and M. Reizbaum (eds), *Ulysses: En-Gendered Perspectives* (Columbia, SC: University of South Carolina Press, 1999).

Duffy, Enda, *The Subaltern 'Ulysses'* (Minneapolis, MN: University of Minnesota Press, 1994).

Eliot, T.S., '*Ulysses*, Order and Myth'. In *Selected Prose of T.S. Eliot*, ed. F. Kermode (London: Faber and Faber, 1975), pp.175–8.

Ellmann, Richard, *James Joyce. New and Revised Edition* (New York: Oxford University Press, 1982). (*JJ*)

Frawley, O. (ed.), *A New and Complex Sensation: Essays on Joyce's 'Dubliners'* (Dublin: Lilliput Press, 2004).

Gibson, A., *Joyce's Revenge: Theory, Politics, and Aesthetics in 'Ulysses'* (Oxford: Oxford University Press, 2002).

Gifford, D. with R.J. Seidman, *'Ulysses' Annotated: Notes for James Joyce's 'Ulysses'* (Berkeley, CA: University of California Press, 1988).

Gilbert, S., *James Joyce's 'Ulysses'. A Study* (1930; rpt. with new preface, New York: Vintage, 1952).

Gordon, J., *'Finnegans Wake': A Plot Summary* (Dublin: Gill and Macmillan, 1986).

—————— *Joyce and Reality: The Empirical Strikes Back* (Syracuse, NY: Syracuse University Press, 2004).

Groden, M., *'Ulysses' in Progress* (Princeton, NJ: Princeton University Press, 1977).

Hayman, D., *The 'Wake' in Transit* (Ithaca, NY: Cornell University Press, 1990).

Henke, S.A., *James Joyce and the Politics of Desire* (London and New York: Routledge, 1990).

Herr, C. *Joyce's Anatomy of Culture* (Urbana, IL: University of Illinois Press, 1986).

Joyce, J., *A First Draft Version of 'Finnegans Wake'*, ed. D. Hayman (London: Faber and Faber, 1963).

Kelly, J., *Our Joyce: From Outcast to Icon* (Austin, TX: University of Texas Press, 1998).

Kenner, H., *Dublin's Joyce* (New York: Columbia University Press, 1987).

———— *Joyce's Voices* (Berkeley, CA: University of California Press, 1978).

Kershner, R.B., *Joyce, Bakhtin, and Popular Literature: Chronicles of Disorder* (Chapel Hill, NC: University of North Carolina Press, 1989).

Leonard, G., *Advertising and Commodity Culture in Joyce* (Gainesville, FL: University of Florida Press, 1998).

Leonard, G. and J. Wicke (eds), 'Joyce and Advertising'. Special issue of *James Joyce Quarterly*, 30, 4/31, 1 (Summer/Fall 1993).

MacCabe, C., *James Joyce and the Revolution of the Word* (London: Macmillan, 1978).

McCourt, J., *The Years of Bloom: Joyce in Trieste, 1904–1920* (Dublin: Lilliput Press, 2000).

McGee, P., *Paperspace: Style as Ideology in Joyce's 'Ulysses'* (Lincoln, NE: University of Nebraska Press, 1988).

———— *Telling the Other: The Question of Value in Colonial and Postcolonial Writing* (Ithaca, NY: Cornell University Press, 1992).

McHugh, R., *Annotations to 'Finnegans Wake'*, 3rd edn (Baltimore, MD: Johns Hopkins University Press, 2006).

Mahaffey, V., *States of Desire: Wilde, Yeats, Joyce, and the Irish Experiment* (New York: Oxford University Press, 1998).

Nolan, E., *James Joyce and Nationalism* (London: Routledge, 1995).

Norburn, R., *A James Joyce Chronology* (New York: Palgrave, 2004).

Norris, M., *The Decentered Universe of 'Finnegans Wake': A Structuralist Analysis* (Baltimore, MD: Johns Hopkins University Press, 1976).

———— *Suspicious Readings of Joyce's 'Dubliners'* (Philadelphia, PA: University of Pennsylvania Press, 2003).

Pierce, D., *James Joyce's Ireland* (New Haven, CT and London: Yale University Press, 1992).

Potts, W., *Joyce and the Two Irelands* (Austin, TX: University of Texas Press, 2000).

Riquelme, J., *Teller and Tale in Joyce's Fiction: Oscillating Perspectives* (Baltimore, MD: Johns Hopkins University Press, 1983).

Scholes, R., *In Search of James Joyce* (Urbana, IL: University of Illinois Press, 1992).

Scholes, R. and R. Kain, *The Workshop of Daedalus: James Joyce and the Raw Materials for 'A Portrait of the Artist as a Young Man'* (Evanston, IL: Northwestern University Press, 1965).

Schloss, C., *Lucia Joyce: To Dance in the Wake* (New York: Farrar, Straus and Giroux, 2003).

Scott, B.K., *Joyce and Feminism* (Bloomington, IN: Indiana University Press, 1984).

Spoo, R., 'Injuries, Remedies, Moral Rights, and the Public Domain'. *James Joyce Quarterly*, 37, 3 (2000), pp.333–51.

Thwaites, T., *Joycean Temporalities: Debts, Promises, and Countersignatures* (Gainesville, FL: University of Florida Press, 2001).

Vanderham, P., *James Joyce and Censorship: The Trials of 'Ulysses'* (New York: New York University Press, 1998).

Wollaeger, M. (ed.), *James Joyce's 'A Portrait of the Artist as a Young Man': A Casebook* (Oxford: Oxford University Press, 2003).

Index

'Eumaeus' episode, 116, 120
'Hades' episode, 114, 115, 116, 148
'Ithaca' episode, 116, 120, 122–3
'Lestrygonians' episode, 115, 116, 118, 125, 183
'Lotus Eaters' episode, 114, 115, 116, 118
'Nausicaa' episode, 16, 36, 85, 92–3, 116, 119, 123, 124, 135, 183
'Nestor' episode, 111, 112, 113
'Oxen of the Sun' episode, 35, 116, 119, 123, 183
'Penelope' episode, 120–1, 122, 184–5
'Proteus' episode, 111, 112, 113, 114
'Scylla and Charybdis' episode, 33, 118, 183
'Sirens' episode, 85, 115, 116, 118
'Telemachus' episode', 111, 112, 124, 182
'Wandering Rocks' episode, 1, 115, 182
censorship and, 36, 37, 68, 135, 170, 183, 203
characters, 20, 26, 27, 29, 35–6, 78, 93, 110–18, 119–23, 171, 182, 183–5
    see also 'Bloom, Leopold' (character in Ulysses); 'Bloom, Molly' (character in Ulysses); 'Dedalus, Stephen' (character in Joyce's fiction)
'classic' status, 106, 107, 108, 126
as counterpart to The Waste Land, 86
critical responses to, 105–6, 107, 123
as difficult to read, 4, 15, 106, 107–9, 112, 125
T.S. Eliot on, 1, 4, 35, 132
as Hegelian work of art, 23
humour in, 87, 100
Joyce on, 109–10, 120, 125
language and, 77, 78, 82, 109
modernity and, 4, 6, 7, 15, 16, 86, 141, 170, 195
mythology and, 1–2, 4, 35, 108, 110–11, 112, 113–14, 115, 116, 165–6
narrative style, 4, 34–5, 100, 108–9, 118–21, 134–5, 183, 184
novel of the century polls and, 71, 105–6, 108, 208–10
obscenity and, 106, 107, 119, 123, 124, 170, 183
physical body and, 16, 113, 114, 120, 125, 170–1, 181, 182–5, 187
plot and structure, 15, 16, 34,

110–18, 119–21, 122–3, 124–5, 134–5
publication of (1922), 36–7, 106–7, 123–4, 155
religion and, 23, 27, 112
serialization in Little Review, 34, 36, 105, 106, 123, 124, 170, 183
sexuality see sexuality: Ulysses and
theoretical approaches to, 121, 156, 157, 158, 162–3, 165–6
Time magazine and, 208–10
Joyce, John Stanislaus, 19–20, 26, 31, 134, 197
Joyce, Lucia Anna, 31, 40, 41
health of, 36, 39–40, 146
Joyce, Mary Jane "May" (née Murray), 19, 20, 26–7
Joyce, Stanislaus, 21, 30, 31, 33, 36, 40, 96
    Chamber Music and, 88, 95
    Finnegans Wake and, 132
Joyce, Stephen, 39, 40
Jung, Carl, 34, 39

K

Kafka, Franz, 141
Kelly, Aaron, 35
Kenner, Hugh, 3, 99, 157
    Dublin's Joyce, 156–7
Kershner, R.B., 99
Kettle, Thomas, 32
Kristeva, Julia, 159

L

Lacan, Jacques, 16, 153, 155, 157, 158, 159–62, 165, 166, 167
Lamb, Charles, Adventures of Ulysses, 110
Lambert, Gregg, 192
Larbaud, Valèry, 36, 124
Leavis, F.R., 156
Léon, Paul, 39, 40
Leslie, Shane, 107
Lessing, Gotthold Ephraim, Laocoön, 23
Levin, Harry, 92
Lévi-Strauss, Claude, 157
Levitt, Morton, 192
Lewis, Sinclair, 189, 203–4
Lewis, Wyndham, 3, 132
linguistics, 76–80, 82
Little Review, 34, 36, 105, 106, 123, 124, 170, 183
Lodge, David, 154
Lowry, Malcolm, Under the Volcano, 208–9
Lyotard, Jean-François, 165–6

INDEX

M

MacCabe, Colin, *James Joyce and the Revolution of the Word*, 158–9, 164
Mahaffey, V., 92
Mangan, James Clarence, 25, 174
Marsden, Dora, 33
Martello Tower, Sandycove, 29, 110, 111, 124
Marx Brothers, *A Night at the Opera*, 142, 143
Mathew, Elkin, 30
Maunsel & Co., 32, 68, 186
McAlmon, Robert, *Contact Collection of Contemporary Writers*, 40
McCann, Phillip, 22
McCormack, Edith Rockefeller, 34
McCormack, John, 27
McGee, Patrick
 Paperspace: Style as Ideology in Joyce's 'Ulysses', 164–5
 Telling the Other: The Question of Value in Modern and Postcolonial Writing, 166
McGinley, Bernard, 63
McHugh, Roland, 38, 146–7
McLuhan, Marshall, 144–5
McMichael, James, *Ulysses and Justice*, 166
Merton, Thomas, 72
modernity, 2–7, 12, 13–17, 140–1, 154–6, 171, 198–9, 204
 T.S. Eliot and, 3, 86
 Finnegans Wake and, 4, 15–16, 37–8, 137, 141–2, 155, 156
 minor works of Joyce and, 14, 86, 101
 A Portrait of the Artist as a Young Man and, 7–12, 13, 14, 75, 140–1
 Ulysses and, 4, 6, 7, 15, 16, 86, 141, 170, 195
Monnier, Adrienne, 36, 155
Monroe, Marilyn, 195
Moore, George, 25, 26, 106, 125, 126
mythology, 1–2, 4–5, 35, 108, 110–11, 112, 113–14, 115, 116, 165–6

N

narratology, 157
New Criticism, 156
Newman, Cardinal, 200, 201, 202
Nietzsche, Friedrich, 82
Nobel Prizes, 17, 189–91, 193, 194, 199, 203–7
 Irish winners, 199, 207–8
Norris, Margot, 55
 The Decentered Universe of 'Finnegans Wake', 135, 137, 157
Noyes, Alfred, 106

O

O'Connell, Daniel, 19
O'Faolain, Sean, 39
Österling, Anders, 204

P

Pamuk, Orhan, 206
Parnell, Charles Stewart, 12, 19, 21, 58, 143
Pater, Walter, 5
Pearse, Patrick, 27
physics, 193–5
Picasso, Pablo, 155
Il Piccolo della Sera (Trieste), 31
Pinter, Harold, 84, 86, 190
Poe, Edgar Allan, *The Purloined Letter*, 153, 160
politics, 25, 37, 40, 58–9, 123
Popper, Amalia, 33, 90
post-structuralism, 16, 153, 156, 157, 158–64, 192
 deconstruction, 164, 165
 ethics and, 158–9, 164–6
Pound, Ezra, 32, 33, 36, 86, 90, 100, 101, 154
 Finnegans Wake and, 39, 132
 Ulysses and, 105, 110, 126, 170, 171, 187
Power, Arthur, 20
Power, Henriette, 84
Prezioso, Roberto, 31
prizes, cultural, 189–92, 194, 195
 Nobel Prizes, 17, 189–91, 193, 194, 199, 203–8
Proust, Marcel, 3, 141, 165
psychoanalysis, 37, 135, 136, 156, 157, 160
Purcell, Henry, *Dido and Aeneas*, 35

Q

Queen's University, Cork, 7, 19, 178–9
queer studies, 167

R

Rabaté, Jean-Michel, 161
Random House, 71, 107, 109
Rasula, Jed, 134
Read, Forrest, 28
reception-aesthetics, 154
Richards, Grant, 30, 33, 34, 45, 52–3, 55, 57, 67, 68, 69
Rickaby, John, *General Metaphysics*, 23
Riquelme, John P., 158
Roberts, George, 32, 45, 68–9, 186
romanticism, 25–6, 76
Rooney, William, 54